I0047810

Building VMware Software-Defined Data Centers

Make the most of software-defined data centers with revolutionary VMware technologies

Valentin Hamburger

Pack<t>

BIRMINGHAM - MUMBAI

Building VMware Software-Defined Data Centers

Copyright © 2016 Packt Publishing

All rights reserved. No part of this book may be reproduced, stored in a retrieval system, or transmitted in any form or by any means, without the prior written permission of the publisher, except in the case of brief quotations embedded in critical articles or reviews.

Every effort has been made in the preparation of this book to ensure the accuracy of the information presented. However, the information contained in this book is sold without warranty, either express or implied. Neither the author, nor Packt Publishing, and its dealers and distributors will be held liable for any damages caused or alleged to be caused directly or indirectly by this book.

Packt Publishing has endeavored to provide trademark information about all of the companies and products mentioned in this book by the appropriate use of capitals. However, Packt Publishing cannot guarantee the accuracy of this information.

First published: December 2016

Production reference: 1061216

Published by Packt Publishing Ltd.
Livery Place
35 Livery Street
Birmingham
B3 2PB, UK.
ISBN 978-1-78646-437-8

www.packtpub.com

Credits

Author

Valentin Hamburger

Reviewer

Daniel Koeck

Commissioning Editor

Kartikey Pandey

Acquisition Editor

Vijin Boricha

Content Development Editor

Rashmi Suvarna

Technical Editor

Gaurav Suri

Copy Editors

Safis Editing

Dipti Mankame

Project Coordinator

Judie Jose

Proofreader

Safis Editing

Indexer

Pratik Shirodkar

Graphics

Kirk D'Penha

Production Coordinator

Shantanu N. Zagade

About the Author

Valentin Hamburger was working at VMware for more than seven years. In his former role, he was a lead consulting architect and took care of the delivery and architecture of cloud projects in central EMEA. In his current role, he is EMEA solutions lead for VMware at Hitachi Data Systems (HDS). Furthermore he works as an advisor with HDS engineering on the Hitachi Enterprise Cloud, which is based on VMware vRealize technology. He holds many industry certifications in various areas such as VMware, Linux, and IBM Power compute environments. He serves as a partner and trusted advisor to HDS customers primarily in EMEA. His main responsibilities are ensuring that HDS's future innovations align with essential customer needs and translating customer challenges to opportunities focused on virtualization topics. Valentin enjoys sharing his knowledge as a speaker at national and international conferences such as VMworld.

I want to personally thank Daniel Koeck for reviewing the technical content of this book and providing such valuable and productive inputs. Besides his technical expertise I am happy to have him as a friend and supporter for this book. Furthermore, I want to thank my beautiful wife and daughter for their patience and understanding while I was writing this book. Without their support and love, this wouldn't have been possible at all. Finally I do want to thank Rashmi Suvarna who had patience with me as an author and supported me wherever she could in order to get all this work done.

About the Reviewer

Daniel Koeck has been working for 15 years in IT. He leaded large scale (more than 20,000 VMs) projects, reaching from Service Provider Clouds, to DevOps enabled large scale software solutions in the last 6 years. He holds a degree for applied computer science and IT-security. Daniel is an IBM Redbook Gold author, and co-authored other many other books and whitepapers about x86 virtualization. He is regularly invited as a speaker to different universities and technology conferences all over Europe and USA, and enjoys sharing his experience there. You can find him on twitter @Cloudsandwakes.

www.PacktPub.com

eBooks, discount offers, and more

Did you know that Packt offers eBook versions of every book published, with PDF and ePub files available? You can upgrade to the eBook version at www.PacktPub.com and as a print book customer, you are entitled to a discount on the eBook copy. Get in touch with us at customercare@packtpub.com for more details.

At www.PacktPub.com, you can also read a collection of free technical articles, sign up for a range of free newsletters and receive exclusive discounts and offers on Packt books and eBooks.

⋀⋀Mapt

https://www2.packtpub.com/books/subscription/packtlib

Do you need instant solutions to your IT questions? PacktLib is Packt's online digital book library. Here, you can search, access, and read Packt's entire library of books.

Why subscribe?

- Fully searchable across every book published by Packt
- Copy and paste, print, and bookmark content
- On demand and accessible via a web browser

Table of Contents

Preface

This book uses the most up-to-date, cutting-edge VMware products to help you deliver a complete unified hybrid cloud experience within your infrastructure.

It will help you build an SDDC architecture and practices to deliver a fully virtualized infrastructure with cost-effective IT outcomes. In the process, you will use some of the most advanced VMware products such as vSphere, vRealize Automation and Orchestrator, and NSX. You will see how to provision applications and IT services on private clouds or IaaS with seamless accessibility and mobility across the hybrid environment.

This book will ensure that you develop an SDDC approach for your data center that fulfills your organization's business needs and tremendously boosts your agility and flexibility. It will also teach you how to draft, design, and deploy toolsets and software to automate your data center and speed up IT delivery to meet your lines of businesses demands. In the end, you will build unified hybrid clouds that dramatically boost your IT outcomes.

What this book covers

Chapter 1, *The Software-Defined Data Center*, discusses principles and basics about the SDDC. Besides the technical aspects, it will also highlight the organizational aspects and that the SDDC is a new way of managing and running a data center and therefore also an architectural change. Also, it will describe the implementation journey and what is necessary to take into account besides the technological aspects.

Chapter 2, *Identify Automation and Standardization Opportunities*, highlights the main principles of automation and standardization. The differences between scripts and workflows are described. Also, it will bring examples how to apply standardization and automation to the data center in order to make the SDDC flexible and agile as possible.

Chapter 3, *VMware vSphere: The SDDC Foundation*, covers important vSphere functions, which will decrease the amount of customization when it comes to automation. Since virtualization is the base of an SDDC, this chapter will focus on examples and configurations for vSphere. This chapter will discuss advanced vSphere functions and their importance for an SDDC.

Chapter 4, *SDDC Design Considerations*, explains the main principles of an SDDC design including detailed examples. Highlighted are also what assumptions, constraints and limits are and how they will influence a design. Furthermore, it will show a simple–to-follow approach to translate business challenges in a technical solution and therefore an agile and efficient SDDC design.

Chapter 5, *VMware vRealize Automation*, introduces vRA (formally known as vCloud Automation Center) and its capabilities. The implementation of the design considerations of the former chapter will be discussed, and it will show other important configuration options, principles, and concepts. Also, it will focus on the creation of so-called *blueprints* and what is needed to prepare a VM template to be deployed.

Chapter 6, *vRealize Orchestrator*, touches on what workflows are and how they can be developed in a controlled and clean manner. It will highlight how to integrate those into vRealize Automation to create powerful services for almost any task in the SDDC. In addition, it will discuss what postdeployment third-party integration can be achieved using vRO (for example, IPAM and CMDB integration).

Chapter 7, *Service Catalog Creation*, brings up the basic service catalog design. Also, it bridges the business case to the service catalog and describes why that is important and how that sync can be achieved. It will explain based on an example how to configure an outcome-focused service catalog in vRealize Automation.

Chapter 8, *Network Virtualization using NSX*, discusses software-defined networking principles. It highlights NSX basic functions and configurations and why it is a game changer within the SDDC. With NSX, broad data center automation can be fully achieved by gaining maximal flexibility and agility for service deployments. It will also cover the base configuration and integration with SDDC based on practical examples and detailed integration descriptions.

Chapter 9, *DevOps Considerations*, describes DevOps in general and what changes it brings to IT and the SDDC. It discusses most of the modern technologies to run DevOps including containers and container frameworks such as Pivotal Cloud Foundry. Furthermore, it describes a DevOps approach to run and manage the SDDC itself using VMware vRealize Code Stream Management Pack for IT DevOps. This will add additional agility and flexibility when it comes to managing and operating the SDDC.

Chapter 10, *Capacity Management with vRealize Operations*, mentions how important a proper capacity management is in a fully automated data center. It will highlight techniques and principles in regard to successfully plan infrastructure expansion. It provides practical configuration examples for resource planning and predictive capacity maintenance.

Chapter 11, *Troubleshooting and Monitoring,* explains the monitoring and analytics methods for the SDDC. Since an automated data center might have different challenges in terms of monitoring, it further highlights the differences to static infrastructure and why it is important to have a smart monitoring and analytics approach for the SDDC. It will describe how to limit the impact of issues with smart and predictive troubleshooting and analytics methods, including the use of vRealize Log Insight.

Chapter 12, *Continuous Improvement,* mentions the importance of continuously working on the services and processes within the SDDC. Once the SDDC is deployed and functions properly it is time to reflect and maybe update the created services. The chapter mentions how important it is to detect possible process flaws or glitches and update those. Furthermore, it summarizes the importance of ITIL in a modern data center and explains that the SDDC is basically the fully automated version of ITIL bringing all its benefits to life without all its drawbacks like the bureaucracy overhead.

What you need for this book

- vRealize Automation
- vRealize Orchestrator
- vRealize Operations Manager
- vRealize Log Insight
- vRealize Code Stream
    - Management pack for IT DevOps
- VMware vSphere
- VMware NSX

Who this book is for

If you are an IT professional or VMware administrator who virtualizes data centers and IT infrastructures, this book is for you. Developers and DevOps engineers who deploy applications and services would also find this book useful. Data center architects and those at the CXO level who make decisions will appreciate the value in the content.

Conventions

In this book, you will find a number of text styles that distinguish between different kinds of information. Here are some examples of these styles and an explanation of their meaning.

Code words in text, database table names, folder names, filenames, file extensions, pathnames, dummy URLs, user input, and Twitter handles are shown as follows: "Provide a meaningful name such as `Backup`."

Any command-line input or output is written as follows:

```
msdtc -uninstall
```

A block of code is set as follows:

```
#!/bin/bash
#Turn off iptables for app server access
/sbin/service iptables stop
```

New terms and **important words** are shown in bold. Words that you see on the screen, for example, in menus or dialog boxes, appear in the text like this: "Click **OK** to store the new property."

Warnings or important notes appear in a box like this.

Tips and tricks appear like this.

Reader feedback

Feedback from our readers is always welcome. Let us know what you think about this book-what you liked or disliked. Reader feedback is important for us as it helps us develop titles that you will really get the most out of. To send us general feedback, simply e-mail feedback@packtpub.com, and mention the book's title in the subject of your message. If there is a topic that you have expertise in and you are interested in either writing or contributing to a book, see our author guide at www.packtpub.com/authors.

Customer support

Now that you are the proud owner of a Packt book, we have a number of things to help you to get the most from your purchase.

Downloading the color images of this book

We also provide you with a PDF file that has color images of the screenshots/diagrams used in this book. The color images will help you better understand the changes in the output. You can download this file from `https://www.packtpub.com/sites/default/files/down loads/BuildingVMwareSoftwaredefinedDataCenters_ColorImages.pdf`.

Errata

Although we have taken every care to ensure the accuracy of our content, mistakes do happen. If you find a mistake in one of our books-maybe a mistake in the text or the code-we would be grateful if you could report this to us. By doing so, you can save other readers from frustration and help us improve subsequent versions of this book. If you find any errata, please report them by visiting `http://www.packtpub.com/submit-errata`, selecting your book, clicking on the **Errata Submission Form** link, and entering the details of your errata. Once your errata are verified, your submission will be accepted and the errata will be uploaded to our website or added to any list of existing errata under the Errata section of that title.

To view the previously submitted errata, go to `https://www.packtpub.com/books/conten t/support` and enter the name of the book in the search field. The required information will appear under the **Errata** section.

Piracy

Piracy of copyrighted material on the Internet is an ongoing problem across all media. At Packt, we take the protection of our copyright and licenses very seriously. If you come across any illegal copies of our works in any form on the Internet, please provide us with the location address or website name immediately so that we can pursue a remedy.

Please contact us at `copyright@packtpub.com` with a link to the suspected pirated material.

We appreciate your help in protecting our authors and our ability to bring you valuable content.

Questions

If you have a problem with any aspect of this book, you can contact us at `questions@packtpub.com`, and we will do our best to address the problem.

1
The Software-Defined Data Center

Originally the term **software-defined data center (SDDC)** has been introduced by VMware, to further describe the move to a cloud-like IT experience. The term *software-defined* is an important bit of information. It basically means that every key function in the data center is performed and controlled by software, instead of hardware. This opens a whole new way of operating, maintaining but also innovating in a modern data center.

But how does a so-called SDDC look like, and why is a whole industry pushing so hard towards its adoption? This question might also be a reason why you are reading this book, which is meant to provide a deeper understanding of it and give practical examples and hints how to build and run such a data center. Meanwhile, it will also provide the knowledge of mapping business challenges with IT solutions. This is a practice which becomes more and more important these days.

IT has come a long way from a pure back office, task oriented role in the early days, to a business relevant asset, which can help organizations to compete with their competition. There has been a major shift from a pure infrastructure provider role to a business enablement function. Today, most organizations business is just as good as their internal IT agility and ability to innovate. There are many examples in various markets where a whole business branch was built on IT innovations such as Netflix, **Amazon Web Services (AWS)**, Uber, Airbnb, just to name a few.

However, it is unfair to compare any startup with a traditional organization. A startup has one application to maintain and they have to build up a customer base.

A traditional organization has a wide customer base and many applications to maintain. So they need to adapt their internal IT to become a digital enterprise, with all the flexibility and agility of a startup, but also maintaining the trust and control over their legacy services.

This chapter will cover the following points:

- Why is there a demand for SDDC in IT
- What is SDDC
- Understand the business challenges and map it to SDDC deliverables
- The relation of an SDDC and an internal private cloud
- Identify new data center opportunities and possibilities
- Become a center of innovation to empower your organization's business

The demand for change

Today organizations face different challenges in the market to stay relevant. The biggest move was clearly introduced by smartphones and tablets. It was not just a computer in a smaller device, they changed the way IT is delivered and consumed by end users. These devices proved that it can be simple to consume and install applications. Just search in an app store, choose what you like, use it as long as you like it. If you do not need it any longer, simply remove it. All with very simplistic commands and easy to use gestures.

More and more people relying on IT services by using a smartphone as their terminal to almost everything. These devices created a demand for fast and easy application and service delivery. So in a way, smartphones have not only transformed the whole mobile market, they also transformed how modern applications and services are delivered from organizations to their customers.

Although it would be quite unfair to compare a large enterprise data center with an app store or enterprise service delivery with any app installs on a mobile device, there are startups and industries, which rely solely on the smartphone as their target for services, such as Uber or WhatsApp.

On the other side, smartphone apps also introduce a whole new way of delivering IT services, since any company never knows how many people will use the app simultaneously. But in the backend, they still have to use web servers and databases to continuously provide content and data for these apps.

This also introduces a new value model for all other companies. People start to judge a company by the quality of their smartphone apps available. Also, people started to migrate to companies which might offer better smartphone integration as the previous one used. This is not bound to a single industry, but affects a broad spectrum of industries today such as the financial industry, car manufacturers, insurance groups, and even food retailers, just to name a few.

A classic data center structure might not be ideal for quick and seamless service delivery. These architectures are created by projects to serve a particular use case for a couple of years. An example of this bigger application environments is web server farms, traditional SAP environments, or a data warehouse.

Traditionally these were designed with an assumption about their growth and use. Special project teams have set them up across the data center pillars, as shown in the following figure. Typically, those project teams separate after such the application environment has been completed.

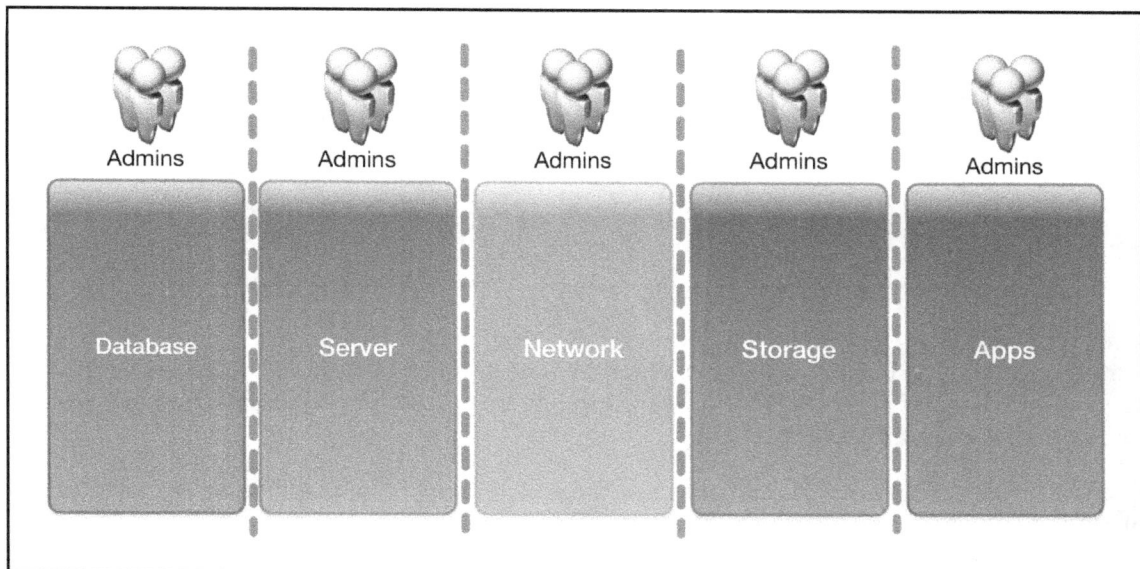

All these pillars in the data center are required to work together, but every one of them also needs to mind their own business. Mostly those different divisions also have their own processes which then may integrate into a data center wide process. There was a good reason to structure a data center in this way, the simple fact that nobody can be an expert in every discipline. Companies started to create groups to operate certain areas in a data center, each building their own expertise for their own subject.

This was evolving and became the most applied model for IT operations within organizations. Many, if not all, bigger organizations have adopted this approach and people build their careers on these definitions. It served IT well for decades and ensured that each party was adding its best knowledge to any given project.

However, this setup has one flaw, it has not been designed for massive change and scale. The bigger these divisions get, the slower they can react to request from other groups in the data center. This introduces a bi-directional issue, since all groups may grow at a similar rate, the overall service delivery time might also increase exponentially.

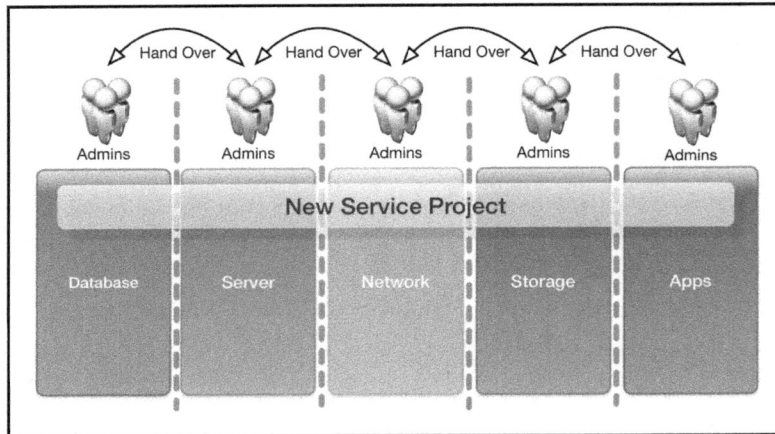

Unfortunately, this also introduces a cost factor when it comes to service deployments across these pillars. Each new service, an organization might introduce or develop, will require each area of IT to contribute. Traditionally, this is done by human handovers from one department to the other.

Each of these handovers will delay the overall project time or service delivery time, which is also often referred to as **time to market**. It reflects the needed time interval from the request of a new service to its actual delivery. It is important to mention that this is a level of complexity every modern organization has to deal with when it comes to application deployment today.

The difference between organizations might be in the size of the separate units, but the principle is always the same. Most organizations try to bring their overall service delivery time down to be quicker and more agile. This is often related to business reasons as well as IT cost reasons.

In some organizations, the time to deliver a brand new service from request to final roll out may take *90 working days*. This means a requestor might wait *18 weeks* or more than *four and a half month* from requesting a new business service to its actual delivery. Do not forget that this reflects the complete service delivery, over all groups until it is ready for production. Also, after these 90 days, the requirement of the original request might have changed which would lead into repeating the entire process.

Often a quicker time to market is driven by the **lines of business (LOB)** owners to respond to a competitor in the market, who might already deliver their services faster. This means that today's IT has changed from a pure internal service provider to a business enabler supporting its organization to fight the competition with advanced and innovative services.

While this introduces a great chance to the IT department to enable and support their organizations business, it also introduces a threat at the same time. If the internal IT struggles to deliver what the business is asking for, it may lead to leverage shadow IT within the organization.

The term **shadow IT** describes a situation where either the LOBs of an organization or its application developers have grown so disappointed with the internal IT delivery times, that they actually use an external provider for their requirements. This behavior is not agreed with the IT security and can lead to heavy business or legal troubles.

This happens more often than one might expect, and it can be as simple as putting some internal files on a public cloud storage provider. These services grant quick results. It is as simple as *Register-Download-Use*. They are very quick in enrolling new users and sometimes provide a limited use for free. The developer or business owner might not even be aware that there is something non-compliant going on while using these services.

So besides the business demand for a quicker service delivery and the security aspect, an organization's IT department has now also the pressure of staying relevant. But SDDC can provide much more value to the IT than just staying relevant.

The automated data center will be an enabler for innovation and trust and introduce a new era of IT delivery. It can not only provide faster service delivery to the business, it can also enable new services or offerings to help the whole organization being innovative for their customers or partners.

Business challenges: The use case

Today's business strategies often involve a digital delivery of services of any kind. This implies that the requirements a modern organization has towards their internal IT have changed drastically. Unfortunately, the business owners and the IT department tend to have communication issues in some organizations. Sometimes they even operate completely disconnected from each other, as if each of them were their own small company within the organization.

Nevertheless, a lot of data center automation projects are driven by enhanced business requirements. In some of these cases, the IT department has not been made aware of what these business requirements look like, or even what the actual business challenges are. Sometimes IT just gets as little information as: *We are doing cloud now*.

It's a dangerous simplification, since the use case is key when it comes to designing and identifying the right solution to the organization's challenges. It is important to get the requirements from the IT delivery side as well as the business requirements and expectations.

Here is a simple example how a use case might be identified and mapped to technical implementation.

The business view

John works as a business owner in an insurance company. He recognizes that their biggest competitor in the market started to offer a mobile application to their clients. The app is simple and allows to do online contract management and tells the clients which products they have enrolled as well as rich information about contract timelines and possible consolidation options.

He asks his manager to start a project to also deliver such an application to their customers. Since it is only a simple smartphone application, he expects that its development might take a couple of weeks and then they can start a beta phase. To be competitive he estimates that they should have something usable for their customers within a maximum of 5 months. Based on these facts, he got approval from his manager to request such a product from the internal IT.

The IT view

Tom is the data center manager of this insurance company. He got informed that the business wants to have a smartphone application to do all kinds of things for the new and existing customers. He is responsible for creating a project and bring all necessary people on board to support this project and finally deliver the service to the business. The programming of the app will be done by an external consulting company.

Tom discusses a couple of questions regarding this request with his team:

- How many users do we need to serve?
- How much time do we need to create this environment?
- What is the expected level of availability?
- How much compute power/disk space might be required?

After a round of brainstorming and intense discussion, the team still is quite unsure how to answer these questions. For every question, there are a couple of variables the team cannot predict.

Will only a few of their thousands of users adapt to the app, what if they undersize the middleware environment?

What if the user adoption rises within a couple of days, what if it lowers and the environment is overpowered and therefore the cost is too high?

Tom and his team identified that they need a dynamic solution to be able to serve the business request. He creates a mapping to match possible technical capabilities to the use case. After this mapping was completed, he is using it to discuss with his CIO if and how it can be implemented.

Business challenge	Question	IT capability
Easy to use app to win new customers/keep existing	How many users do we need to the server?	Dynamic scale of an environment based on actual performance demand.
	How much time do we need to create this environment?	To fulfill the expectations the environment needs to be flexible. Start small – scale big.
	What is the expected level of availability?	Analytics and monitoring over all layers. Including possible self-healing approach.
	How much compute power/disk space might be required?	Create compute nodes based on actual performance requirements on demand. Introduce a capacity on demand model for required resources.

Given this table, Tom revealed that with their current data center structure it is quite difficult to deliver what the business is asking for. Also, he got a couple of requirements from other departments, which are going in a similar direction.

Based on these mappings, he identified that they need to change their way of deploying services and applications. They will need to use a fair amount of automation. Also, they have to span these functionalities across each data center department as a holistic approach, as shown in the following diagram:

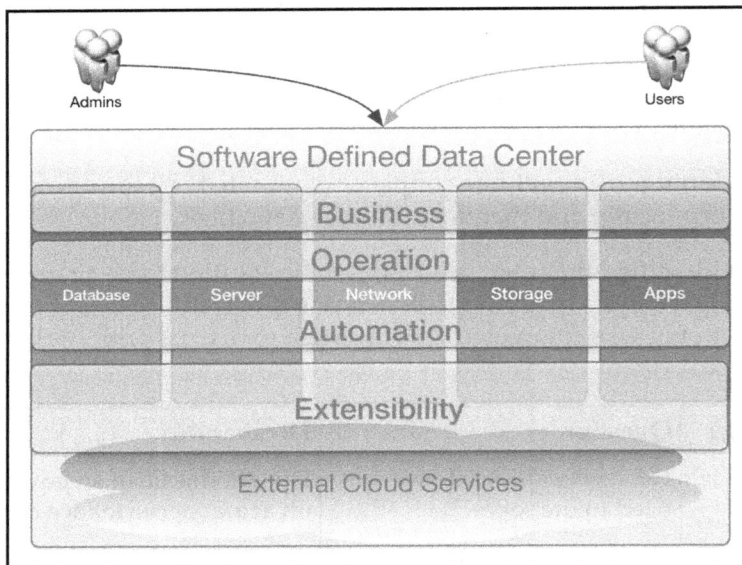

In this example, Tom actually identified a very strong use case for SDDC in his company. Based on the actual business requirements of a *simple* application, the whole IT delivery of this company needs to adopt. While this may sound like pure fiction, these are the challenges modern organizations need to face today.

> It is very important to identify the required capabilities for the entire data center and not just for a single department. You will also have to serve the legacy applications and bring them onto the new model. Therefore it is important to find a solution, which is serving the new business case as well as the legacy applications either way. In the first stage of any SDDC introduction in an organization, it is the key to keeping always an eye on the big picture.

Tools to enable SDDC

There is a basic and broadly accepted declaration of what an SDDC needs to offer. It can be considered as the second evolutionary step after server virtualization. It offers an abstraction layer from the infrastructure components such as compute, storage, and network by using automation and tools as such as a self-service catalog In a way; it represents a virtualization of the whole data center with the purpose to simplify the request and deployment of complex services. Other capabilities of an SDDC are:

- Automated infrastructure/service consumption
- Policy based services and applications deployment
- Changes to services can be made easily and instantly
- All infrastructure layers are automated (storage, network, and compute)
- No human intervention is needed for infrastructure/service deployment
- High level of standardization is used
- Business logic is for chargeback or showback functionality

All of the preceding points define an SDDC technically. But it is important to understand that an SDDC is considered to solve the business challenges of the organization running it. That means based on the actual business requirements, each SDDC will serve a different use case. Of course, there is the main setup you can adopt and roll out, but it is important to understand your organization's business challenges in order to prevent any planning or design shortcomings.

Also, to realize this functionality, SDDC needs a couple of software tools. These are designed to work together to deliver a seamless environment. The different parts can be seen like gears in a watch where each gear has an equally important role to make the clockwork function correctly.

It is important to remember this when building your SDDC, since missing on one part can make another very complex or even impossible afterward.

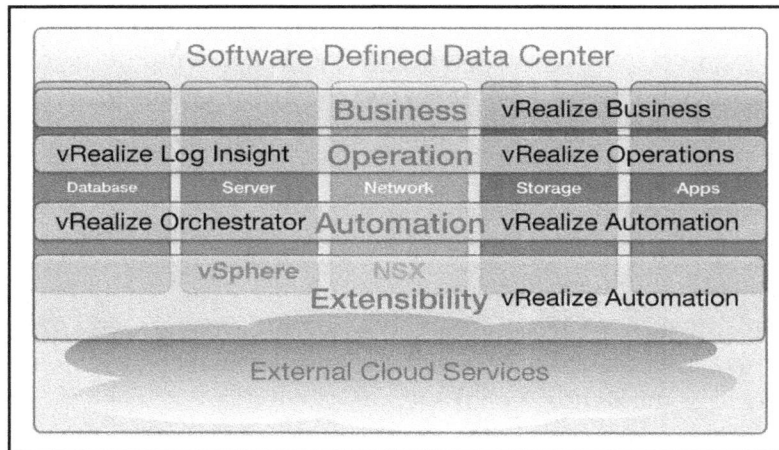

This is a list of VMware tools building an SDDC:

- vRealize Business for Cloud
- vRealize Operations Manager
- vRealize Log Insight
- vRealize Automation
- vRealize Orchestrator
- vRealize Automation Converged Blueprint
- vRealize Code Stream
- VMware NSX
- VMware vSphere

vRealize Business for Cloud is a chargeback/showback tool. It can be used to track the cost of services as well as the cost of a whole data center. Since the agility of an SDDC is much higher than for a traditional data center, it is important to track and show also the cost of adding new services. It is not only important from a financial perspective, it also serves as a control mechanism to ensure users are not deploying uncontrolled services and leaving them running even if they are not required anymore.

vRealize Operations Manager is serving basically two functionalities. One is to help with the troubleshooting and analytics of the whole SDDC platform. It has an analytics engine, which applies machine learning to the behavior of its monitored components. The another important function is capacity management. It is capable of providing what-if analysis and informs about possible shortcomings of resources way before they occur. These functionalities also use the machine learning algorithms and get more accurate over time. This becomes very important in a dynamic environment where on-demand provisioning is granted.

vRealize Log Insight is a unified log management. It offers rich functionality and can search and profile a lot of log files in seconds. It is recommended to use it as a universal log endpoint for all components in your SDDC. This includes all OSes as well as applications and also your underlying hardware. In an event of error, it is much simpler to have a central log management which is easily searchable and delivers an outcome in seconds.

vRealize Automation (**vRA**) is the base automation tool. It is providing the cloud portal to interact with your SDDC. The portal it provides offers the business logic such as service catalogs, service requests, approvals, and application life cycles. However, it relies strongly on vRealize Orchestrator for its technical automation part. vRA can also tap into external clouds to extend the internal data center. Extending an SDDC is mostly referred to as *hybrid cloud*. There are a couple of supported cloud offerings vRA can manage.

vRealize Orchestrator (**vRO**) is providing the workflow engine and the technical automation part of the SDDC. It is literally the orchestrator of your new data center. vRO can be easily bound together with vRA to form a very powerful automation suite, where anything with an **application programming interface** (**API**) can be integrated. Also, it is required to integrate third-party solutions into your deployment workflows, such as **configuration management database** (**CMDB**), **IP address management** (**IPAM**), or ticketing systems via **IT service management** (**ITSM**).

vRealize Automation Converged Blueprint was formally known as **vRealize Automation Application Services** and is an add-on functionality to vRA, which takes care of application installations. It can be used with pre-existing scripts (like Windows PowerShell or Bash on Linux), but also with variables received from vRA. This makes it very powerful when it comes to on-demand application installations. This tool can also make use of vRO to provide even better capabilities for complex application installations.

vRealize Code Stream is an addition to vRA and serves specific use cases in the DevOps area of the SDDC. It can be used with various development frameworks such as Jenkins. Also it can be used as a tool for developers to build and operate their own software test, QA and deployment environment. Not only can the developer build these separate stages, the migration from one stage into another can also be fully automated by scripts. This makes it a very powerful tool when it comes to stage and deploy modern and traditional applications within the SDDC.

VMware NSX is the network virtualization component. Given the complexity some applications/services might introduce, NSX will provide a good and profound solution to help solving it. The challenges include:

- Dynamic network creation
- Microsegmentation
- Advanced security
- Network function virtualization

VMware vSphere is mostly the base infrastructure and used as the hypervisor for server virtualization. You are probably familiar with vSphere and its functionalities. However, since the SDDC is introducing a change to you data center architecture, it is recommended to revisit some of the vSphere functionalities and configurations. By using the full potential of vSphere it is possible to save effort when it comes to automation aspects as well as the service/application deployment part of the SDDC.

This represents your toolbox required to build the platform for an automated data center. All of them will bring tremendous value and possibilities, but they also will introduce change. It is important that this change needs to be addressed and is a part of the overall SDDC design and installation effort. Embrace the change.

The implementation journey

While a big part of this book focuses on building and configuring the SDDC, it is important to mention that there are also non-technical aspects to consider. Creating a new way of operating and running your data center will always involve people. It is important to also briefly touch this part of the SDDC. Basically, there are three major players when it comes to a fundamental change in any data center, as shown in the following image:

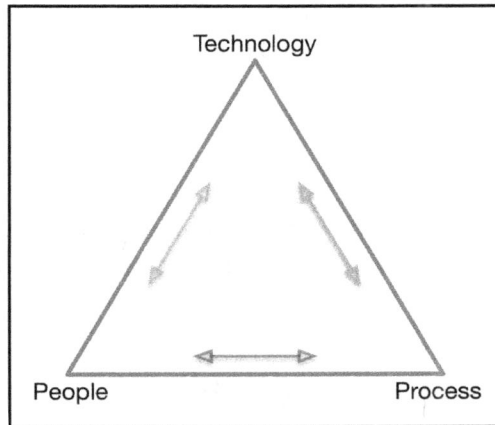

Basically, there are three major topics relevant for every successful SDDC deployment. Same as for the tools principle, these three disciplines need to work together in order to enable the change and make sure that all benefits can be fully leveraged.

These three categories are:

- People
- Process
- Technology

The process category

Data center processes are as established and settled as IT itself. Beginning with the first operator tasks like changing tapes or starting procedures up to highly sophisticated processes to ensure that the service deployment and management is working as expected they have already come a long way. However, some of these processes might not be fit for purpose anymore, once automation is applied to a data center. To build an SDDC it is very important to revisit data center processes and adapt them to work with the new automation tasks. The tools will offer integration points into processes, but it is equally important to remove bottlenecks for the processes as well. However, keep in mind that if you automate a bad process, the process will still be bad, but fully automated. So it is also necessary to revisit those processes so that they can become slim and effective as well.

Remember Tom, the data center manager. He has successfully identified that they need an SDDC to fulfill the business requirements and also did a use case to IT capabilities mapping. While this mapping is mainly talking about what the IT needs to deliver technically, it will also imply that the current IT processes need to adapt to this new delivery model.

The process change example in Tom's organization

If the compute department works on a service involving OS deployment, they need to fill out an Excel sheet with IP addresses and server names and send it to the networking department. The network admins will ensure that there is no double booking by reserving the IP address and approve the requested hostname. After successfully proving the uniqueness of this data, name and IP get added to the organization's DNS server.

The manual part of this process is no longer feasible once the data center enters the automation era, imagine that every time somebody orders a service involving a VM/OS deploy, the network department gets an e-mail containing the Excel with the IP and hostname combination. The whole process will have to stop until this step is manually finished.

To overcome this, the process has to be changed to use an automated solution for IPAM. The new process has to track IP and hostnames programmatically to ensure there is no duplication within the entire data center. Also, after successfully checking the uniqueness of the data, it has to be added to the **Domain Name System** (**DNS**).

While this is a simple example of one small process, normally there is a large number of processes involved which need to be reviewed for a fully automated data center. This is a very important task and should not be underestimated since it can be a differentiator for success or failure of an SDDC.

Think about all other processes in place, which are used to control the deploy/enable/install mechanics in your data center. Here is a small example list of questions to ask regarding established processes:

- What is our current IPAM/DNS process?
- Do we need to consider a CMDB integration?
- What is our current ticketing process? (ITSM)
- What is our process to get resources from the network, storage, and compute?
- What OS/VM deployment process is currently in place?
- What is our process to deploy an application (handovers, steps, or departments involved)?
- What does our current approval process look like?
    - Do we need a technical approval to deliver a service?
    - Do we need a business approval to deliver a service?
- What integration process do we have for a service/application deployment?
    - DNS, **Active Directory (AD)**, **Dynamic Host Configuration Protocol (DHCP)**, routing, **Information Technology Infrastructure Library (ITIL)**, and so on

Now for the approval question, normally these are an exception for the automation part since approvals are meant to be manual in the first place (either technical or business). If all the other answers to this example questions involve human interaction as well, consider to changing these processes to be fully automated by the SDDC.

Since human intervention creates waiting times, it has to be avoided during service deployments in any automated data center. Think of it as the robotic construction bands today's car manufacturers are using. The processes they have implemented, developed over ages of experience, are all designed to stop the band only in case of an emergency.

The same comes true for the SDDC; try to enable the automated deployment through your processes, stop the automation only in case of an emergency.

Identifying processes is the simple part, changing them is the tricky part. However, keep in mind that this is an all-new model of IT delivery, therefore there is no golden way of doing it. Once you have committed to change those processes, keep monitoring if they truly fulfill their requirement.

This leads to another process principle in the SDDC: **Continual Service Improvement (CSI)**. Revisit what you have changed from time to time and make sure that those processes are still working as expected, if they don't, change them again.

The people category

Since every data center is run by people, it is important to also consider that a change of technology will also impact those people. There are some claims that an SDDC can be run with only half of the staff or save a couple of employees since all is automated.

The truth is, an SDDC will transform IT roles in a data center. This means that some classic roles might vanish, while others will be added by this change.

It is unrealistic to say that you can run an automated data center with half the staff than before. But it is realistic to say that your staff can concentrate on innovation and development instead of working a 100% to keep the lights on. And this is the change an automated data center introduces. It opens up the possibilities to evolve into a more architecture and design focused role for current administrators.

The people example in Tom's organization

Currently, there are two admins in the compute department working for Tom. They are managing and maintaining the virtual environment, which is largely VMware vSphere. They are creating VMs manually, deploying an OS by a network install routine (which was a requirement for physical installs – so they kept the process) and then handing the ready VMs over to the next department to finish installing the service they are meant for.

Recently they have experienced a lot of demand for VMs and each of them configures 10 to 12 VMs per day. Given this, they cannot concentrate on other aspects of their job, like improving OS deployments or the handover process.

At a first look, it seems like the SDDC might replace these two employees since the tools will largely automate their work. But that is like saying a jackhammer will replace a construction worker.

Actually, their roles will shift to a more architectural aspect. They need to come up with a template for OS installations and an improvement how to further automate the deployment process. Also, they might need to add new services/parts to the SDDC in order to fulfill the business needs continuously.

So instead of creating all the VMs manually, they are now focused on designing a blueprint, able to be replicated as easy and efficient as possible.

While their tasks might have changed, their workforce is still important to operate and run the SDDC. However, given that they focus on design and architectural tasks now, they also have the time to introduce innovative functions and additions to the data center.

Keep in mind that an automated data center affects all departments in an IT organization. This means that also the tasks of the network and storage as well as application and database teams will change. In fact, in an SDDC it is quite impossible to still operate the departments disconnected from each other since a deployment will affect all of them.

This also implies that all of these departments will have admins shifting to higher-level functions in order to make the automation possible. In the industry, this shift is also often referred to as **Operational Transformation**. This basically means that not only the tools have to be in place, you also have to change the way how the staff operates the data center. In most cases organizations decide to form a so-called **center of excellence (CoE)** to administer and operate the automated data center.

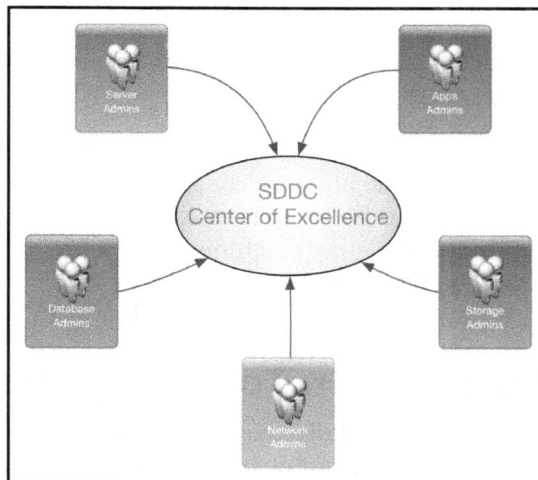

This virtual group of admins in a data center is very similar to project groups in traditional data centers. The difference is that these people should be permanently assigned to the CoE for an SDDC. Typically you might have one champion from each department taking part in this virtual team.

Each person acts as an expert and ambassador for their department. With this principle, it can be ensured that decisions and overlapping processes are well defined and ready to function across the departments. Also, as an ambassador, each participant should advertise the new functionalities within their department and enable their colleagues to fully support the new data center approach.

It is important to have good expertise in terms of technology as well as good communication skills for each member of the CoE.

The technology category

This is the third aspect of the triangle to successfully implement an SDDC in your environment. Often this is the part where people spend most of their attention, sometimes by ignoring one of the other two parts. However, it is important to note that all three topics need to be equally considered. Think of it like a three-legged chair, if one leg is missing it can never stand.

The term technology does not necessarily only refer to new tools required to deploy services. It also refers to already established technology, which has to be integrated with the automation toolset (often referred to as **third-party integration**). This might be your AD, DHCP server, e-mail system, and so on.

There might be technology which is not enabling or empowering the data center automation, so instead of only thinking about adding tools, there might also be tools to be removed or replaced. This is a normal IT lifecycle task and has been gone through many iterations already. Think of things like a fax machine or the telex; you might not use them anymore, they have been replaced by e-mail and messaging.

The technology example in Tom's organization

The team uses some tools to make their daily work easier when it comes to new service deployments. One of the tools is a little graphical user interface to quickly add content to AD. The admins use it to insert the hostname, **organizational unit** (**OU**) as well as creating the computer account with it. This was meant to save admin time since they don't have to open all the various menus in the AD configuration to accomplish these tasks.

With the automated service delivery, this has to be done programmatically. Once a new OS is deployed it has to be added to the AD including all requirements by the deployment tool. Since AD offers an API this can be easily automated and integrated into the deployment automation. Instead of painfully integrating the graphical tool, this is now done directly by interfacing the organization's AD, ultimately replacing the old graphical tool.

The automated deployment of a service across the entire data center requires a fair amount of communication. Not in a traditional way, but machine-to-machine communication leveraging programmable interfaces. Using such APIs is another important aspect of the applied data center technologies. Most of the today's data center tools, from backup all the way up to web servers, do come with APIs. The better the API is documented, the easier the integration into the automation tool. In some cases, you might need the vendors to support you with the integration of their tools.

If you have identified a tool in the data center, which does not offer any API or even **command-line interface** (**CLI**) option at all, try to find a way around this software or even consider replacing it with a new tool.

APIs are the equivalent of handovers in the manual world. The better the communication works between tools, the faster and easier the deployment will be completed. To coordinate and control all this communication, you will need far more than scripts to run. This is a task for an orchestrator, which can run all necessary integration workflows from a central point. This orchestrator will act as a conductor for a big orchestra. It will form the backbone of your SDDC.

Why are these three topics so important?

The technology aspect closes the triangle and brings the people and the processes parts together. If the processes are not altered to fit the new deployment methods, automation will be painful and complex to implement. If the deployment stops at some point, since the processes require manual intervention, the people will have to fill in this gap.

This means that they now have new roles, but also need to maintain some of their old tasks to keep the process running. By introducing such an unbalanced implementation of an automated data center, the workload for people can actually increase, while the service delivery times may not dramatically decrease. This may lead to an avoidance of the automated tasks since the manual intervention might be seen as faster by individual admins.

So it is very important to accept *all three* aspects as the main part of the SDDC implementation journey. They all need to be addressed equally and thoughtfully to unveil the benefits and improvements an automated data center has to offer.

However, keep in mind that this truly is a journey. An SDDC is not implemented in days but in months. Given this, also the implementation team in the data center has this time to adopt themselves and their process to this new way of delivering IT services. Also, all necessary departments and their lead need to be involved in this procedure.

An SDDC implementation is always a team effort.

Additional possibilities and opportunities

All the previews mentioned topics serve the sole goal to install and use the SDDC within your data center. However, once you have the SDDC running the real fun begins since you can start to introduce additional functionalities impossible for any traditional data center. Let's just briefly touch on some of the possibilities from an IT view.

The self-healing data center

This is a concept where the automatic deployment of services is connected to a monitoring system. Once the monitoring system detects that a service or environment may be facing constraints, it can automatically trigger an additional deployment for this service to increase the throughput.

While this is application dependent, for infrastructure services this can become quite handy. Think of ESXi host auto deployments if compute power is becoming a constraint, or data store deployments if disk space is running low. If this automation is acting too aggressive for your organization, it can be used with an approval function. Once the monitoring detects a shortcoming it will ask for approval to fix it with a deployment action.

Instead of getting an e-mail from your monitoring system that there is a constraint identified, you get an e-mail with the constraint and the resolving action. All you need to do is to approve the action.

The self-scaling data center

A similar principle is to use a capacity management tool to predict the growth of your environment. If it approaches a trigger, the system can automatically generate an order letter, containing all needed components to satisfy the growing capacity demands.

This can then be sent to finance or the purchasing management for approval and before you even get into any capacity constraints, the new gear might be available and ready to run. However, consider the regular turnaround time for ordering hardware, which might affect how far in the future you have to set the trigger for such functionality.

Both of this opportunities are more than just nice to haves, they enable your data center to be truly flexible and proactive. Due to the fact that an SDDC is offering a high amount of agility, it will also need some self-monitoring to stay flexible and usable and to fulfill unpredictable demand.

Summary

In this chapter, we discussed the main principles and declarations of an SDDC. It provided an overview of the opportunities and possibilities this new data center architecture provides. Also, it covered the changes which will be introduced by this new approach. Finally, it discussed the implementation journey and its involvement with people, processes, and technology.

In the next chapter, we will dive deep into identifying tasks and processes for automation within the data center. It will discuss in more detail what level of automation an SDDC requires and why standardization is very important for automated services deployment.

2
Identify Automation and Standardization Opportunities

"A journey of a thousand miles must begin with a single step."
— Lao Tzu

In this case, it is the journey of building the SDDC and fully automating your data center. Automation is the key word and it is very worthwhile to spend a fair amount of time to identify tasks for automation. The difficult part is automating the right things, efficiently and helpful for the daily operations of a modern data center.

Automation itself is not a new topic within a data center. There has always been automation present in form of scripts called by date controlled task managers. In the Linux world, it is usually *crond* calling command-line scripts. In Windows, this can be done using the task manager.

However, the SDDC automation approach is bigger than a local task based automation. It needs to introduce automation across many different tools, infrastructure, and departments. Therefore it needs to be controlled and managed by a central instance, which often is referred to as an **orchestrator**. Also, there needs to be one place where this automation is controlled and managed, otherwise it will become very difficult to implement changes and updates.

Before you start and automate each and every manual task in the data center it is important to think about what makes sense and what does not. Also, the partner of automation is standardization. Without standards, it will be impossible to automate, since workflows will have no sense for exceptions. It is important to define a path for certain tasks and then rigidly follow it. Therefore the important step is to make sure this path is valid and well working before automating it.

This chapter will cover the following topics:

- Automation principles and best practices
- Comparison of a script versus a workflow
- Identify processes to find a path for automation
- Identify your IT delivery framework
- Standardization of repeatable tasks
- Examples of applied standardization and automation approach

Automation principles

Automation is a topic, which seems quite simple and straightforward at a first glance. Mostly it is seen as simple as:

1. Find a repeatable task.
2. Create a script or program to replace the manual steps.
3. Add it to a trigger or scheduler for repeated execution.

While this is true for the actual scripting the first point is maybe the most important. There are many tasks in a modern data center, but not all are gold candidates for automation.

Day two automation

Automating daily manual tasks which are important to run and operate the data center and often performed by admins are so-called *day two operations*. Normally each data center has quite a few of them happening in the back to keep running. The very first step into the automation world should be to proper identify and define those tasks, as well as find a repeatable and clear way of executing them. Therefore you should think of a few criteria to successfully identify those tasks:

- Often repeated per work day
- Execution is straight and linear
- Does not require pattern recognition
- Do not relate to other tasks to finish
- Optional criteria: Follow a runbook to be executed

Based on these criteria there might be already a lot of tasks which can be automated to just reduce the amount of manual time to run a data center. In the SDDC, it is all about increasing the efficiency. Also, those tasks are often not the admins favorite and most probably there might be already scripts to support the admins with their monotone task worker role.

The 80:20 rule

This is an older principle which basically describes the amount of work versus the value add a task or project can bring.

Here are a few examples of typical 80:20 rule claims:

80 percent of work is needed to finalize the last 20 percent of a project.

80 percent of tasks can be easily automated but 20 percent are real difficult to tackle

This is a very important rule to follow, pick the right tasks for automation at the right time. As simple as that. Based on real SDDC project experience, a lot of implementations fail because this rule was completely ignored. It is important to pick the 80% of tasks which are easy to accomplish and there are multiple reasons for following this strategy.

First of all, it is a new IT project so everybody will watch closely what is happening. It is much better to have a lot of little successful things going on, than one big sophisticated project where the outcome may be unclear for a couple of months.

Second, it grows confidence in the team and with the manager that this whole SDDC project is the right thing to do. Succeeding in small automation chunks is translated to succeeding with the bigger complex orchestration tasks, which will come.

Third, it is important to gain all this experience with these smaller tasks since the most complex ones will definitely require every lesson learned from the former automation projects.

This leads to the second important principle when it comes to automation and any SDDC itself.

Think big, start small

This is as important as the 80:20 rule. Keep an eye on the big picture, but start small to get quick wins. As mentioned before, quick wins are important to make everybody believe in the project itself. Also, it helps to advertise the value of the overall SDDC in smaller chunks and success news. Those two principles play very well together when it comes to automation and should be kept in mind for all upcoming automation requests/tasks. For this to work properly, there are a few practices, which may help to ease the work on complex and big tasks:

- Break big tasks into smaller chunks
- Use the 80:20 rule (again) on this chunks
- Communicate each successful completion of a chunk as win
- Rebuild the big tasks by recombining the smaller chunks

However, cutting a big task into smaller pieces to automate the whole thing is only one aspect of this principle. It is also a metaphor for keeping the whole complexity of a data center in mind and identifies realistic and efficient ways to automate processes as well as increase the efficiency. Think big in terms of how many tasks are required to succeed in order to deploy a service into your data center. How many tasks are required to just add resources or even change a resource allocation to an existing service?

The efficiency bottleneck

Efficiency and bottlenecks are normally not two things which have too much in common. But when it comes to automation, these two can add up which normally has the side effect that it completely zeroes out any efficiency or time benefits. There are a few examples when this happens, a lot of these examples are because of communication issues or because of a lack of standardization.

There is a good chance that each department looks at their own tasks and tries to automate as much as possible to make them smoother and quicker. But this is actually quite difficult if the whole process is also dependent on other departments. So they might keep working on *their end of the process* to make it as efficient as possible.

There is one very prominent example of this *efficiency bottleneck*. It was used to introduce virtualization and was used a lot to show its greatness.

Create a server (VM) in 5 minutes instead of an hour!

Wow, you save nearly an hour by using virtualization and it takes just 5 minutes to create a new server. This is an improvement of 92.6%!

But how long does it take to deploy the whole service across all departments?

If the overall deployment time of a service might take up to 90 work days, the improvement on the server installation is only 0.02% (rounded) of the overall process.

So it is important to know the scale of a task or process and then start improving it. There might be areas which are consuming a lot of time because of manual work, automating them might be adding more value to the overall time savings.

However, this does not mean that the time improvements due to automation (virtualization) are not important. It does only mean that they are a piece of the overall puzzle. The think big approach addresses the whole service delivery process, the start small step in the overall process might be to introduce virtualization to install a server in 5 minutes. But the big picture needs to be kept in mind to realize the whole process. However, automating the entire data center needs a solid basis and therefore a lot of these small steps are required to form the bigger process. The better these work on their own, the easier they can be handled by automation later on.

Bringing it all together

These four principles should help and guide everyone who is willing to introduce an SDDC and start automating their data center. They are relevant for the whole data center and all departments. A single player cannot accomplish this, all have to be aboard ready to revolutionize the way IT is delivered. In a typical SDDC project, it is important to start by identifying the scope first. The scope contains the main functionalities of the SDDC, which might also be translated to the most important automation functionalities an SDDC should deliver.

It contains at least one service or application and the complete rollout of this service. All tasks and necessary steps are documented and known by each party who is involved in the overall automation. The service has been chosen by applying the 80:20 rule, so it should be one which is easy enough to be accomplished in a reasonable amount of time (quick win). All steps between departments (process) are known and can be automated. Also, third-party integration is understood and can also be done by using workflows and automation principles.

Congratulations, you have successfully chosen the starting point for your SDDC!

Script or workflow

It is important to understand the differences between a workflow and a script. As mentioned earlier, scripts are well established in the IT and originally were created to complete smaller tasks faster than a human could. Typically, scripts provide a single scripting language like Bash scripts in UNIX or PowerShell scripts in Windows. They can also be used to address complex tasks calling other scripts introducing multiple layers of relations to successfully complete a task. By following this logic, it can get very confusing very soon.

These scripts have to have logic to wait for their subscripts to come back with status information (success/failure/idle). This status queries are not as simple as it sounds and sometimes requires an own script, just to take care of all the subscripts running. Also, they can't simply be stopped since they have no control over the subscripts running in the background.

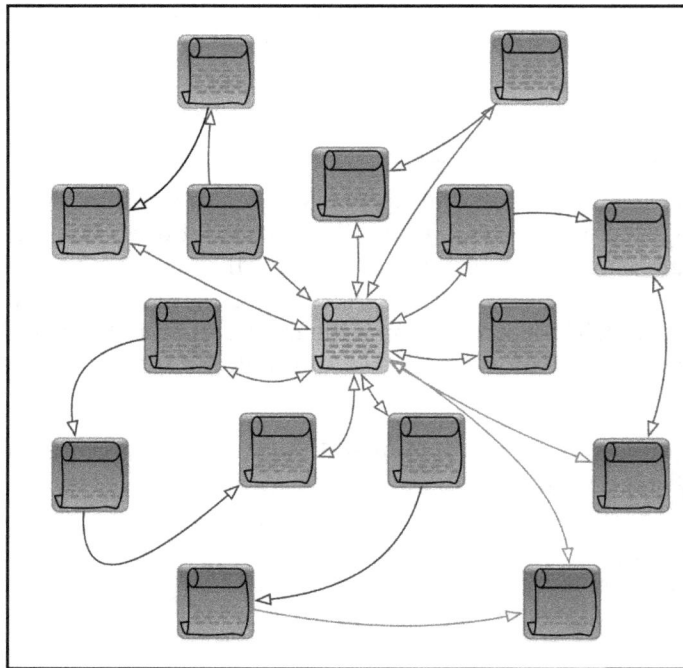

Often scripts are maintained by a single admin, who is aware of their logic and functions. The scripts can be run without the admin, but he might be required to do troubleshooting or to add additional features. It is best practice to have a central scripting host running all required scripts. But this might only be true for the solution/scripting language the script is using.

The Linux team might have a central Linux host, the Windows admins do it from a Windows system, the network admin may have their complete own integration and the storage admin has some runbook like instructions to configure a given storage array. Finally, the SAN admins might use some SSH combination to access their fiber channel switches and create/change the zoning once in a while.

All this might have worked perfectly in the past, but once you enter the SDDC era, these concepts cannot keep up with the massive scale. That does not mean that their logic and hard work is automatically lost. But there needs to be a central system which is calling and managing all automation takes over all required departments. This is what most software vendors call an orchestrator.

Typically, an orchestrator is running workflows in order to automate tasks. The orchestrator takes care of the scheduling and makes the workflows also *triggerable* if they need to run on demand. It can call a workflow from a workflow, but keep the relation and track to quickly show what is currently running. It keeps track of all the referenced workflows and their status and provides a framework to easily make the status of different workflows available to the overall workflow, without a complex logic to think of!

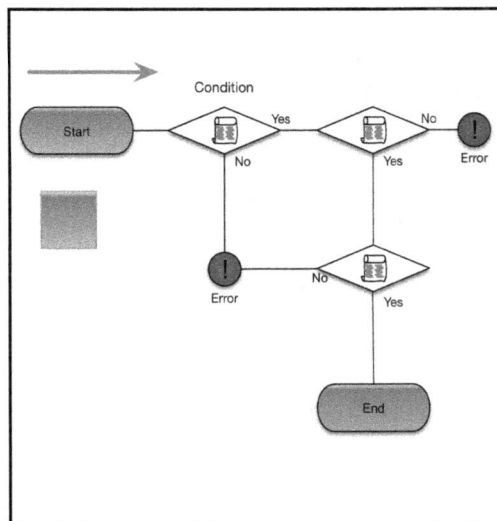

So the orchestrator's job is to keep track of its running workflow and their status. This enables some great functionality, which is only limited available for scripts. You can pause a workflow including its subworkflows. You can stop a workflow and automatically know what changes have been made already. You might even be able to roll back changes from a workflow. This provides a lot more flexibility than a script could. Also, if a workflow fails you could troubleshoot and run it from where it stopped. This provides great flexibility in terms of developing and quality checking automation.

Besides that, all your workflows stay in one place, being able to run end edit by multiple users. Normally an orchestrator also applies a versioning model in order to make sure that each workflow is using its most recent version including all its changes and added functions. Changing between versions is a simple mouse click and updates the entire workflow library.

Within a workflow, there is typically scripting elements responsible for calling certain automation function with target infrastructure. The brilliant thing about a workflow is, it is not limited to a single scripting language, it can call whatever is required at this step. The workflow can start by doing the REST call, continue to talk to vCenter and end by providing data via SQL into a database. That offer a very high level of flexibility, plus you can use existing scripts and calls. All you need to do is adapt it into the workflows by ensuring that data can be shared across these workflow steps.

Since this will build the backbone of your SDDC, it is important to create simple and smooth running workflows. There are a couple of best practices to follow when you create workflows:

- Pick a simple task to start with (80:20 rule)
- Keep the scripting within the workflow steps as short and simple as possible
- If a series of steps is used multiple times in a workflow, think of creating a subworkflow containing these steps
- Keep in mind that it will be easier to maintain to break complex workflows in smaller workflows to call
- For every substantial change, change the version of the workflow
- Use reasonable and understandable status messages for workflow steps
- Think of possible errors and implement the error handling in the workflow

To leverage all functionalities an orchestrator with workflows has to offer it is important to follow that rules. At the beginning, it might feel strange to have only 10 lines of code in a scripted element, but that quickly becomes normal and familiar when creating a workflow. If you are doing a lot of scripting already, this might possibly be the biggest change, try to prevent yourself from writing long and complex steps in a workflow.

An example workflow could look like:

1. Query a VMs associated data center via vSphere API.
2. Query a VMs associated cluster via vSphere API.
3. Compose the information into variables.
4. Create an SQL statement using these variables to inject into to a CMDB database.
5. Provide status message (success/failure).
6. End workflow.

Now each of this can be done with a single line of code. This is just a simple example of a possible ITIL automation functionality. With the mix of languages (vSphere API and SQL code) and the possibility to share variables across steps, it makes it quite easy to accomplish this task.

An orchestrator and workflows, in general, should make complex automation tasks easy to create, but keep in mind that it highly depends on the way the workflows are created. This is why you need to apply the automation principles to the workflows in order to fully leverage all workflow benefits.

Identifying processes and how to automate them

This is one of the main discussion points when it comes to an SDDC. The concept of automation across departments is dependent on the pre-existing processes. The first step of automating them is actually identifying all their stages and requirements. This might be a tricky task but is very important for applying all SDDC benefits later on.

How would a perfect process look like to be automated?

- Clear defined steps and stations
- The execution of the process is preapproved; no approvals required during runtime
- Well defined requirements and outcomes for each station

- All used tools are programmable (API, scripts, CLI, and so on)
- All endpoints/tools can be reached from a single location
- All (yet) manual tasks can be automated using workflows

Again, this reflects the description of a perfect candidate. There might be a chance that you have processes, which fulfill only parts of these criteria. If that is the case, it is very important to be able to change the part of the process, which does not fit into the automation criteria. This happens from time to time since processes are less often changed than tools. Also, some practices in a process might be proven but haven't been revisited for a long time and can be therefore outdated.

Here are examples where it becomes quite difficult to automate a process because of such steps:

Manual data entry: Some organizations manage their internal IT assets by Excel. Sometimes they even track IP addresses and host names using this versatile tool. The big problem with Excel is, it is not programmable from the outside.

> **Recommended change**: If the process requires manual data entry steps, it is highly recommended to rethink these steps. By having all process steps automated, the need for manual data entry might already be irrelevant. Since an orchestrator takes care of all data entries it can also provide the process outcome to any programmable interface.

No programmable tools: There are tools in the data center, which may lack an API or simply have no documentation for their API. However, they might be used for important steps within a process. Some of these may be used as CMDB and others may be simply used to track the progress and the current stage of the process.

Recommended change: First revisit the purpose of the tool and prove that it is still valid and required to complete the process. If this is the case try to find a way to ingest or extract data from the tool even without an API. Think out of the box and explore all feasible possibilities for these tools. If a database is used, maybe SQL commands can be leveraged. Some tools support ingestion of data via XML files. Others may have an import or export functionality for CSV or feature a command line to be used.

If there is absolutely no way to program the tool without a GUI, it might be necessary to either change the process to work without this tool or replace the tool with one which features an API or any other programmable interface (file import).

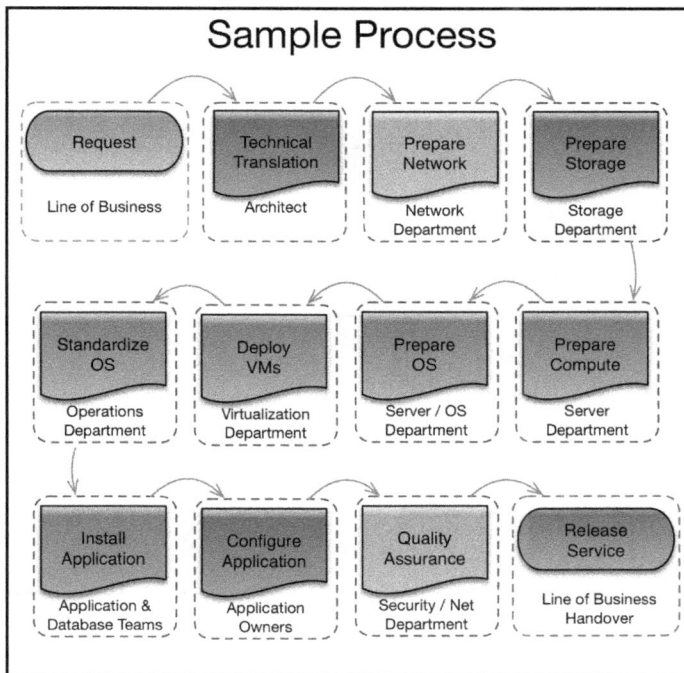

Sample Process

Request	Technical Translation	Prepare Network	Prepare Storage
Line of Business	Architect	Network Department	Storage Department
Standardize OS	Deploy VMs	Prepare OS	Prepare Compute
Operations Department	Virtualization Department	Server / OS Department	Server Department
Install Application	Configure Application	Quality Assurance	Release Service
Application & Database Teams	Application Owners	Security / Net Department	Line of Business Handover

Once you have identified all steps of the process and all tools and actions required, it is ready for the automation. Try not to create a giant workflow to cover everything, break it in smaller workflows. Maybe one workflow for each tool to integrate, or one for each major process task or step. By using this method it will be quite easy to replace a tool or change a step in the process, simply change the corresponding workflow and let the *Uber* workflow call it.

This is also called **modular approach** and should be applied to keep the workflow automation simple and maintainable.

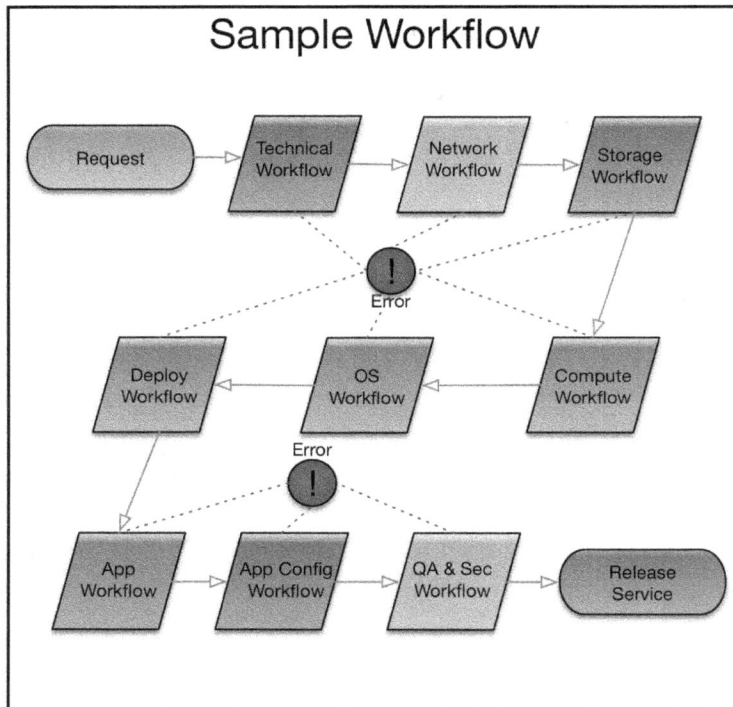

By applying the modular approach, you also ensure that you can accomplish the automation of even complex processes. It is basically the use of all best practices discussed earlier for automation. This approach will also grant that you can communicate every small success as a big win, every time one step of the overall process runs as a workflow, that is a win. Do not forget to communicate it, since good news will help the entire IT to successfully finish an SDDC project.

IT delivery frameworks

Each IT has its own **delivery frameworks**. Even if it is a tiny company, there are some tools and actions which need to be performed to successfully deliver any application or service. The term framework means basically that it is a predefined routine or set of tools which should make its delivery easier. These normally consist out of installation tools used for application delivery, deployment tools for OSes and configuration tools for infrastructure. All together they form your delivery framework.

IT is important to understand what function each tool is covering. Sometimes there are tools which already cover a part of a process or an entire process. Then it is important to understand how to interact with those tools and at which point the automation has to handover the task to this tools. A very popular example is ticket managing systems. In bigger companies, they are typically part of the delivery process, even though they serve a rather passive role. However, they do cover normally quite a big part of other processes such as change management, release planning as well as tracking service deployments.

There is a misbelieve that ITIL plays no role in a modern SDDC, that is actually not true. ITIL is still valid, with the difference that the integration can now be done completely automatically. This guarantees its completeness over manual data entry and also helps to relieve some tedious tasks from the administrators. This is a typical example of an IT delivery process taking care of all the technical orchestration, handing over all necessary information to the ticketing system and then, if it got a successful return, continuing the task and closing the ticket.

> If this is already in place, respect the ticketing and change process and concentrate on the technical handover within your automation workflows.

The same comes true for CMDB. This is a typical ITIL requirement and contains and maintains all software and hardware configurations within a data center. It is meant to hold this information in order to keep track of changes as well as knowing what is deployed and running in the data center. You might not find this in smaller data centers, but in bigger ones, with thousands of servers and hundreds of applications, it might become necessary to maintain a CMDB. To keep theses CMDBs accurate is often one of the less popular things to do for an administrator. Sometimes they are already using data out of the ticketing system. Sometimes a complete configuration dataset has to be provided plus the ticketing system is required to file a change/support/deployment request.

However, with the power of automation, also this data entry can be taken care of by the technical deployment workflow. All we need is to know which data is required to go into the CMDB and if we can use an API to simply hand the data over. Also, each time somebody requests a change we can update the record to keep the data accurate. Finally, once a user has decided to remove a workload/application, automation can eventually mark the record in the CMDB as *application deleted*.

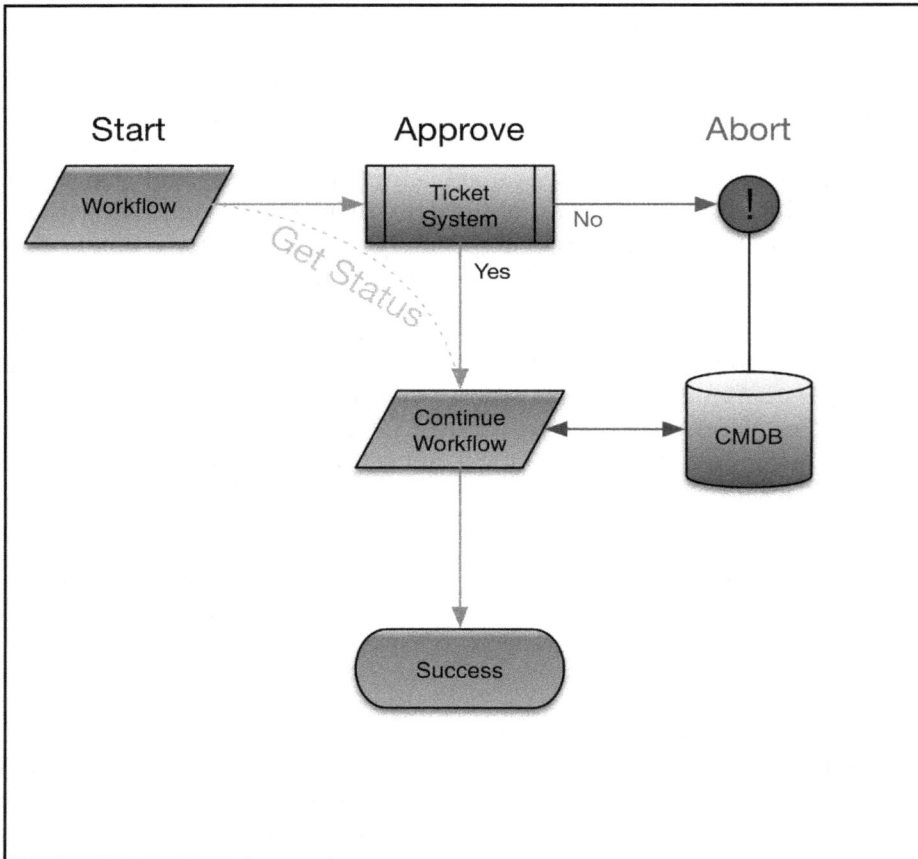

These are steps of the IT delivery framework which typically form a bigger picture. Since all departments have to add their data to a CMDB or use the ticket management system. This means that automation within the data center makes the job of the teams easier to keep this kind of information accurate. But it is important to know when and where these tools are used and what data goes into them.

What if no CMDB or ticket management is in place

On the other hand, if your organization is not using a CMDB or ticket management system yet, the good news is that a lot of the SDDC functions and features are quite similar to these frameworks. Therefore, you do not need to specifically introduce these concepts all together with the SDDC. You could simply declare the way the SDDC management handles deployments as your change and configuration management standards. Since introducing a proper ticket management system might be as complex as introducing an SDDC, you might consider using the SDDCs options first and then decide if it is fulfilling your requirements. However, there are some regulations which might still require a CMDB or ticket system, to ensure compliance standards.

All this is part of your framework, by identifying your internal data center processes you might also identify how your delivery framework looks like. Always keep in mind that this is relevant for all involved parties and departments. It does not make sense to have it fully documented for the server department, but the processes and tools for any other departments are mostly unknown. Always keep in mind that the SDDC will touch each and every part of your data center, even if it might have a big share in the server unit, it can and will not work without the participation of every other department in the data center.

Achieving standardization

This is maybe the big topic when it comes to the SDDC or automation itself. For scripts and workflows, it is paramount to adhere to a standard in doing things. If all deployments consist of some exceptions it might be impossible to use automation to deploy. Normally there are a few tasks in a data center, which have already been standardized. There are a few factors, which point out that something is already following a standard:

- There is a form to request the service
- The service is deployed according to preset choices
- These choices will modular fit most requirements
- There might be runbooks to create any config/deploy any service
- There is a catalog of services

Typically any of these things describe the standardized setup of a service. Standardization basically stands for easily repeatable actions, based on predefined data entry forms. This is why standardization goes hand in hand with automation. If every deployment is different and every OS is custom, if every network setting is unique and every storage requirement is different, it will be impossible to automate it in a straight forward manner. Workflows are perfect for applying standards, but only limited usable for exceptions and customized installations.

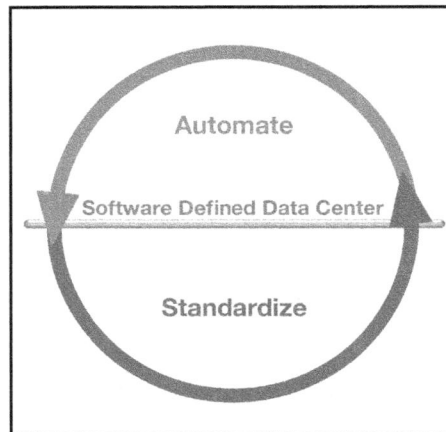

Therefore, one of the most important things to do before creating an SDDC is ensuring standardization is in place. The good news is a lot of organizations already have some kind standardization in place.

There are areas where standardization is transparent for the end user:

- In the storage team, the pool size, **logical device** (**LDEV**) size or **logical unit number** (**LUN**) size can be set in chunks (for example, 100 GB steps)
- In the network team, IPs/networks may be requested at a pool or range level (for example, 20 addresses)
- In the server department, VMs can be requested using predefined compute and memory value
- 1 vCPU with 2 GB RAM, 2 vCPU with 4 GB RAM, and so on

However, there are standards, which might influence the user more than the infrastructure standards. Mostly, those are OS to application combinations. Or only certain OS types are supported for deployment. Typically, organizations try to keep the zoo of OSes and applications as small as possible and as big as necessary. Therefore, mostly they support some versions of Windows as well as some specific Linux distributions.

These are often set by the IT group itself. Just keep in mind that for every OS/application you want to support, you need to have somebody who can help you troubleshoot and fix problems which may arise on these platforms.

Deployment standards

Also, sometimes standardization can lead to the introduction of so-called **runbooks**, which are needed to install an OS or any application on top of it. These runbooks need to be as up to date as possible to stay relevant. So somebody needs to prove all the steps over and over and update them as the OSes/applications develop. This often is a full-time job and consumes a lot of time. Therefore, some IT departments try to keep this at a low profile, to prevent their staff from constantly updating those runbooks.

A runbook typically is a detailed step by step guide which is easy to follow by an administrator. Normally, they are written in a way that even a new employee can follow their instructions. Bigger organizations can have multiple runbooks for tens or hundreds of use cases. However, since this is a *read and copy* exercise, this work might be quite error prone for administrators who are doing it for the first couple of times.

The good news is that with automation, this is taken over by the orchestrator running the workflows. The workflow replaces the runbook and is way quicker than a human in completing the steps. Also, it has no issues in doing the same steps over and over again. This is why standardization and automation go so well together.

Instead of maintaining the runbooks, administrators or service designers now keep the workflow up to date.

By following the modular approach, this should be quite simple to do. Once the workflow is updated it can be run to recheck its functionality. No one will have to sit through all the steps and copy on the screen what's written in a book.

Before automation, standardization was limiting your service portfolio but enhancing your efficiency. With the SDDC you can actually broaden your portfolio while still keeping standardization with the power of automation. Indeed, you will be able to accomplish more tasks than before, with enhanced efficiency and diversity.

Organization automation examples

Many things have been covered already, but this section should give an overview what to think about when it comes to automation and standardization. Also, it will highlight how actual projects dealt with challenges and requirements which were discovered during the workflow creation.

Often, not all requirements for a deployment or delivery task in a data center may be known by all administrators. This is because traditionally, everyone is focusing on their own tasks until they hand it over to another group or department.

Simple VM deployment

The mission sounds quite simple: Deploy a VM in a data center out of a portal. The server administrator in of us might think: Easy, just create a template for the OS, add some customization (hostname, IP) and that's it.

Indeed, the first step was to create a template containing the OS. But there is also a requirement to use the most recent version of the OS for each deployment.

> The first side task was to create a workflow which ensures that the OS template is as up to date as possible. This was necessary to prevent the installation of a huge amount of patches, which may slow down the overall setup process.

Once this has been created, the organization decided that it is best to have multiple storage performance classes. This was already introduced for the manual installation of VMs and must be available for automated installations as well.

> The second side task was to use a workflow to identify the right data store to put the VM onto, based on the selected performance class. Also, It needed to be ensured that the workflow is not simply filling up one data store but distributing the VMs across all possible matches.

After that has been accomplished, the journey continued. This organization has an IP address management tool in place. These tools typically reserve IP addresses out of a pool and also work as an organization-wide DNS server.

> The third side task was that the IP address request has to be forwarded to that tool to enter the VMs hostname and create the proper reservation record. Also, this workflow has to remove IP address and hostname reservation, once the VM is deleted.

After this was successfully accomplished, the OS has to be brought into the right AD **organizational unit** (**OU**). The OU is actually dependent on the user/department who requested the VM, also the user should be entitled to the VM to actually log in to the OS with its AD account. It was also requested that the user can specify a group or other users who should have access to the VM.

> The fourth side task was to get all the information either automatically or by a form from a requestor to put the VM in the right OU. Then create a workflow which adds a computer account in this OU and entitles the requestor as well as additional users/groups to be able to log into the new OS. Also, this workflow needs to remove the computer account and the user entitlements, once the VM is eventually deleted.

Furthermore, the organization is using a CMDB to track all deployments and changes. For each and every new created server there has to be a specific dataset entered into the CMDB.

> The fifth side task was to capture all required CMDB data like the CPU, RAM, and disk of the VM. But also on which cluster it is deployed and in which data center it is going to reside. Again, all this was done in a workflow which also has the possibility to add *deleted* to the created dataset once the VM gets removed.

There where multiple sites and the requestor should have the chance to actually chose in which data center the VM will be deployed. Also, they should have the chance to choose a disaster recovery option for the VM. Also, a backup retention policy should be offered to the requestor.

> The sixth side task was to identify and offer the different data centers. Also, a workflow was created to instantiate replication for select VMs (if the requestor chooses this option).
> Backup integration was done using an XML file interface to the backup system, telling it about the retention policy (a preset standard policy) and the VM name and data center location. The XML file is dynamically created by the workflow.
> Again, everything to be removed once the VM gets deleted.

Once all these workflows have been completed the VM deployment can actually run. This was mainly requirements from the compute department and the network requirements were rather easy (predefined VLAN to deploy into).

However, it may illustrate how quickly simple looking tasks can get complicated.

So the typical things to ask when it comes VM deployments are:

- Are there any special AD requirements?
- Are there any performance options (SLAs, classes) required?
- Is there any IPAM or DHCP reservation system in use?
- Is multi data center deployment required?
- Is replication of the VM required?
- Is backup integration a requirement?
- Does the retention policy for backup needs to be selectable?
- Does the deployment data need to go into a CMDB?

Additional things to think of:

- Virus scanner integration
- Is workflow based backup restore a requirement?
- Possible network and routing configuration requirements
- OS update and template requirements
- Security requirements (hardening, creating/obtaining certificates, and so on)
- Integration of a monitoring tool
- Any possible third-party management tool integration?

There are many more things which might come up during this kind of deployments. Remember this is still a VM with an OS only installation. Once an application is added to this, or multi VM / service installations the whole requirements get even more complex.

However, this example should illustrate that there is often more behind a simple sounding task then one might expect. Be open to asking these type of questions upfront even if the answer might be unknown for the moment. The better the preparation is for such tasks, the easier it is to put everything in an orchestration framework.

The hybrid cloud deployment

This is another good example of an organization, looking to deploy one of their key applications into a hybrid cloud. Typically, the term **hybrid cloud** describes a cloud setup where an organization's data center is virtually connected with a cloud provider. Therefore, services can simply either be deployed in the local data center, or in the hybrid cloud environment.

The goal was to have the key application running in the hybrid cloud with all necessary supporting systems. After a workshop to identify the applications requirement, it turned out that it consists out of a couple of application servers, some web frontend servers, two database servers, and some additional helper servers for maintenance and orchestration of the application. It was a little more than 15 VMs all with different functions and OSes (Linux and Windows) but all form together one application.

> An application does not typically only consist out of one VM with an OS and some software installed. Often VMs and software are only components of bigger applications. A good example for that is company web pages. These typically consist out of web servers, application servers as well as database servers for the content. There are many applications which require multiple servers to function in a data center.

In order to bring all these VMs to the hybrid cloud, it has been decided to create a giant virtual container. This container is basically offering a virtual network infrastructure (AppServ, DB, and web server are all required to run in different VLANs). This application container is automatically created (per API/workflow) to be tested in the local data center. Once all this is successful, the hybrid deployment shall be tested.

Multiple weeks were spent on finalizing the container creation and deployment automation. This is already a quite complex and high sophisticated use case, but it is doable through automation and workflow orchestration.

Eventually, everything was ready and could be automatically deployed in the local data center. So the decision was made to put the whole deployment into the hybrid cloud.

Since this application is very much self-contained, the hybrid cloud does not have to have a VPN tunnel into the local data center. This was also rejected due to security reasons.

The deployment went fine and after a couple of hours, the application with all its 15 VMs and database was running on the hybrid cloud.

However, unfortunately, it was not usable. No admin could log into the VMs, all accounts and users appeared to be locked. Also, the application servers could not communicate with the database servers.

The analysis of the hybrid cloud deployment

A lot of work was put into the automation and container creation of this application. The approach was fine from a technical point of view. But the problem was that the application team was not involved with all this work. It was a 100% infrastructure project. Once the application was deployed, the VMs tried to reach an AD server to verify the user accounts. Since there was no AD server deployed in the hybrid cloud, nobody could log onto the VMs.

Also, there was an external service bus used to instantiate the communication from the application servers to the database systems. This service bus was not present as well in the hybrid cloud.

So if it comes to hybrid cloud deployments, it is important to think about every aspect of it. Keep in mind that if there is no direct connection into your data center, there might be no AD or DNS or DHCP server available for the deployed VMs.

Keep the big picture in mind and ask questions which might be obvious but knowing is always better than guessing.

The better approach

Hybrid cloud is a good way in order to provide resources for bursting or for capacity which is required once for an application. There are good examples that this concept makes a lot of sense and also that it can work flawlessly.

In order to ensure that this works, be aware of the requirements of these applications and provide a valid solution for them. An example could be to clone some AD server to run in the cloud, or to have a very solid *site-to-site* VPN line in place, which serves the advanced needs of the application.

There are many global organizations successfully leveraging the benefits of such an approach. Besides the performance or capacity reasons, some do so in order to have the service located closer to the end user.

Imagine that an airline provides a map service to their pilots. This service might include the maps and directives for every airport they operate. Wouldn't it be great if the data can be derived from a local source instead of always traveling the entire world to get to these pilots? This is a perfect use case for hybrid cloud and makes the application even better and more responsive for the end users.

When it comes to hybrid cloud, think out of the box to add capabilities to your application, which has not been possible in a traditional data center!

Summary

In this chapter, we discussed the main principles of automation and standardization. Also, the differences of workflows and scripts have been highlighted. Finally, two examples have been described to give a better insight how automation and standardization might be applied in a real-world use case.

In the next chapter, we discuss the foundation of the SDDC which is built on VMware vSphere. It will be much more technical and provide a detailed description of useful vSphere features and functionalities fit for the SDDC. We will also recap some vSphere automation basics round workload deployment, storage management, and management best practices.

3
VMware vSphere: The SDDC Foundation

VMware vSphere is the foundation for the SDDC. It is the hypervisor to build the rest of the automation and management functionally upon. Consider it as the basement for your data center automation. vSphere is often seen as the *given infrastructure provider*. Like a real basement, it is sometimes not seen as the important bit of a cloud or SDDC environment.

However, this does not mean that it is unimportant, as every support or basement installation; if you make mistakes here, your whole SDDC might be weak and loose. Also, vSphere is offering automation, which is built already into the hypervisor. While some of these functions might be not as important for traditional environments, they are a huge time saver for an SDDC. Every vSphere functionality, which is offering time and effort savings should be strongly considered for the SDDC.

If you haven't already considered an Enterprise Plus license for vSphere, you may do so now. **Enterprise Plus** is the most feature-rich licensing option for VMware vSphere supporting a lot of helping and sometimes necessary features for an SDDC. If you want to see a full overview of features and functionalities please visit http://www.vmware.com/licensing.

Keep in mind that each build in functionality which eases the operation of your SDDC saves you from creating workflows to accomplish exactly this. Automation is important, but you do not need to reinvent the wheel and program everything yourself. The principle we are applying here is: *Keep it as simple as possible*.

This chapter will touch on the following topics:

- vSphere basics in an SDDC
- vSphere configuration considerations for the SDDC
- Availability and resiliency
- Recap of recent SDDC relevant vSphere features
- Best practices and good practices to configure your vSphere environment for the SDDC
- Build in vSphere automation capabilities

Basics and recommendations for vSphere in the SDDC

This chapter is not discussing general vSphere basics, the title might be slightly misleading. You should already have a profound vSphere knowledge and know your way around in vCenter server. Also, you should know how to setup and configure an ESXi server. However, in a traditional vSphere environment, some features might not be as important and therefore they might not be considered to be used. This chapter is to touch some basic features, which will help you in efficiently setting up your SDDC on top of vSphere.

All these recommendations are based on good practice, but they will not replace the need for a design of the vSphere infrastructure to meet your SDDCs requirements. The vSphere design is a very important point and should not be underestimated.

Besides that, here are some vSphere prerequisites for a successful SDDC installation:

- Check the interoperability matrix for all used VMware products
- Ensure the most recent version of vSphere and vCenter is used
- Update automation for vSphere (update manager) is in place
- Fully working DNS; all components can be registered and resolved
- Access from vCenter and SDDC components is possible into the ESXi management LAN
- vSphere certificates are all valid and not self-signed (including PSC)
- **Network Time Protocol (NTP)** service is available and used by all ESXi hosts
- vCenter role-based access is prepared accordingly (service user, read-only roles, and so on)

By following these recommendations, you will save time and effort within an SDDC implementation. A lot of them have been designed and introduced by VMware with the SDDC idea in the background. Every function, which saves you from designing and creating it from scratch for the SDDC, should be used.

Distributed Resource Scheduler

Distributed Resource Scheduler (DRS) is one of the oldest features of VMware vSphere and has received a long list of updates and enhancements since its introduction. Its job is to keep the cluster balanced in terms of resource usage. This does not mean to keep the same amount of VMs on each host, this is a popular misbelief. It will continuously monitor VM resource demands like CPU and memory and decide which host might be perfect to fulfill those. It is an automation routine to manage the VM distribution within a cluster and also to apply *self-healing* vMotion once the resource demand can't be met anymore. DRS is being configured in the vSphere cluster settings and has a couple of different modes it can support:

- Grade of automation
- Level of aggressiveness
- VM groups
- Host groups
- Affinity rules
- Anti-affinity rules
- Host affinity rules
- Resource pools

Mostly, DRS gets enabled and sometimes there are a couple of affinity rules configured. Most organizations apply the defaults and let DRS do Its thing. Some set the automation level to manual, in that case, an administrator can decide what happens to a VM to be migrated. DRS will ask if the VM can be moved, and more important, also where to power on new VMs.

One of the other major things DRS takes care of is **admission control**.

This means that, based on the utilization and resource availability, DRS decides where to start/deploy a VM. This is a very important feature if you want to deploy VMs automatically.

It is highly recommended to set DRS to **Fully Automated** in any SDDC environment. This enables vSphere to choose the right host for deploying or powering on VMs. The aggressiveness might be set to mediocre, dependent on your average workload profile. If you ignore this setting, your cluster or hosts might be unbalanced which can lead to severe performance issues!

The affinity setting is a more complex topic. Any SDDC will also work without setting affinity to VMs or host groups. However, there might be applications where you require affinity groups or VM anti-affinity. Just to recap what affinity/anti-affinity means:

- A VM should run on the same host as another: *VM = VM affinity*
- A VM should not in on the same host as another: *VM != VM anti-affinity*
- A VM should run on a specified group of hosts in the cluster: *VM = host group affinity*
- A VM should not run on a specified group of host in the cluster: *VM != host group anti-affinity*

The `ForceAffinePowerOn` setting in advanced DRS should also be reviewed. This switch can control what should happen to VM-to-VM affinity if there is a resource issue. If it is set to 0, it means the VMs can still power on without respecting the affinity rule. If it is set to 1, the VMs cannot be powered on if the affinity rule cannot be respected. However, this setting has nothing to do with VM-to-VM anti-affinity!

For host groups, there is a difference between *should run* and *must run*. Be very careful if you choose the latter one. It means the VM cannot violate its host group affinity policy, even if it's original host group has an outage!

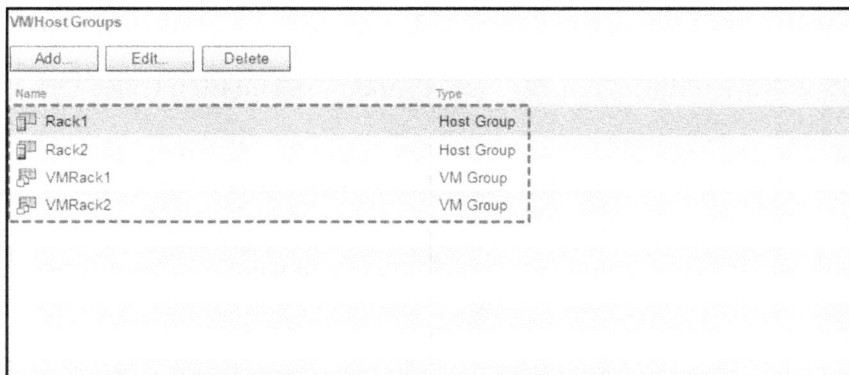

Affinity rules can also affect vSphere **High Availability** (**HA**), be very careful if you use **Must run on hosts in group** settings, remember to configure HA accordingly and allow it to violate the affinity rules in case of an HA event, otherwise these VMs will not be restarted on surviving hosts if they are outside of their configured host group.

Host groups are useful if you have a cross-rack or cross server room or even metro cluster in use. They can be used to ensure that not all VMs end up in one place. They can easily be integrated into vRealize Automation, which will save a lot of time and effort if this level of control is required. Mostly this is done for cross-data center deployments to support a metro cluster. The requestor could decide where the VM needs to run (DC1 or DC2); vRealize Orchestrator is then using the vSphere API to place the VM in the right host affinity group.

This host group affinity/anti-affinity is also often used to separate VMs between different data center rooms or sections. All hosts in one room or section form a host group and vRA can then use a location parameter to match those groups of hosts.

Resource pools

Resource pools are a major part of DRS and help DRS to share and distribute resources amongst hosts in a cluster. However, they are probably one of the most discussed and misunderstood concepts in the entire VMware ecosystem.

> Do not use resource pools as folders or to structure the look and feel of your environment. Even if they are not configured they will follow their function and limit or enable resources for all VMs contained. Also, never place VMs side-by-side to a resource pool, this will degrade performance for all VMs under the resource pool!

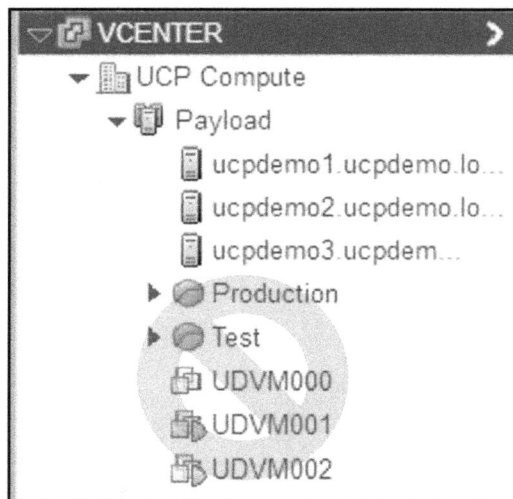

In a cloud environment, resource pools can be used to only provide a share of your available infrastructure to a tenant. However, be aware that you have to use resource pools for all workloads once you get started, since having VMs outside of resource pools (in the root folder of the cluster) will lead to performance constraints.

Generally, it is not necessary to use resource pools for a vRealize Cloud, but in a bigger environment, it might be useful to carve out a specific amount of resources. The best practices for the usage of these features is: Keep it as simple as possible and only as complex as necessary.

There are some good blogs available to discuss the way resource pools work in great detail. One of the best resources is the blog of Frank Denneman, he did a brilliant series to describe how all the shares, reservation and limitation functionalities work together. Also, on the topic of advanced vSphere HA and how it works in harmony with DRS, Duncan Epping has his blog called *Yellow Bricks*, which is definitely worth a read!

Before you decide to use resource pools you should make sure that you have all information required to create crisp and functional configurations. Also, resource pools need maintenance too. If your cluster grows or your resources change, these changes need to be reflected in the resource pools.

Storage DRS

Storage DRS is not as long around as DRS itself, but it can be seen as one of the vSphere's standard functionalities. Basically, it creates a DRS-like automation across **Virtual Machine File System** (**VMFS**) data stores. Those are added to so-called *data store clusters* and every VMFS added will be providing more capacity and performance to the entire data store cluster.

Often, if Storage DRS is mentioned, people think immediately of the **I/O load-balancing** capabilities of this function. While they might be an option to prevent a noisy neighbor problem, sometimes they cannot be fully leveraged since the storage array might have similar features, typically referred to as *auto-tiering* or *dynamic tiering*.

Once the array has such a capability, the Storage DRS I/O load-balancing may be disabled, dependent if the array will support it or now. With VASA 2.0 VMware added the capability to support such arrays and give Storage DRS more insights before migrating workloads based on their I/O pattern. Make sure you storage vendor is supported; otherwise it might lead to confusion and a degraded performance. If the vendor does not support it, it can be turned off individually.

Please refer to your storage vendor to find out if storage I/O load-balancing can be enabled even if the array is using auto-tiering or dynamic tiering functions.

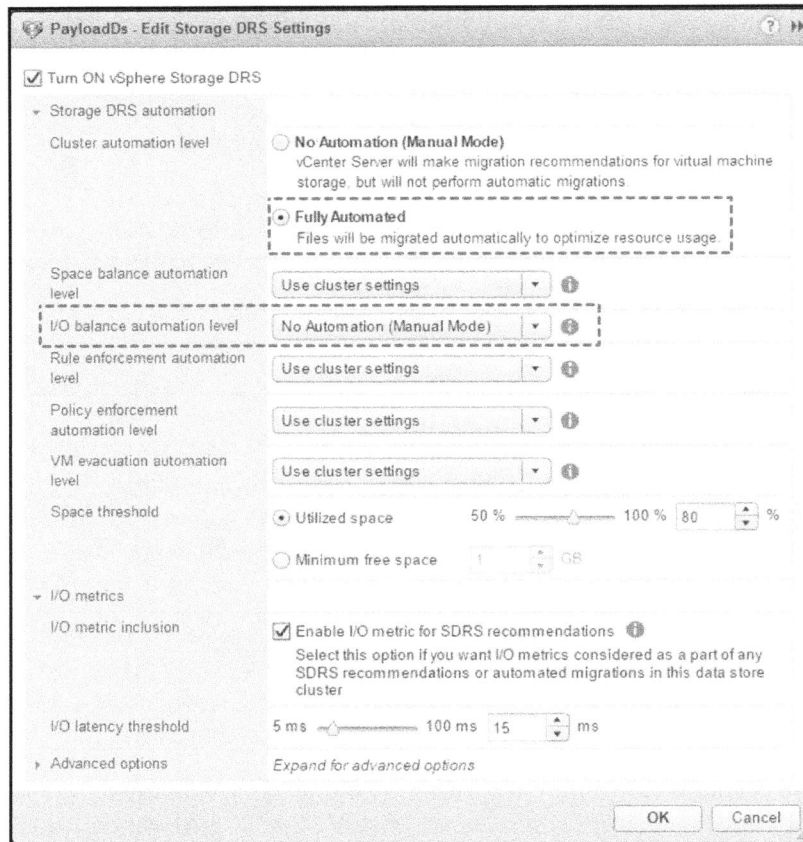

```
PayloadDs - Edit Storage DRS Settings                              ?  ▶▶

☑ Turn ON vSphere Storage DRS

 ▾ Storage DRS automation

   Cluster automation level        ○ No Automation (Manual Mode)
                                     vCenter Server will make migration recommendations for virtual machine
                                     storage, but will not perform automatic migrations.
                                   ┌─────────────────────────────────────────────────────────────────┐
                                   │ ⦿ Fully Automated                                                 │
                                   │   Files will be migrated automatically to optimize resource usage.│
                                   └─────────────────────────────────────────────────────────────────┘

   Space balance automation
   level                           [ Use cluster settings            ▼ ] ⓘ

   I/O balance automation level    [ No Automation (Manual Mode)      ▼ ] ⓘ

   Rule enforcement automation
   level                           [ Use cluster settings            ▼ ] ⓘ

   Policy enforcement
   automation level                [ Use cluster settings            ▼ ] ⓘ

   VM evacuation automation
   level                           [ Use cluster settings            ▼ ] ⓘ

   Space threshold                 ⦿ Utilized space        50 % ───△─── 100 %  [ 80 ] ⌃⌄ %

                                   ○ Minimum free space      1  ⌃⌄  GB

 ▾ I/O metrics

   I/O metric inclusion            ☑ Enable I/O metric for SDRS recommendations ⓘ
                                     Select this option if you want I/O metrics considered as a part of any
                                     SDRS recommendations or automated migrations in this data store
                                     cluster

   I/O latency threshold           5 ms ─△──── 100 ms  [ 15 ] ⌃⌄ ms

 ▸ Advanced options                Expand for advanced options

                                                              [ OK ]  [ Cancel ]
```

In the preceding screenshot, we see a Storage DRS configuration set to **Fully Automated**. However, the **I/O balance automation level** is set to **No Automation (Manual Mode)** to ensure that this setting goes well with the used storage array.

Another useful function of Storage DRS clusters is the auto placement of **Virtual Machine Disks** (**VMDKs**). Basically, as soon as a data store cluster is chosen to house a VMDK, it determines the best fitting data store in terms of IOPs and balance (number of VMDKs already present) to place that new disk. This is similar to the admission control function of DRS to determine on which host a VM is best to be powered on.

In an SDDC environment, where VMs get dynamically provisioned, this is a very useful function since the system basically balances the storage deployment itself and determines the best data store to be used for a VMDK placement. Before this functionality was available in vSphere, all this had to be done using scripts or workflows. Enabling it should not only provide a time-saving factor but also adds valuable and practical automation to your environment.

Another important feature of Storage DRS is the out of space avoidance move functionality. It is a threshold, which can be configured to move VMDKs to different data stores in case the original data store is running out of free space. This should avoid that the VMs are forced to pause, which is a standard vSphere behavior if data stores run out of space. It will move the VMDK to a different data store instead with enough free space before an impact might happen. So it can be seen like a pro-active downtime prevention, which is offered by Storage DRS out of the box.

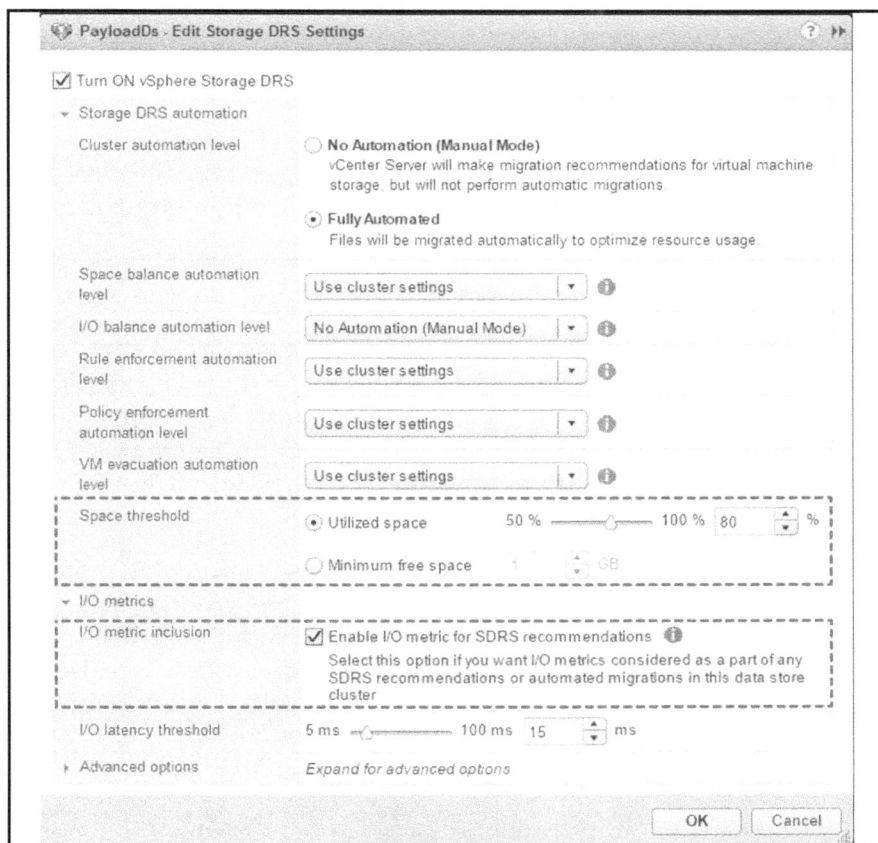

In the Storage DRS cluster config, this is set to **80%** per default. In that case, SDRS will try to find another data store to move some VMs onto to free up space before any impact will hit other VMs. Also, **VM evacuation automation level** needs to be enabled for this to take effect. In this case, it is using the cluster setting, which is set to **Fully Automated**

The **I/O metric inclusion** function is another useful setting at an SDRS cluster. Setting a SDRS cluster to **Fully Automated** means that it will apply recommendations immediately. The setting will provide information about the general I/O behavior of data stores and workloads and use its findings for any SDRS recommendation. It will also prevent a data store from being filled with too many high profile I/O VMs.

> It is highly recommended to use the auto placement and the space avoidance move functionality in an SDDC environment. These two Storage DRS features will basically ensure that your environment stays healthy and ease the deployment of VMs on data stores.

Distributed Virtual Switch

The vSphere **Distributed Virtual Switch (DVS)** is ensuring that each and every host in a cluster or even a vCenter is having the same network configuration as well as port group settings. It is a logical layer which ensures that once you add a port group centrally; all other hosts will also have the same configuration instantly available.

In an SDDC environment, this is an important and time-saving function which also ensures a common configuration across all hosts in a given cluster/data center or vCenter.

Basically, the switches can be set up on a vCenter level and different hosts from different clusters can be added to each switch via their physical uplinks. It also offers some other helpful functionality like **Network I/O Control**, which is controlling the preference of specific traffic types, for example, **Virtual Machine Traffic, vMotion, VADP** (data protection), management, and so on.

This is useful to ensure that the Virtual Machine Traffic is always getting preferred over other services on the available bandwidth, even if for example, vMotion is using a high amount of resources to migrate a VM. It is recommended to use the shares to set the preference. Although it is also possible to set static reservations, these can also harm an environment. Shares will only kick in once there is bandwidth congestion. If there is none, any traffic type can use as much bandwidth as it needs. This enables a very dynamic and fair traffic management on the **vSphere Distributed Switch (VDS)**.

Reservations will be deducted from the overall bandwidth, even if there is no congestion. This means other services will not be able to use the reserved bandwidth, even if the traffic type holding a reservation is not fully utilizing it. This principle is very similar to resource reservations and shares management for computing.

> **TIP**
>
> Network I/O Control is only available with the DVS.

Network shares in NIC work similar to compute shares in resource pools or VMs. They will only enforce if there is congestion on the network. This is why shares are the better tools to prevent congestion. If there is none, they will not enforce any protocol to slow down.

In this example, there are 500 shares for the entire network available. All ESXi based traffic types got 50 shares, while the VM traffic type got 100. This means that in the case of congestion, 500 Mbit (1/5th) of the bandwidth will be available exclusively to the VM traffic. If the other traffic types are not used in your environment, you can set their shares to zero, but remember that this changes the overall outcome of all other traffic types as well.

If we set VSAN and iSCSI to 0, we would end up having 400 shares for the whole system, so we promoted every other protocol more bandwidth in case of a congestion. Our VM traffic type can now use up to 750 Mbit (1/4th) of the overall bandwidth. However, just to be clear, if you use VSAN or iSCSI it might not be wise to set their shares simply to zero. The whole idea is to balance wisely, so be careful when changing these settings!

> Do not misinterpret shares as some kind of maximum settings. If there is no congestion, each traffic type can consume as much bandwidth as available. However, if vMotion would saturate the entire connection, shares will kick in and provide fairness of traffic types.

Often multiple DVS are used in an environment, to separate the management network switch from the payload network switch. This is also done to prevent human error since all port groups of a DVS can be seen on any participating vSphere host. However, this is dependent on your chosen vSphere design and good practice. But typically, organizations tend to run their own DVS for management, separated from the one running all payload VMs.

For an SDDC environment, the DVS is very valuable since it can be easily extended to added hosts. Also, it can span multiple clusters and data centers in vCenter. Since the DVS is running at the vCenter level, it is a very versatile and easy to maintain virtual network switch. Given an automated data center might be extended more often as a traditional data centers, this can be a time saver as well as a good practice for automation and standardization.

Also, if NSX is an option, a VDS is a prerequisite for any network virtualization.

Host Profiles

VMware **Host Profiles** are a configuration template for vSphere hosts. The principle is to configure a baseline host and then use this host to create a Host Profile from its settings. These profiles can be attached to either any individual ESXi host or to a cluster.

This functionality eases the process of adding resources to a cluster. As soon as the host will be put into the cluster it will run a compliance check. After that, the host can be brought into maintenance mode to remediate the Host Profile, which will set all the configuration changes according to the baseline host.

Host Profiles are a great way to keep a common configuration for all ESXi Hosts in a vCenter. Their use will enhance the flexibility as well as the scalability of the environment.

If a changed configuration needs to be pushed to all hosts in an environment (DNS change, network settings, and so on) this can easily be accomplished by creating or editing a Host Profile.

Host Profiles are also enabling another vSphere feature, which is called **Auto Deploy**. Auto Deploy is a service, which can install and set up vSphere hosts automatically once they boot. It can either fully install ESXi on the local disk/USB stick/SD card, or it can do a full network boot of ESXi. In the case of the network boot, Host Profiles are needed to ensure the host is ready and fully configured once it is up and running. Since every reboot makes the host a *fresh install*, Host Profiles are required to ensure all connection and cluster information are available to the Host.

Auto Deploy is typically used in a very large environment to support rapid scalability and growth of the data center. In an SDDC it can be useful to make the add-on of a host as simple and standardized as possible.

vSphere configuration considerations

The SDDC will influence the way you might configure and setup vSphere in a data center. While any vSphere environment can be the base for an SDDC, it might make sense to revisit some of its settings and make them fit for the SDDC. Basically, there are two major approaches to think about:

- The management cluster and all the management relevant VMs and applications
- The environment running all your production/development or test VMs often referred to as *payload*

Both configurations are important and need to be well thought through. In a classic vSphere only environment, the need of a management cluster might be not as strong as in an SDDC environment, since all it runs is vCenter and maybe some virtual desktop managers (if applicable). So it can often be run on small vSphere hosts with a low-performance configuration. If you add monitoring like vRealize Operations and Log Insight the performance requirements of this cluster will rise since these two tools will require intense memory and CPU power to serve medium or large environments.

Separate management cluster

This is a general recommendation from VMware. Every bigger vSphere environment should have its separated manager cluster where all management VMs are installed onto. In an SDDC environment, all the required tools to run the SDDC will be added into the management cluster as well. Therefore, it is important to plan accordingly and provide it with all necessary resources.

So the requirements of your management cluster will change dramatically in an SDDC. If you also intend to add NSX to the picture, you need to run the NSX manager as well as think about a separate **NSX Edge cluster**.

Here is a list of VMs you will have to fit in your management cluster for a medium size SDDC installation:

- 2x vRealize Automation appliance
- 2x DEM worker for vRealize Automation
- 2x IaaS server for vRealize Automation
- 1x (or 2x) vRealize Orchestrator
- 1x (or 2x) vRealize Operations Manager
- 1x (or 2x) vRealize Log Insight
- 1x vRealize Business for Cloud
- 1x NSX Manager (if applicable) 3x NSX controller nodes
- 1x vRealize Code Stream (if applicable)
- 1x vCenter server

This means that your SDDC management server will have at least 16 management servers with different resource and performance requirements to host. Some of these services require extensive resources such as disk space or heavy CPU and memory workloads. Especially vRealize Operations and vRealize Log Insight can easily consume a couple of terabyte of storage and require high-performance CPU and memory configurations.

Because of this added duties, the management cluster gets more important and therefore needs well thought through high availability settings. vSphere HA should be configured to protect all necessary VMs to run and manage your SDDC. However, keep in mind that other management servers can run on this cluster as well. It is not exclusively reserved for VMware products.

If you plan to introduce a campus or metro cluster setup with shared storage between two data centers, this concept needs to be extended to the management cluster as well. This might be less important in a pure vSphere environment, but for the SDDC it is imperative to make sure the portal is high available and reachable. Just keep in mind that all consumers will have to go through the portal to manage their VMs and other ordered objects. If the portal is down, they have no option to interact with their installation.

Another important point here is the **HA Restart Priority**. The SDDC components may require a special restart order after an outage. Otherwise, they might be up but the portal is not running because of missing connection requirements. In the following screenshot, you will find a sample how to configure the restart priority for an SDDC management cluster:

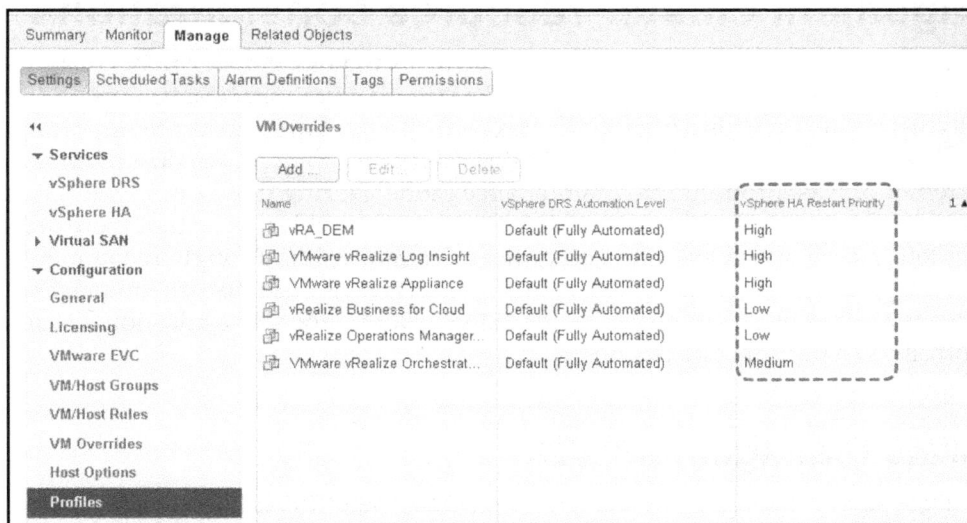

Obviously, vCenter is also important to be up and running as one of the first VMs, but that should be a given in any environment. Besides that, the logic for this startup priority is the following:

1. Start vRealize Automation portal and **Distributed Execution Mangers** (**DEM**) first to bring up the portal and general functionality.
2. Start vRealize Log Insight with the same priority in cases logs needs to be analyzed.
3. Start up vRealize Orchestrator to make sure that any additional workflows or the XaaS components can work. Orchestrator can start and register itself fine if vRA is already running.

4. Start up vRealize Operations and vRealize Business to restore capacity and analytics monitoring as well as chargeback and showback functionalities.

> In the case of two data centers and a stretched management cluster, it might be very helpful to set an affinity rule to have all components running in the same data center. This will prevent random outages in case one of the data center sites has an issue. However, if you use a clustered vRA setup (as well as other components) make sure that each site runs one instance of it, instead of having both on one site!

Management cluster resource considerations

It is strongly recommended to have at least three hosts in your management cluster. If you are using a campus or metro cluster setup, make sure that you use host groups and VM groups to distribute the VMs across both sites accordingly. Three hosts are important to also cover maintenance events. If vSphere upgrades need to be applied, the host often needs to be restarted or at least brought into maintenance mode. During these times your cluster resiliency is diminished. If you would only have two hosts, this means that there are no resources left in case of a failed of the other host. Therefore, it is strongly recommended to have at least a *2+1 configuration* in place. However, in an NSX use case, the management cluster needs to have at least 6 hosts (3 per site) in order to house the additional required NSX controllers (3 per site, one per host).

Separate management VDS

Besides the separate management cluster, it might be useful to also create a separate management VDS. One of the reasons to do this is to limit the failure domain.

A VDS is nothing more than a software component to give access to the physical **Network Interface Card** (**NIC**) of a vSphere host. This is done by creating failover (NIC teaming) configurations as well as through adding so-called port groups. But such a switch also represents its own failure domain, which means in case something is going wrong with this VDS, it will only affect the management cluster. Limiting your failure domain is a passive move which will enhance your overall resiliency.

Another reason is often to add security. Since all port groups in a VDS can be used on all participating ESXi hosts, it might be possible to accidentally add a VM in the wrong port group. If this port group is part of the overall management network – severe harm could be done by accessing this network. To prevent this situation a separate management VDS helps to logically separate all the production networks from the management networks. Basically, it can also all be done with one single VDS, but some organizations may restrict this due to security regulations and force to have a separation of VDS.

The payload cluster

The main principle of an SDDC is to share workloads on a general purpose infrastructure. This is done by using logical software constructs to create the impression that a select area is providing resources for deployed application. Typically, this can be done by either creating own clusters to host different use cases, or by creating resource pools to carve out resources and performance from a bigger cluster.

vSphere provides high flexibility in what technique to use, but there are differences, pros and cons with each approach.

The resource pool approach

Resource pools are one option in vSphere to reserve and limit resources. They also offer shares to ensure a fair prioritization of CPU and memory. Resource pools can be used to create a tiering approach for different workloads. They can also be used to separate workload classes from each other. Some organizations use resource pools to separate test/dev from production workloads. The resource pools act as a resource broker and ensure that each class gets the resources it demands. However, if one class is exceeding its resource requirements, they can ensure that the other class still gets the required resources.

In an SDDC they can be used as a reservation (or multiple reservations) for a tenant. Meaning all workloads of that tenant will be deployed in these specific resource pools.

Although they can also be configured to set a limit, this limit would be permanent. This means that even if the resources might be available, the limit will prevent all VMs in the resource pool to consume more than the allowed resources. This is not to be underestimated since a memory limit in a resource pool can lead to VMs swapping out their memory pages since there is no more RAM available. A CPU limit can lead to the artificial slowdown of the VM to ensure the boundary is kept. This is a very forceful way to ensure that an environment is staying in its boundaries.

Resource shaping should be done by using shares within resource pools. This way grants that the resource pool will provide the necessary resources in case of congestion by using the shares. If there is no congestion, the VMs can use more resources than the pool is configured for. As soon as this conflicts with another resource pool in the system, the shares are used to determine the priorities of the pools/VMs to get to resources.

This grants that, if there is no congestion in the system, VMs can use as many resources as available. If there is congestion, the shares ensure that the different classes get exactly as many resources as configured in the resource pool. This means that shares offer a much more flexible way of resource management than limits.

However, these shares need to be adjusted if you add a resource pool to the cluster. You should come up with a formula to add shares to a pool based on what it should deliver.

A simple example might be:

- *Development = 30% of cluster resources*
- *Test = 10% of cluster resources*
- *Production = 60% of cluster resources*

Since you can define shares yourself, they can be easily used to represent these values. To further add to this example, the following shares might be added:

- *Development = 3 shares per vCPU/GB memory* (more vCPUs means more shares to add)
- *Test = 1 share per vCPU/GB of memory*
- *Production = 6 shares per vCPU/GB of memory*

Some people simply add a static number of shares to a resource pool, but that can lead to the opposite, performance degrade. Let's look at an example of static shares in pools:

- Pool test has 1000 shares and houses 50 VMs
- Pool production has 6000 shares and houses 600 VMs

First glance seems that production has much more resources (shares) available than test. But if you break it down to the VM level, a test VM gets 20 shares, a production VM gets only 10 shares.

This means that in a congestion event, test VMs get twice as often access to resources than production VMs.

This is an important principle to understand. By applying the easy percentage approach, the shares per resource pool must be calculated on a per VM level. If you add VMs to a resource pool, also the number of shares has to be changed, every time!

This is maybe one of the downsides of resource pools, they are flexible and agile, but they need to be configured accurately. This is also one of the main reasons why it is very harmful to use them as a folder structure, even if you never configure their shares, they will force VMs to align to their configuration. Typically this can either be done by using vRealize Orchestrator or by using vSphere PowerCLI scripts which are checking and changing shares per pool on a regular (hourly/daily) basis.

Pros and cons:

- + Dynamic and agile approach to grant resources to VMs
- + Easy works with multiple cluster sizes
- + No wasted capacity
- – Needs continuous adoption if new VMs are added
- – Needs well-structured resource tiering model
- – Needs additional automation

The cluster approach

Pooling resources across your data center can also be done by putting certain workloads on certain clusters. If your environment is big enough this might be an attractive way to ensure that different tiers of workloads do not affect other tiers. Also, this approach is very attractive from a licensing perspective. Similar software might be licensed more effectively when running on the same cluster. In this case, this setup is very common.

Typically this is done by creating tier based clusters such as test, dev, or production. Each cluster represents one workload class/tier and will only host the respective tier. This is easy to handle since you physically separate the workloads by letting them run on distinct vSphere hosts. In an SDDC environment, a tenant can have one or multiple clusters as a reservation. Workloads deployed by that tenant will then always end in one of these clusters.

Basically, the cluster can be seen as giant resource pools, the difference is that there is no need to configure any shares or resource reservation.

However, keep in mind that each cluster must meet all resiliency and availability requirements. If this example is used in a campus or metro cluster environment, you need enough hosts to distribute across both sides. The minimal configuration for each cluster is similar to the management cluster requirements: *2+1*. Otherwise, you can't ensure resiliency during maintenance windows. Of course, this might be done differently in test and dev environments. In this case, a two-node cluster might be acceptable in order to act in the interest of budget. However, keep in mind that the resiliency is diminished with this setup. If the test or dev clusters serve a production purpose (can't work productively without these environments) the three-node setup might be more appropriate.

This implies that each of your tiers is running on their very own cluster. So in the test/dev /production example, one cluster is needed for each group. So even if you start small, you would need at least nine ESXi host, to begin with. This is one of the downsides of the cluster approach; it requires more resources than the resource pool shaping. Also, keep in mind that you need to map different VMFS volumes to a different cluster to stay within VMware's best practices. So it will also increase your storage mapping effort as well as your overall storage consumption. Typically this approach is chosen for large environments, where hundreds or thousands of VMs run in the select tier. In this case, it might make a lot of sense to use separate clusters. But in a smaller environment, it simply isn't much cost attractive.

Pros and cons:

- + Easy approach to classify using hardware resources
- + Good and easy scalability since no changes need to be made
- – Possible waste of resources, licenses, and therefore cost.
- – Needs well-structured resource tiering model
- – Each tier needs its own cluster

Both options work well with vRealize Automation. In the end, it is up to the requirements you have to fulfill which way is more appealing to you. In terms of scalability, both options scale very well. The biggest difference is though that the resource pool option scales beginning with 3 hosts for 3 tiers.

It scales dynamic and efficiently as you add hosts if you always change the resource pool settings to accommodate new VMs and resources.

The cluster option scales beginning with 9 hosts for 3 tiers, so it added three times the cost. You scale the individual tiers by adding hosts to their clusters without any change or task to complete.

Both options can scale very well up to VMware provided maximums for vSphere

> vSphere 6.0 scales easily up to 64 hosts per cluster and 10,000 VMs as well as 1,000 hosts per vCenter

Storage Policy Based Management

Storage Policy Based Management (**SPBM**) is relatively new to the vSphere world. It got introduced with vSphere 5.0 and has been quite enhanced since then. The basic principle of SPBM is to manage the storage in form of VMFS data stores based on precreated policies instead of trying to figure out their function by their name.

Typically, organizations picked a distinct name scheme to apply to the data stores to identify their capabilities. Such a name could look like:

```
S1PDR040
```

This is a code to identify what this VMFS data store has to offer. Translated it means:

- `S1` = site 1
- `P` = production
- `DR` = disaster recovery/replicated data store
- `040` = LUN ID to identify in ESXi/storage system

All the admins have to know all this abbreviations and codes to *quickly* identify where a VM should be deployed. While Storage DRS adds one simplification for that since all VMFS of a kind and site could be put together in a big storage cluster, SPBM adds another solution. It can create storage policies and match VMFS data stores or data store clusters toward that policies.

The interesting thing with SPBM is, they can be applied on a per VMDK level. So each disk of a VM can have its very own storage policy attached. Instead of trying to decrypt complex data store names all the admin has to do know is picking the fitting policy per the VMDK and the compatible data store will be shown in the deployment wizard.

For a manual deployment that is a time saver and also prevents deployments errors (wrong data store picked because of *lost in translation* issue).

In an SDDC where storage tiering might be a requirement, this functionality is not just nice to have, it is a much-needed functionality.

SPBM definition

SPBMs can be defined in various ways. This description is highlighting two easy to maintain ways to create storage policies to be used in either vSphere or vRealize Automation for tiering purposes. This is one of vSphere integrated automation functionalities which should not be underestimated for an SDDC since it added valuable features without much effort to configure.

Static SPBM configuration

In this configuration, you can select the data stores which should be compatible with the policy based on tags. These tags have to be added to the data stores before you can create the policy. To add a tag to a VMFS data store:

1. Click on **Home** in the vCenter Web Client.
2. Go to the **Storage** overview in vCenter Web Client.
3. Right-click on the data store you want to add the tag to and select **Assign Tag**.
4. If no tags are available click on the *new tag* sign to create a new tag.
5. Create a new tag category if needed (for example, `Storage`).
6. Select the newly created tag to assign it to the data store.

In our previous example, tags can be:

- **Production**
- **Replicated**
- Performance class (**Gold**, **Platinum**, **Ultra**)

These tags can either be assigned to individual VMFS data store or to an entire data store cluster. After you tagged all your data stores you can use this tags in the storage policies to match their requirements.

In our case, that would be a storage policy called `Production` which requires the tags, **Replicated**, **Production**, and **Ultra**. To create this policy, do the following tasks:

1. Click on **Home** in the vCenter Web Client.
2. In the overview screen, click on **VM Storage Policies**.
3. Click on the *Create a new VM storage policy* icon at top left.
4. Give it a name and a description.
5. Under **2a Rule-Set 1** select **Add tag-based rule....**.
6. Add all required tags to the policy.

7. Provide a valid description what this policy is including.
8. Check the compatible data stores in the overview.
9. Click **Finish**.

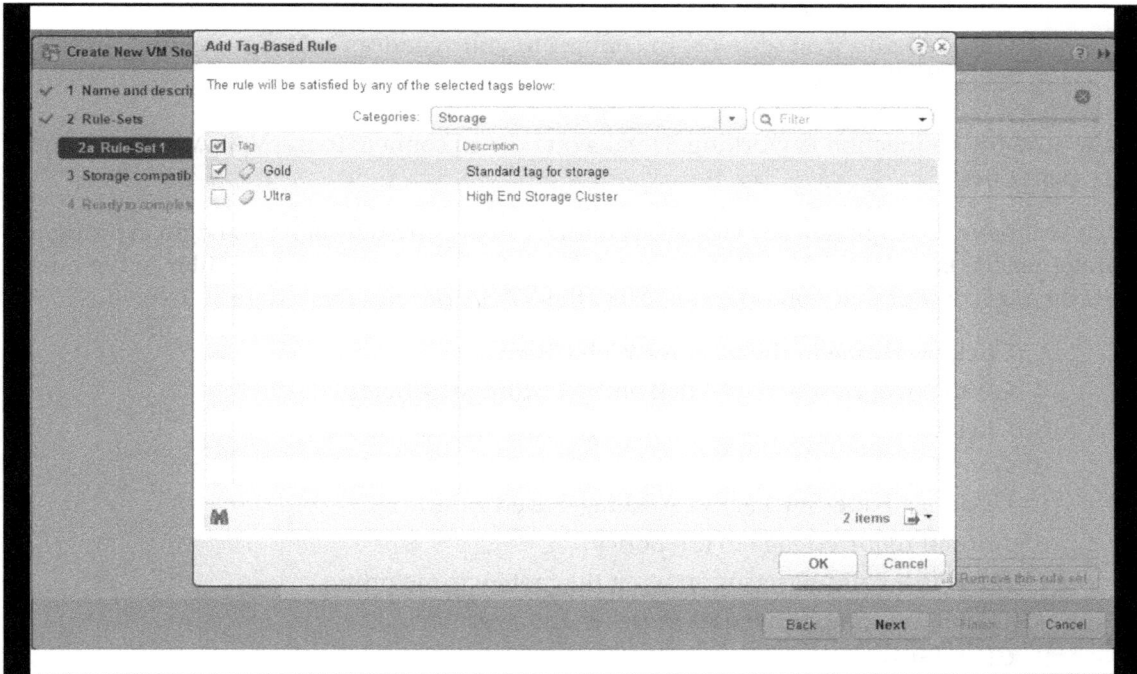

You just created a valid storage policy based on tags. If this policy is selected with a VM deployment, it will only show compatible VMFS data stores for the VM deployment.

Dynamic SPBM configuration

Besides, the SPBM configuration based on tags this can also be done on live array data. This brings the advantage that the storage policy can be created based on capabilities delivered by the storage array. It could include requirements such as **Max Latency** or **Max IOPs** based on real data provided by the array.

To make this work you need to install a so-called **vSphere API for Storage Awareness** (**VASA**) provider from your array vendor. Each vendor has their own provider, typically they are either a **vApp** to download, or they are already running on one of the array controllers. In any case, you need to connect vCenter to the VASA provider before you can create such a dynamic storage policy.

Follow these steps to enable the VASA provider in vCenter:

1. Go to the *tree view* in vCenter.
2. Click on **vCenter** at the top.
3. Select the **Storage Provider** tab on the far right in the main window.
4. Click the add icon (*green +*) to connect to your vendors VASA provider.
5. Click **OK** and save the connection.

Make sure the connection is working. Details on how to connect to the VASA provider may vary per vendor.

Once you have configured your storage vendors VASA provider, you can begin creating a storage profile based on actual storage capabilities. The configuration is similar to the one with the tags, except that you now can select the VASA provider as a data source:

1. Click on **Home** in the vCenter Web Client.
2. On the overview screen, click on **VM Storage Policies**.
3. Click on the *Create a new VM storage policy* icon at top left.
4. Give it a name and a description.
5. Under **2a Rule-Set 1** select **Add tag-based rule...**.
6. Add all required tags to the policy.
7. Provide a valid description what this policy is including.
8. Check the compatible data stores in the overview.
9. Click **Finish**.

Done, you just created a storage policy based on storage capabilities. The beauty of this is that the VASA provider and SPBM will automatically detect compatible VMFS volumes/LUNs.

In vRealize Automation 7, these policies can be leveraged in IaaS blueprints or even selected while ordering a VM. In this case, the VM will only be deployed onto the policy compatible VMFS volumes. Before SPBM was built into vSphere and vRA; these requirements could only be realized based on complex vRealize Orchestrator workflows often custom created for each scenario.

Now, this functionality can be simply preconfigured in vSphere and leveraged in vRA. This simplifies the implementation of the SDDC a lot and grants that each VM is running on the right storage tier.

Integrated vSphere automation

vSphere already comes with very rich and built-in automation functionality. Initially, all this was added to make the administrators lives easier. Ultimately it was meant to ease the daily operation of medium and large vSphere deployments. Over time, the SDDC evolved and brought up new possibilities to deploy workloads in a vSphere environment.

With this new possibility also requirements are raised regarding basic SLAs like tiering, performance classes, security, and so on.

For the SDDC, the features which made the vSphere administrators live easier have become a huge time saver for any SDDC deployment. Think about the effort savings you get by using all of this automation vSphere provides per default.

These functionalities can save weeks of custom workflow scripting or implementation work. Just remember that VMware's engineers spent a fair amount of time developing all their functionality to blend in perfectly in the vSphere environment. DRS, Storage DRS, vMotion, HA, SPBM work together in perfect unison to make a good vSphere environment a perfect base installation for the SDDC.

It is important to leverage the already integrated automation features vSphere brings with it's out of the box functionalities. All functions which can be configured and used in vSphere are a huge time saver for the SDDC since they do not have to be created and programmed in vRealize Orchestrator with big efforts.

DRS and Storage DRS is just one big example of making maintenance and initial placement of VMs an automated task of vSphere. Without this functionality, it would require quite an effort to place VMs or to support host maintenance. Since vMotion takes care of evacuating VMs from hosts planned for maintenance mode, this is transparent to the SDDC and therefore also to the end user of the service.

Storage DRS is a good helper in preventing unplanned downtime by using the out of space avoidance move functionality; this is not just a nice feature, it can be a live saver. Besides that, it also takes care of placing VMs onto the right data store out of a data store cluster. This is another functionality which has not been available in the past and therefore created quite an effort in vRealize Orchestrator (or with PowerShell scripts) to choose the right data store for a VM to be deployed onto.

Finally, resource pools provide a great option to shape the environment in the most efficient way but need some attention on their own. If you are not completely sure that your resource pool design is exactly doing what you want it to do, review it or think of changing to the cluster shaping approach. Resource pools can be quite a complex topic, that is also why Duncan Epping and Frank Denneman created a complete series of books about vSphere HA and DRS. This is a highly recommended read if you want to learn all the details about vSphere resource pools and how they work.

All vSphere automation functionality should be taken into account to ease

Best practices and recommendations

A healthy and well configured vSphere environment is a perfect base for any SDDC installation. Check your environment and see if you can either add the automation features discussed or enhance your current use of them. In an SDDC there is not too much space for manual tasks, therefore anything which can be solved with automation and is required for the SDDC to work probably should be considered.

Spend enough time to evaluate your vSphere environment if it is actually ready for cloud. If you identify manual tasks or very static settings which are complex to replicate on added hosts, try to solve these by using the provided toolset of vSphere. It is important to identify roadblocks before they are getting dead ends in an SDDC deployment.

An SDDC is about enhancing agility in your data center and fulfilling your businesses IT demands in a quick and straightforward way. It will need some customization for integration into third-party management tools in your data center. But this effort should not be spent on vSphere integration.

Before you identify a task which might need to be customized in vRealize Orchestrator, think twice if this can be fulfilled with standard vCenter functionality.

Saving license cost by sacrificing some of this features is actually rather burning cost than saving it. The problem is, even if you find a quick way and reproduce some of these features in vRealize Orchestrator, every time you change a thing in your environment you have to recheck if your vSphere Orchestrator workflow is still working. This may become a huge effort and time factor while operating your SDDC.

This is why using built-in vSphere automation is one of the most important best practices to follow when preparing your environment for installing an SDDC.

Summary

In this chapter, we discussed the main principles of build in vSphere automation and some of its advanced features. From basic HA and resiliency topics, all the way to vSphere integrated resource shaping options are valid functions for the SDDC. By leveraging all these included functions in vSphere and by ensuring that your clusters are meeting HA and resiliency standards this will form a healthy and capable infrastructure layer for your SDDC.

The next chapter will highlight SDDC design considerations to take into account. It will discuss the tools required for the SDDC based on the requirements. Furthermore, it will help you to map business requirements to actual SDDC design elements and to form proper decisions which tools are required. It will touch all components required for an SDDC as well as components to enhance the SDDC possibilities. Also, it will guide you to basic design principles which include assumptions, risks as well as constraints you have to take into account.

4

SDDC Design Considerations

If you have never done any design before, this chapter should give you a good starting point and some useful insights about what is good and proven practice. It will talk about the basic principles you want to put into your design as well as how to document any assumptions constraints and limitations.

The design is probably one of the most important things in any SDDC implementation. However, the design itself will be formed out of the actual requirements and business cases. This is one of the reasons why a business case or at least a use case for an SDDC is very important.

The use case or business case will influence the way the SDDC is configured and shaped, therefore you should put as much effort in documenting the business and use cases, as in creating the initial SDDC design itself.

Another important task is the translation from a business case into a functional design as well as how any technical requirements are directly or indirectly related to a business case.

Besides the specific use case mapping, the SDDC needs to be versatile, scalable, and capable for future undertakings. There should be room for additional functionalities as well as room for adding resources as needed for the future. In the end, an automated data center needs to scale transparently from the user's point of view. Therefore, it needs also to be designed to scale easily and unnoticed for any portal users or programmatic consumption using its API.

This chapter will cover the following points:

- Business needs and the design equivalent
- General logical design principles
- Best practices on taking assumptions
- Scalability of the environment
- Do's and don'ts when designing automation
- Example design considerations
- What must or what can be in the design

The business use case

This is also often referred to as **business use case** and should describe an IT need from a business perspective. Many organizations have such cases, but some lack of translating them into IT needs. Sometimes, there is simply no communication between the lines of business and the IT. This often ends in a bad relationship between those two departments. Often the business thinks IT is too slow, complex and ancient to understand their needs and deliver what they ask for. On the other hand, the IT often gets just a fraction of the problem, but then it has already escalated a few times and now only complaints reach the IT department.

Since a successful SDDC is about communication (people, processes, technology) it is important to understand the business needs of an organization to create a solution which is capable of supporting them and even give them an advantage over the competition. The first step of creating your SDDC design is to document and question that business need. Then you can translate it into a technical design and implement it, therefore.

Let's do a sample business case just to give you an impression what the flow of this translation might look like.

The business challenge

XYZ Corp is a well-known insurance company. They are around for quite some time with an established and broad customer base. Their services are based on personal contact with their customers as well as well-trained and experienced employees. Since a few months, another company is taking their business away by approaching their customers and making them change over to them. It has been identified that this new company offers a rich mobile application as well as some add-on services XYZ has not been considered yet.

The application from the competitor collects all insurance reports and can identify and alert its termination. Also, it can identify duplicate contracts and therefore save money for the clients. All this is included for free in this mobile app.

The CIO challenge

They identified this as a risk to lose more customers and instructed their **chief information officer (CIO)** to find a solution and come up with their own app including the functionality of the competitor. The CIOs task now is to find out if and how the IT department can deliver this ask. Based on their last meeting, they use virtualization for quick VM deployment. However, all these actions are done manually. The installation of services is handled by a different department and then there is the operations unit who runs all production services. All over all it takes them a little more than 1-5 months to bring a new web server farm up. Not to speak about changing the capacity of a running web server farm and incorporating all the various security and regulatory restrictions.

> This is not an unusual use case, although many organization might have their own app, not all are using it as a strategic asset to actively attract customers. There are various reasons why this might be complex, but in the end, there is always someone who has done it and earns all the customer credit with that.

Now, the task for the CIO and his team is to match the business requirement to a technical requirement/IT deliverable. Therefore, the important bits must be extracted and technically translated:

- A web server farm for the mobile app is required
- It needs to be scalable
- Number of users and adoption is unknown
- Other services need to exchange information with this application
- Needs to be joined with existing customer base
- Dynamic deployment of additional services might be required

All these are aspects of an SDDC. The scope seems to be the mobile app, which should possibly serve all existing customers of XYZ Corp. Also, there should be a way to put in new functionality over time and feature enhancements without disrupting the users or long development times.

Besides that, the service should be pre-configured and easy to deploy. Once it is running, there should be an option to either grow it manually or add a monitoring which adds systems based on its usage. This should all happen automatically and without interrupting the service. This is a major factor since application performance is always seen critical by end users.

The **Cloud Management Portal** (**CMP**) should be capable of deploying this service automatically. But this will only be used by a limited set of users in XYZ Corp. Probably from the IT engineers, developers and operations groups only. So the design needs to fit for a small set of users.

Also, in order to setup a web server farm, the OS deployment has to be automated. The CMP should be capable of deploying **Infrastructure as a Service** (**IaaS**) for OS only, but also to install an application after this deployment has happened.

Also, XYZ Corp has a couple of third-party systems where any new service deployment needs to register into. The automation should fully integrate into those systems to prevent any manual intervention. And finally, a predictive resource analysis might be required, to prevent any shortage of compute, network, or memory resources. This system should work alert based and inform about a possible bottleneck before it occurs. This could then be worked into the procurement planning to make sure additional resources are orders and available before any impact is hitting the running services.

All this should run automated including a basic self-service portal where new services can be ordered/maintained and removed by the portal users.

This was the first step of identifying what might be required to solve this business case efficiently. The next step would be to document all facts and possibilities to further create a design which takes all this into account.

Constraints, assumptions, and limitations

These three components will shape the way you set up and install your SDDC. Let's briefly touch on what each of this terms means in a design and how to identify and document these terms.

Constraints

A **constraint** is something you cannot influence nor change in the data center. Since it is non-changeable it should be documented as a constraint to explain why you might have chosen the design you did. Constraints can be various things, they do not need to be only technical, also processes or people can be a constraint. Since a constraint will massively influence the chosen path of installation and configuration, they should all be documented in a table at the beginning of the design.

Here is a sample constraint table:

Constraint ID	Description	Impact
C001	DMZ and production must be physically separated	More hosts as well as a complex deployment method are required to ensure no DMZ workload can be run on production or vice versa
C002	All IP addresses must be obtained from a central IPAM	IPAM needs to be integrated into the cloud management solution
C003	All deployed VMs need to be registered with the CMDB	CMDB must be programmable (API) and will be integrated with the automatic VM deployment
C004	Every non-standard change needs to be approved and documented	Approval policies need to be used and implemented for possible service changes in the portal
C005	No VM template deployment is allowed to be used	Service deployment has to be configured to do **Preboot Execution Environment** (**PXE**) boot for VMs to install an operating system

This is just an example, there can be various other things and those depend on the organization's processes and operation structures. However, if there is a chance to eliminate a constraint it should be done. Since every constraint might limit your SDDC capabilities.

The documentation of constraints also often helps to get aware of them. Sometimes one might think, *that is how it is*, or my favorite quote, *it has always been like that*. Think out of these patterns to identify if some of the constraints are still valid. While eliminating a constraint can sometimes be very difficult (politics, people, processes) it can also be a key factor in making the SDDC successful. So the second part of documenting constraints is, find those which can be eliminated.

Too many constraints can put the whole SDDC at risk since it might end in a non-functioning or non-beneficial state. The third step of getting aware of your constraints is making sure they are not preventing any major SDDC functionality. Data center automation means change and change mean that many tasks or processes need to be revisited if they still make sense in an SDDC environment.

> One weird process for a cloud environment was to open a ticket for deploying a service. Not to document its configuration in a CMDB or ticketing system, but because of the operators had the mandate to do so. If they didn't, their manager will get an alert about their productivity. So they requested that each portal action (deploy a service, change a service, and so on) is opening in a ticket under their names and closes it after it's done. This is a typical example of a legacy process which is not fitting into the automated data center world. While it was possible to integrate this, it was quite a high effort to automate that. So the project was more expensive than initially though. This is the impact of a constraint which might have been able to be eliminated.

Once all the constraints have been identified let's move on to the next topic.

Limits

A **limit** can be physical or logical and describes a circumstance which can't be simply changed. Limits are often technical, but can also be organizational or process related. An organization which has only one data center has this as a limit. It cannot easily stand up a second data center. While this is a somewhat extreme example, there are many limits which sound easy to solve but are as difficult to resolve as the data center example.

The process for the limits is the same as for the constraints. However, limits and constraints can be related to each other. A constraint can create a limit and vice versa, a limit can be present due to a constraint.

A simple example for that is:

The project has a fixed budget, which is a cost limit and cannot easily overcome.

This creates a constraint describing additional costs cannot be covered. The impact would be to keep the design simple and remove some of the planned integration work.

Here is a sample limits table:

Constraint ID	Description	Impact
L001	The core network cannot deliver more than 10 Gbit.	In order to prevent congestion, multiple nice will be used to separate management, backup, and production traffic.
L002	PXE network cannot support more than 10 simultaneous deployments.	Global service deployment needs to be configured to not exceed 10 simultaneous service deployments if PXE boot is involved.
L003	Link speed to the secondary data center is 100 Mbit.	Asynchronous replication needs to be considered in order to configure DR prevention.
L004	Pre-defined project deadline, set before the design/project plan was created to handover the fully installed and running system.	Scope needs to be re-visited and a reverse project plan needs to be created. Some features might not be implemented due to this deployment time limit.
L005	Only two FTEs will support this project.	Implementation time might be longer given the limited resources.

In this table, you will notice that C005: No VM template deployment is actually related to L002: PXE limit on simultaneous OS installs. This is an example how constraints and limits might impact each other. If the constraint would move away, the limit would also be gone at once. This would actually make the platform more comprehensive and capable.

Limits are normally quite hard or impossible to eliminate, except they are related to constraints. Therefore a good design has to acknowledge them and trying to work around them. It is important to have a full understanding of all limits before you start your design, otherwise, you might plan for features and then notice that they cannot be used. It is always easier to be well prepared and aware to create your design around that, than trying to improvise later on without jeopardizing the whole integrity and functionality of the SDDC.

Documenting the limits opens up the same opportunity as documenting constraints. They can be re-visited, discussed and maybe there is already a solution to overcome them in the data center. As with the constraints, the important factor is that based on the documented limits it is much easier to follow up than if there is nothing but guessing.

Assumptions

Even the best and well-prepared design team or SDDC architect needs to be educated guessing sometimes. It is just impossible to be aware of every aspect and every requirement before you create your design. Therefore, as well as with the other two, document your assumptions and their impact. Assumptions can be re-visited any time and corrected whenever possible. However, some of them will only reveal once the data center automation has been set up, or once the first couple of services are running. Therefore, assumptions should not lead to absolute design decisions. They should give you a direction and an idea what might be required. Creating a non-reversible configuration which might limit your later use of the platform should be prevented.

However, assumptions are an important part of the design since they will underline why certain things in the system might be configured as they are. It is important to relate them to design decisions since they will help the reader of your design to understand why you took certain decisions. This makes it much easier to form a sound design and also to defend the configuration if required.

Assumptions can cover all sorts of things, beginning from technical assumptions to process based assumptions or application/service based assumptions. Often assumptions are already a big part of any data center. In a bigger organization, the admin sometimes does not know what will be installed on a VM, so they create those VMs based on assumptions and best practices.

In an automated data center there is a lot which can be assumed: Growth, deployments per day, portal users, services, service requirements, service scalability, resource availability, resource constraints, and so on.

This list could get very long. In order to relate that to a design, it is important to list only relevant assumptions which also have a measurable impact on the design and setup of the SDDC.

Here is a sample assumptions table

Constraint ID	Description	Impact
A001	The application supports dynamic scale-out.	The service needs to be designed to support adding VMs on demand.
A002	Only one department/group is using the CMP.	Only one tenant and business group need to be set up to support this.

A003	Backup is done separately and will not be configurable in the CMP.	Easier integration of services without advanced customization requirements.
A004	No advanced networking/firewall rules are required by the application.	Easier integration of services without advanced customization requirements.
A005	Mix of different subnets/VLANs per vSphere host is allowed due to logical network separation.	Less cost and effort with the vSphere implementation. No custom service design in the portal required.

> **TIP**
>
> A004 is a good assumption, but might be very unusual for most projects. VMware's NSX could help to address possible requirements and further automate the deployment of complex applications. If so, consider it to be part of the initial SDDC design.

While some of these assumptions might sound obvious to you, it is important to understand that in huge projects there is always a chance of misunderstandings. So assumptions can also be used to document soft requirements. If you look at A002, it states that only one department might be using the portal. The design decision, therefore, is to create only one tenant. This saves effort and project time. Also, the decision of creating one tenant is tied to the assumption, which makes it quite easy to understand. Sometimes people change their mind in the middle of a project. This often leads to missed milestones and deadlines. Often there can be a discussion that this change hasn't had any impact on the design. If all the assumptions and therefore the scope is well defined in the beginning, those discussions do not need to happen.

So assumptions are good to keep track with design decisions and also to deliver a valid point why this decision has been taken. Besides of that, they help to guess what impact a change of this assumptions might have on the SDDC implementation/configuration.

Also, all assumptions in this table are linked to specific settings. Those settings can be changed anytime. However, the impact might be configuration/project time as well as costs, but the system is not limited to these configurations. Try always to keep the limiting factor of assumptions and its linked decisions as low as possible. Since assumptions can change rather quickly you might need to re-visit the configuration and adapt it to the new requirements.

While these are some worst-case examples, they are all from real SDDC implementations. A good design is keeping track of these aspects. It is also a good practice to create an ID for each design decision and map it to any of these three descriptions. It will improve the readability and understandability of your design if all decision can be tracked back to a constraint, limit or assumption.

Scalability and future growth

If you are about to design your VMware SDDC you should always have growth and scalability in mind while doing so. There is a lot of options to install the needed VMware components for small, medium or even large environments, but it is important that all of them are having their own requirements and limitations.

Keep in mind that albeit there is a very good implementation of a self-service portal in vRealize, the whole SDDC can also be consumed programmatically using APIs. There is APIs for vRealize Automation and its plugins as well as for the vRealize Orchestrator. This might include a scenario where application servers get deployed on a specific day to prevent additional power. After their task is done they are simply removed from the environment to free up the resources for the other existing workloads. The programmatic consumption of the whole SDDC also needs to be considered in a good design document.

Before starting creating a design or even deploying the tools it might be important to explore and understand each of the components of the SDDC. Typically the following components will be required to build the data center automation foundation.

vRealize Automation

This serves as the central front end. Often it is also referred to as the CMP where end users or administrators can request services to be deployed. But this is one of its obvious functions, actually, it is doing much more than that. It also uses so-called **Distributed Execution Managers (DEM)** to monitor and execute workflows. vRealize Automation takes care of the basic automation tasks as well as workflows for deploying VMs and even applications. Also, it can leverage and integrate with advanced features like NSX. It will also be the interface where all the service templates, called blueprints, will be created and designed. These can be simple, like a single VM, or complex like a couple of VMs including a software deployment.

This is the core of the SDDC and therefore quite important to be designed and sized correctly.

vRealize Code Stream

This serves as a good addition to vRealize and makes the SDDC fit for DevOps tasks. It can automate the staging of applications. Furthermore, it features the creation of custom development environments including VMs, application installation, and gating rules. This is called a **pipeline** in vRealize Code Stream. The rules can describe if and when an application can reach the next stage. All this can be automated by integrating either a developer tool like Jenkins or by leveraging scripts or even vRealize Orchestrator workflows. While this addition might not be relevant for the business end users, it will have an impact how developers can make use of the SDDC and speed up their work too. This makes it a very useful tool to speed up application deployment and discover new ways of deploying enterprise grade services.

vRealize Orchestrator

This is the hidden star amongst all SDDC components. VMware is even offering **vRealize Orchestrator** (**vRO**) included in the vCenter license for every customer. However, this is not heavily advertised so not too many customers are aware of this brilliant tool.

Its role is to run workflows and orchestrate their executions from a central point. This sounds not exciting, but actually, it is exciting. It is a true orchestrator, that means that it can do this for all and everything which has an API for its control. The reason to have it in an SDDC is to integrate into the non-VMware software. This can be a ticketing system, an IPAM or even external load balancer or storage systems. All these actions can be created in separate workflows, these can also be called from other workflows (nested execution).

The second big add on with the vRealize Orchestrator is the ability to create orderable services in vRealize Automation based on workflows. This means that it is even possible to provide innovative workflows in the vRealize Automation portal which have not too much to do with virtualization or VMware itself. An example of this is AD automation, where a user could actually request a user account for another user.

The orchestrator is as important as vRealize Automation itself. Since many workflows might run also simultaneously in a big environment, it is important to also reflect this in the design for this tool.

vRealize Operations Manager

vRealize Operations Manager (vROps) has two primary functions. One is the ongoing analytics and monitoring of the SDDC environment, the other is the capacity planning options and possibilities. Both of these tasks are not directly impacting the function of the SDDC, but still critical for the environment. Especially the capacity management aspect should not be underestimated. Since a cloud environment is in constant change, it is important to know and understand how much more load an environment can take until it needs further resources.

Besides that, if there is anything not working as expected, it is important to be able to quickly identify the failing component and how it might be related to other processes and tasks in the system. That can be done using the analytics part of vRealize Operations Manager. This provides more than just metrics, it understands relations and provides a relational mapping and even creates a possible root cause analysis. All this is not seen by the end user on the portal, but it is important to guarantee a healthy and fully functional cloud environment.

vRealize Business

This is the showback or financial part of the SDDC. It takes care of the cost of VMs and makes sure that these are seen by the end user once the VMs get ordered. It also does cost comparison between different cloud offerings if applicable. Basically, the sizing and design of vRealize Business should match the design and sizing for vRealize Automation.

This is again one of the services which will not harm the production, but it will have an influence on the overall system. If requestors do not know how expensive a request is, it might highly irritate them. Certainly, it will for approvers, if they need to sign off a VM request and they have no idea of the cost. So it is another example of a tool in the SDDC which is not technically blocking any tasks or workflows, but from a process point of view, it can be a show stopper issue if it does not run.

vRealize Log Insight

Similar as vRealize Operations Manager, **vRealize Log Insight** (vRLI) is not an active component in the request/deploy process. vRealize Log Insight is an advanced log collecting and searching tool. It is meant for quickly finding messages in logs. These logs can literally come from everywhere, as long as they are text based, vRLI will be able to parse and search them in a very powerful way.

But it is not only hypervisor logs, all management components in an SDDC should log into vRealize Log Insight. This means all the systems/tools/VMs running the SDDC send their messages and log files straight into vRealize Log Insight. This has the huge advantage that all logs are central and easily searchable. In a complex cloud environment, this can be key in order to speed up troubleshooting or even to find the failing component. An SDDC has many moving parts, so a solution like this is required in order to be able to do troubleshooting and monitoring.

Therefore, vRealize Log Insight has to be sized and designed to support the rest of the SDDC as good as possible.

NSX

NSX is VMware's network virtualization layer. It can enable true on-demand networking including security functionality. It also features advanced routing and protocol management features. It is not just a nice to have if the SDDC should be truly elastic and agile NSX is a must to support the different needs of the deployed services. Mostly it is known for microsegmentation, which means multiple services can sit on the same network without being able to influence each other on the network segment.

An example of this might be a web server and a database server sitting on the same network. But the web server can only contact the database server through port 80. However, NSX needs also to be designed correctly to provide the needed performance and availability for the entire SDDC. Since this is an entire task of its own there will be an own chapter of NSX discussing all the options and possibilities of this amazing piece of technology. NSX should be in the equation for the entire SDDC design, even though it needs its own design as well. The requirements, limits, and assumptions will ultimately also affect the NSX design.

An SDDC is the sum of its components and more than just a single application/infrastructure, each and every component should be designed for the size and the growth according to the estimate for the entire environment. This means, if one decides to design a large installation of vRealize Automation, this also needs to be reflected in vRealize Operations Manager, vRealize Orchestrator as well as vRealize Business and finally vRealize Log Insight. Since all of these are core cloud management components and automation systems, all of them need to be adopted for serving a large environment.

Design and relations of SDDC components

These are best practices and proven practices how a design for all components in the SDDC might look like. It will highlight a possible cluster layout including a detailed description want needs to be put where and why a certain configuration needs to be made like that.

Typically, every design should have an overview to quickly understand what the solution is going to look like and how the major components are related. In the SDDC one could start drawing the used vSphere Clusters including their functions.

Logical overview of the SDDC clusters

This following image describes an SDDC that is going to be run on the three cluster approach:

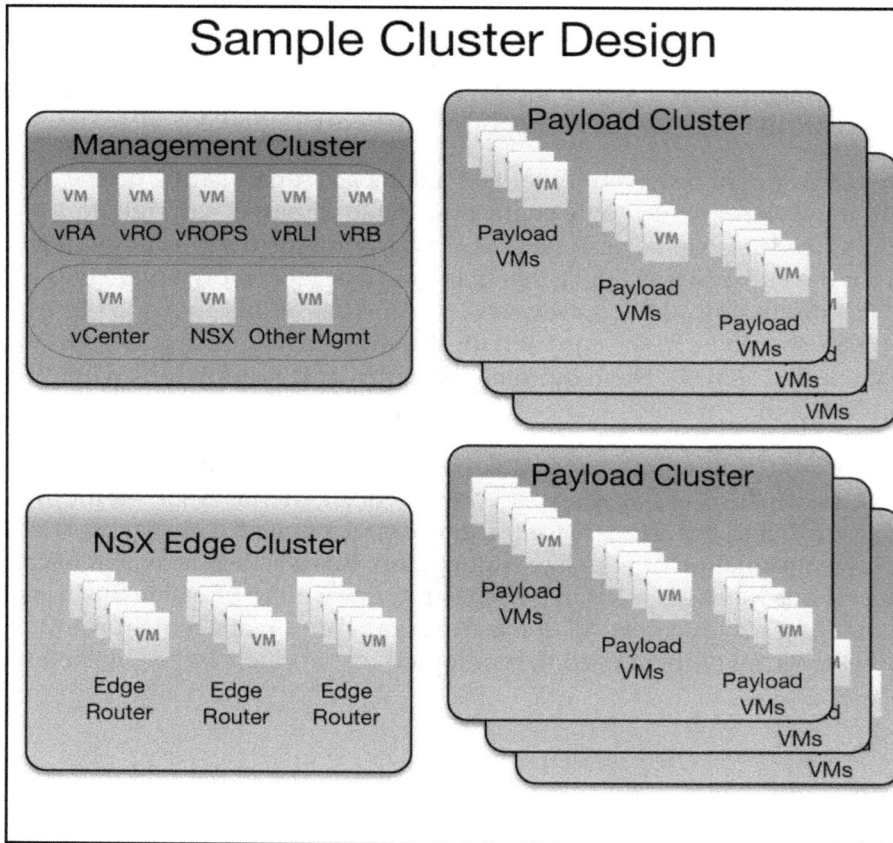

The three clusters are as follows:

- The management cluster for all SDDC managing services
- The edge for NSX cluster where all the north-south network traffic is flowing through
- The actual payload cluster where the production VMs get deployed onto

> Newer best practices from VMware, as described in the **VMware validated designs (VVD)** version 3.0 also propose a two-cluster approach. In this case, the edge cluster is not needed anymore and all edge VMs are deployed directly onto the payload cluster. This can be a better choice from a cost and scalability perspective. However, it is important to choose the model accordingly to the requirements and constraints found in the design.

The detail of this overview should be only as complex as necessary since its purpose is to give a quick impression over the solution and its configuration. Typically, there are a few of these overviews for each section.

This forms a basic SDDC design where the edge and the management cluster are separated. According to the latest VMware best practices, payload and edge VMs can also run on the same cluster. This basically is a decision based on scale and size of the entire environment. Often it is also a decision based on a limit or a requirement (for example, edge hosts need to be physically separated from management hosts)

Logical overview of the solution components

This is as important as the cluster overview and should describe the basic structure of the used SDDC components including some possible connections to third-party integration like IPAM.

Also, it should provide a basic understanding how the relationship between the different solutions is.

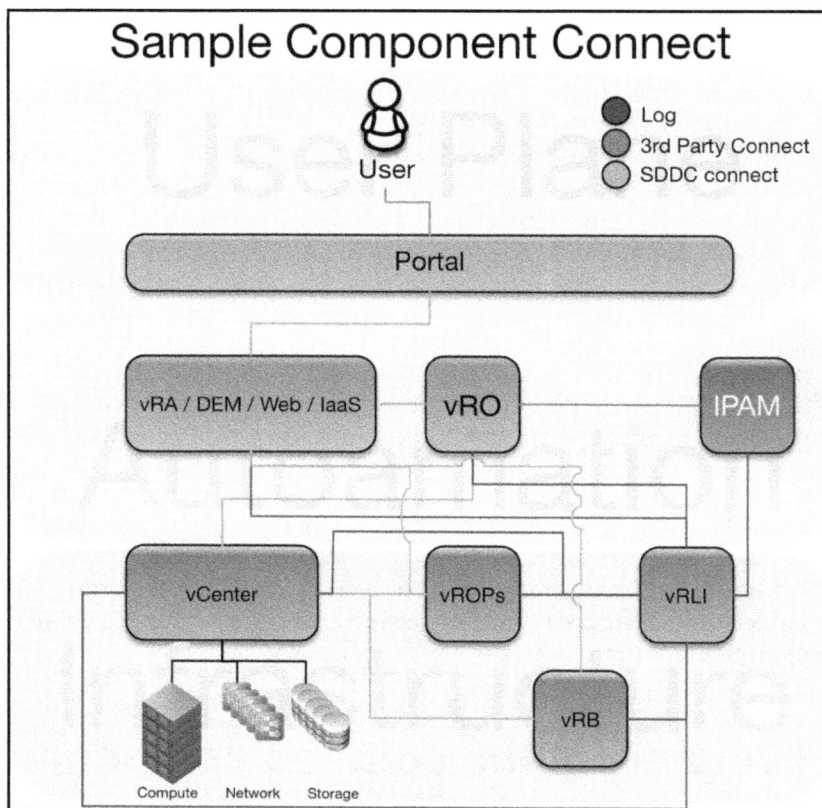

It is important to have an understanding of these components and how they work together. This will become important during the deployment of the SDDC since none of these components should be left out or configured wrong. Especially for the vRealize Log Insight connects that is important.

> If not all components are configured to send their logs into vRealize Log Insight, there will be gaps which can make troubleshooting very difficult or even impossible. A plan, which describes the relation, can be very helpful during this step of the SDDC configuration.

These connections should also be reflected in a table to show the relationship and control if everything has been set up correctly. The better the detail is in the design, the lower the chance that something gets configured wrong or is forgotten during the installation.

The vRealize Automation design

Based on the decision and the use case there are two setup methods/designs vRealize Automation 7 supports when being installed.

Small

Small stands for a very dense and easy to deploy design. It is not recommended for any enterprise workloads or even for production. But it is ideal to be used in a **Proof of Concept** (**PoC**) environment, or for a small dev/test environment to play around with SDDC principles and functions.

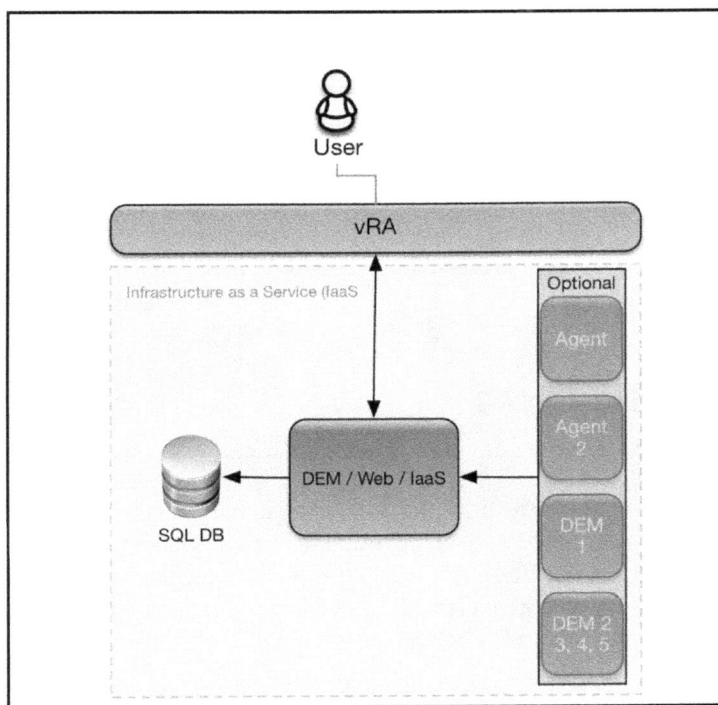

The clue of the small deployment is that all the IaaS components can reside on one single Windows VM. Optional there can be additional DEMs attached which eases future scale. However, this setup has one fundamental disadvantage: There is no built-in resilience or HA for the portal or DEM layer.

This means that every glitch in one of these components will always affect the entire SDDC.

Enterprise

Although this is a more complex way to install vRealize Automation this option will be ready for production use cases and is meant to serve big environments. All the components in this design will be distributed across multiple VMs to enable resiliency and high availability.

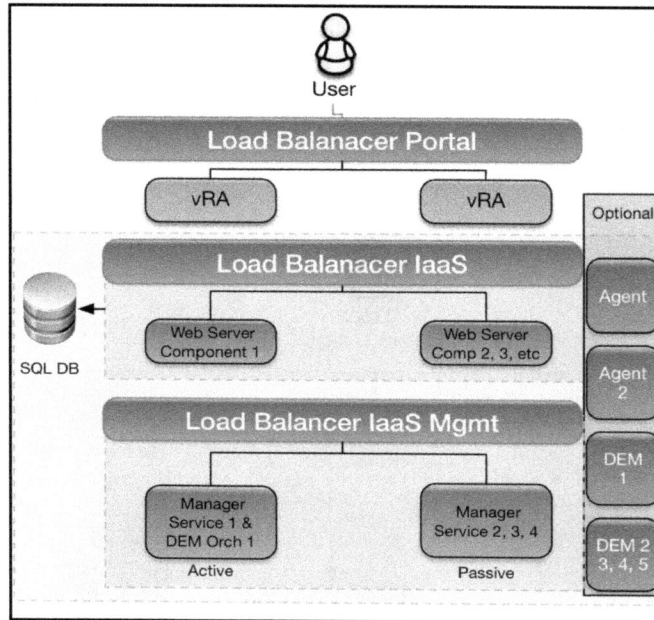

In this design, the vRealize Automation OVA (vApp) is running twice. To enable true resilience a load balance needs to be configured. The users access the load balancer and get forwarded to one of the portals. VMware has a good documentation on configuring NSX as a load balancer for this purpose, as well as **F5 load balancer**. Basically, any load balancer can be used, as long as it supports HTML protocol checks.

DNS alias or MS load-balancing should not be used for this, since these methods cannot prove if the target server is still alive. According to VMware, there are checks required for the load balancer to understand if each of the vRA Apps is still available. If these checks are not implemented the user will get an error while trying to access the broken vRA

In addition to the vRealize Automation portal, there has to be a load balancer also for the web server components. Also, these components will be installed on a separate Windows VM. The load balancer for this components has the same requirements than the one for the vRealize Automation instances.

The active web server must only contain one Web component of vRA, while the second (passive) web server can contain component 2, 3, and more.

Finally, also the DEM workers have to be doubled and put behind a load balancer to ensure that the whole solution is resilient and can survive an outage of any one of the components.

> If this design is used, the VMs for the different solutions needs to run on different ESXi hosts in order to guarantee full resiliency and high availability. Therefore, VM affinity must be used to ensure that never both DEMs, web server or vRA appliances run on the same ESXi host. It is very important to set this rules, otherwise, a single ESXi outage might affect the entire SDDC.

This is one of VMware's suggested reference designs in order to ensure vRA availability for users requesting services. Although it is only a suggestion it is highly recommended for a production environment. Albeit all the complexity, it offers the highest grade of availability and ensures that the SDDC can stay operative even if the management stack might have troubles.

> vSphere HA cannot deliver this grade of availability since the VM would power off and on again. This can be harmful in an SDDC environment. Also, to come back up operations, the startup order is important. Since HA can't really take care of that it might power the VM back on at a surviving host, but the SDDC might still be unusable due to connection errors (wrong order, stalled communication, and so on).

Once the decision was made for one of this designs it should be documented as well in the setup section. Also, take care that none of the limits, assumptions, or requirements are violated with that decision.

Another mechanism of resiliency is to ensure that the required vRA SQL database is configured as an SQL cluster. This would ensure that no single point of failure could affect this component. Typically big organizations have already some form of SQL cluster running, where the vRA database could be installed on. If this possibility is not existent, it is strongly recommended to set up such a cluster in order to protect the database as well. This fact should be documented in the design as a requirement when it comes to the vRA installation.

Infrastructure design examples

The SDDC design should also include the logical infrastructure design descriptions. This should cover the compute sector, storage as well as the approach to the network design. All these decisions and descriptions should be taken with the business case in mind and ultimately enable this case.

In this example, the business case was a new mobile app which should be flexible and quick to deploy and scale. Since there is no data, how many users will actually leverage this app should also be flexible in terms of performance. The important question to solve for now is: What might the infrastructure need to provide in order to serve this use case.

Network

The SDDC will use NSX as a software-defined network provider. This is relevant for the use case for various aspects:

- The web application will need multiple networks with firewall and security needs
- These networks might need to be provisioned on-demand
- The firewall rules need to be attached to the application and removed if the application is scaling down/added if scaling up
- Since it is impossible to predict the user number, the actual network requirements can't be forecasted

Since the edge cluster is already in the design the NSX functionality needs to be added to vRealize Automation. When setting up (designing) NSX it is important to stick to this requirements.

In vRealize Automation, these functions can be added to a blueprint (a service template) and therefore there is no need to pre-define them in the SDDC design itself. If there is a separate section for the blueprint design, this is where the network functions need to be documented and managed.

Storage

There might be different performance classes available regarding the storage in the data center. vSphere can differentiate storage classes by using the SPBM, which was described earlier in this book.

By using the SPBM functionality, vRA can create SLA or rate card service classes, which can be used by blueprints. The design should highlight these classes and decisions so they can easily be configured once the base installation of vRA is done.

This is an example of defining theses storage classes:

Policy name	Disk drives used	Performance guarantee
Ultra	All flash drives	500 IOPs/TB
Gold	SAS drives	100 IOPs/TB
Capacity	SATA drives	15 IOPs/TB

> **TIP**
> For easier configuration, these classes should be defined in vSphere using SPBM and matching data stores (or VASA). If those rules are present they can be leveraged within vRealize Automation by simply adding them to the infrastructure configuration.

In our business case, the application might run the web servers from the Capacity tier, but the databases might all run on the Ultra tier. This can also be set right within the blueprint. If this is done like this, the user will not have to choose the right storage. Also, an automation, which might deploy more instances, is always doing the right setup.

Based on requirements or business case there might be many more storage classes to be defined. There could also be extra classes like Ultra Replication or, what is more common, that the most expensive class features also replication and HA capabilities. While the most affordable tier might be simply storage without any resiliency or availability guarantee.

> This is a favorite option used by public cloud providers in order to make their offer look much more affordable. If one digs deeper into that, it might be discovered that the offered storage is not even persistent.

Compute

Like the other two resources, there are ways to carve out compute resources. This is less common but can be done using vRealize Automation. As described earlier, it either uses a whole vSphere cluster as compute resource or resource pools.

By using resource pools performance classes could be introduced. This might be very helpful for the business case we are looking at since the app needs to be developed somewhere. And this app development workload should most certainly not influence the production workload.

Therefore, a test/dev resource pool could be added to the available vRealize Automation resources, or a separate test/dev cluster. This highly depends on the volume. In this case, the volume of the app is not known, so also the resource needs for test/dev and production are unknown. The most efficient way would be to use pre-configured resource pools in order to provide flexible but fair resources to the two different workloads.

The definition of these could look like this:

Policy name	Resource pool	Shares	Performance
Production	Prod	10000	Unlimited/shares controlled
Development & Test	Test/dev	2000	Unlimited/shares controlled

All these vSphere resources can be transformed to resource reservations which then can be used in vRealize Automation to form the usable infrastructure.

Designing the tenants

One of the build in functionalities of vRealize Automation is the separation of clients. This is often referred to as multitenancy and describes a logical separation of resources, users, and services.

Smaller organizations are often using one single tenant and organize the separation of departments, if applicable, in so-called business groups. Bigger organizations might have the need for a stricter separation and therefore use tenants to separate different subsidiaries from each other. This might be required since all these subsidiaries can have different ADs containing the users.

In the SDDC design, it is necessary to describe these tenants and how they relate to each other. Again, it depends on the business case and the use case driving the SDDC installation. In our example, there might only be one tenant required but multiple business groups, as follows:

- XYZ Corp's tenant, connected to the AD

- Test and dev business group with dedicated resources
- Production business group with dedicated resources

This would fit the business case but is also based on the assumption that all requires users are in the same AD or that there is at least a trust between ADs. If that is not the case another tenant might be required for test and development.

From a security aspect, it is not recommended to separate in tenants, business groups are meant for that purpose. Each tenant comes with its own administration and role-based access structure. The more tenants the more complex this configuration get and the more operational effort an SDDC needs. The golden rule is, as less as possible as much as needed.

Tenants, business groups, and infrastructure fabrics

The tenancy and business group configuration needs to be described in the SDDC design. Sometimes it might be necessary to also give a short explain the action of what is what and why it is needed. Like for all other design decisions, it is recommended to link the assumptions, limits, and requirements also to the tenant layout.

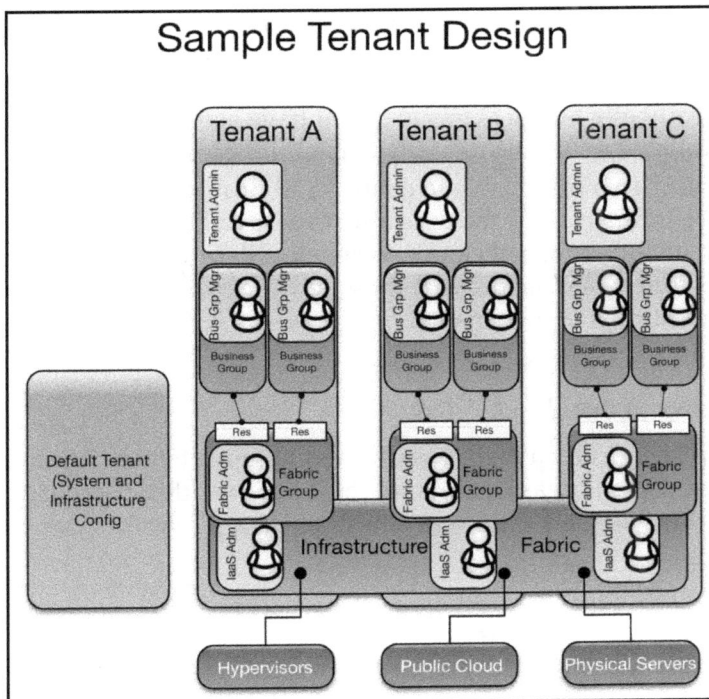

Sample Tenant Design

This is a sample image with three different tenants and should explain how separation is accomplished in the SDDC.

What is a tenant?

A tenant is a logical separation and can be assigned to an organization. Typically it connects to a specific AD to import user roles and access rights. Each tenant can be connected to a different AD, also this AD's do not have to relate to each other. This is important since it might be that all these organizations also do not relate to each other. A very prominent example of tenants is *Coca Cola* and *Pepsi* running in separate tenants but on the same SDDC infrastructure.

Each tenant has also an own tenant admin, this role can define and administer the business groups and assign roles to different users in the tenant. Those roles are as follows:

- **Business Group Manager**: Is reliable of managing resources and services within the business group as well as user privileges. This role can nominate other users to be a designer, an approval manager or a simple consumer
- **Fabric admin**: Is reliable of taking care of the infrastructure (called fabric) the tenant can access. This role will also take care of the reservations, which are created for each business group. A reservation is a smaller logical separated part of the available resources for the entire tenant. This is helpful to control how many resources a business group might have access to. Often not all resources are made available to be able to easily expand if necessary.
- **IaaS admin**: This role is able to control and provide the so-called *infrastructure fabric*. The infrastructure fabric is a set of all available resources to the SDDC. This can even include external clouds to enable a hybrid mode or physical machines. The IaaS admin makes sure that these resources are available and can be used by the fabric admins of the tenants.

What is a business group?

The business group is basically a logical separation within a tenant. It is meant to give different departments in an organization their own space within the tenant. To stay in our example, there might be a `Production` business group and one for `Test and Development`.

In the Coke example, the business groups might be "Finance, Development, IT, Legal". However, it is important to design this again according to the business case and to your organizational processes. business groups should be designed with the same rule in the background as tenants: Keep it simple, as much as needed, as few as possible.

Users can be part of multiple business groups and can see and deploy different services as a result of this. A user could be part of Dev & Test and Production and could deploy services in both groups. Services can be assigned to a specific group or to multiple business groups to be available in a global form. This makes sense for default IaaS services like a deployment of a VM including an OS.

What is a fabric group?

This is the logical part of the IaaS fabric a business group can consume. The fabric group is further divided (if applicable) in so-called *reservations*. As described in the previous image, a business group can hold a reservation for their tenant's fabric group

As described earlier in our example, these reservations would actually reflect the resource pools previously created in vSphere. However, in vRealize Automation, reservations can be further granular configured:

- Max number of CPU power and memory can be defined per reservation
- Max number of available storage space can be defined per reservation
- General VM quota (limit) can be defined per reservation

This setting might be important to ensure the flexibility and availability of the SDDC. A quota can make sure that the environment is not brought down by mass deployments. Furthermore, a limit on memory, CPU, and disk can ensure that the physical resources will not be overloaded. In case the limit is reached it can be simply reset. If a physical resource is fully loaded it will be more difficult to resolve this condition.

In our example, it is a bit difficult to set a limit since the actual resource usage is not known. Therefore, the design should assume a big reservation providing most of the resources. Also, a flexible approach will be needed, in case the deployed services will require more resources than originally configured.

What is the infrastructure fabric?

The so-called *infrastructure fabric* is a combination of all resources available to the SDDC. These resources will be attached to vRealize Automation by so-called *endpoints*. Those endpoints will give vRealize Automation direct access to the attached resources. This is a list of default endpoints for cloud and hypervisors:

- Infrastructure:
  - vCenter
  - KVM (REVM)
  - Microsoft Hyper-V
- Cloud:
  - vCloud Air
  - vCloud Director
  - Amazon Web Services
  - Microsoft Azure
  - OpenStack

For each of these endpoints, resources can be added to the infrastructure fabric. These can be further used within the reservations of the fabric groups.

There are also resources, which might not need or use an endpoint and can still be used. This might include the provisioning of physical servers using an API call. Such services are typically created by using vRealize Orchestrator workflows and will be included in vRealize automation by using the XaaS functionality.

In this case, no endpoint is needed since vRealize Automation is triggering the workflow in vRealize Orchestrator to actually provision the service. However, with this type of service, it is also required to think about reservation on the workflow/blueprint level, since business group reservations cannot be applied to XaaS services.

The purpose of all this is to describe it in your design and include every decision made in that document. It is also important to further briefly describe a functionality and the design decision so that this can still be understood if read years later, or by maybe, less technically focused people.

What must be included in the design

In a good SDDC design, all configurations and decisions are documented and can be easily defended. It will also include all other components besides for vRealize Automation if there are any design decisions made which influence their standard deployment.

If resilience is a requirement, it should be included and described through the entire design. Since an SDDC has quite a lot of moving parts, the design should be the baseline how they are installed and working together. Finally, the business case should be described at the very beginning of a design. Also, the mapping of constraints, limits and assumptions is important and should be reflected in every design decision.

Also, it will make sense to design a test or development environment at a smaller scale. These environments can be used to rehearse updates or upgrades as well as to develop new services and introduce them to the production environment at a later stage. Especially if it comes to upgrades, the procedure should be tested before doing it in the production environment. In the interest of budget and resources, those environments do not need to be as complex and resilient as the production, but they should be as similar as possible in order to get reasonable results. This is an important aspect and should not be underestimated when it comes to the overall design!

What if the vSphere environment is already running?

If an SDDC is created on top of a running vSphere environment, it is important to either include the old vSphere design as an attachment. If there are new clusters created to house either payload, edge or even the management, all these changes should be documented as well in an extra section. It is OK to refer to the already created design, but it should be easily understandable.

A lot of external references to an attachment will distract the readers flow. Also, it might be difficult to keep the overview if there are a lot of pointers to an external document. Use brief descriptions of the original design and only point to it to make the reader aware that there might be more information available.

Summary

In this chapter, we covered the main principles of a design including some examples. We looked at a fictive business case and learned how its requirements could be translated into a technical SDDC setup. Also, we touched some important design principles around assumptions, constraints, and limits as well as got a glimpse of what vRealize Automation might have to offer.

The next chapter will provide deep dive knowledge regarding vRealize Automation and further discuss its possibilities and functionalities. Beginning from tips for its installation it will highlight how to realize service deployments, approval workflows as well as external process integration. Also, service definitions called blueprints will play a big part.

5
VMware vRealize Automation

The CMP of the SDDC is one of the most important components in the entire installation. It is the first point of interaction for users, admins, and even applications if they order/request new services. Also, it needs to be easy to consume, quick, and scalable, as well as responsive and intuitive to use. In a VMware SDDC, this tool is called **vRealize Automation** (**vRA**) and it tries to combine all of these assets into a single portal. Also, behind the curtain, it needs to fulfill several other requirements such as multitenancy as well as business and technical approvals for service requests and their policy-based placement.

The another strong deliverable of a self-service portal or a CMP is the abstraction of complex tasks into simple requestable services which do not require any technical skills from the user. Think of it like your organization's *App Store* which simply enables the deployment of complex and less complex applications. All the user has to do is click on an icon and provide minimal input, and the service gets deployed automatically.

Besides that, vRA might also work as a cloud broker, where services can not only be deployed on premises, they can also be deployed on one of the various public cloud offerings. All this can be controlled and enabled by configuring vRA according to the design and use case you identified for your organization. Since there is a lot of customization and configuration which can be done using vRA, it is recommended to stick to the created design for the initial configuration to not get lost in all the options.

This chapter will explain the most important options and configurations for vRA in an SDDC environment. Also, it will further explain settings and configuration based on the identified use case from earlier chapters.

The following points will be covered:

- Installation tips and tricks
- Description of vRA concepts
- Configuration examples

vRA installation

In vRA version 7, VMware made the installation one of the simplest in the history of the tool. Before that, it was not a simple installation. Sometimes even **VMware Professional Services Organization** took more than a day to install the tool. Thanks to the engineering effort VMware put into the shiny and new installation routine, this can be accomplished in a couple of hours, depending on the chosen setup (small lab or enterprise).

The very nice thing about the new installer is that it guides the admin through all the steps and events, and provides a controlled way of rolling back after an error by using VMware snapshots, just follow the suggested procedure of the installer and there should be no bad surprises.

First things first

To get started, vRA needs to be downloaded (the vApp) from VMware. The vApp can then be imported into the separate vSphere management cluster. The import will bring up a configuration wizard where the most important specs for the deployment need to be put in:

- IP address
- Admin password
- DNS name
- Default gateway
- Search domain

> Before the deployment of the vRA appliance(s), the DNS should be set up. Name resolution is very important for this tool and can make the difference between success and failure. It is very important to check both forward and reverse lookup before proceeding.

Based on the chosen setup, vRA will need one or more Windows VMs to deploy the DEM and IaaS components into. It is recommended that these VMs also get provisioned up front to be ready to use once the vRA vApp has been fully deployed. Besides the very straightforward setup guide, VMware also renewed the installation guide for vRA to cover all the necessary steps to make sure that vRA gets deployed successfully. In the case of enterprise deployment, additional configuration outside of vRA is required to be able to use this deployment; this mainly includes the configuration of the load balancer for the IaaS, DEMs, as well as for the vRA instances themselves.

The IaaS server(s) needs a Microsoft SQL database to work properly. Either a separate database instance or at least a database registered on an existing MS SQL server. The vRA installation wizard will take care of setting up the database including the required data schema.

Every Windows VM in the vRA ecosystem needs to have MS DTC enabled/installed in order to function properly. Sometimes it is required to reregister/reinstall this on the DEM workers or on the SQL database:

1. Open an administrator command prompt.
2. Run the following command: `msdtc -uninstall`.
3. Reboot the virtual machine.
4. Open a separate command prompt and run the following command:
   `msdtc -install <manager-service-host>` (manager service host is optional).

Once everything is prepared, the deployment can begin, from this point on, it will be guided and should be well followed until the *validation* step.

To get the installation started, a web browser is needed to access the newly deployed vRA vApp.

To access the vRA 7 web installer, open a browser and connect to the freshly installed vRA appliance using this format:
`https://vra-a.yourdomain.local:5480`

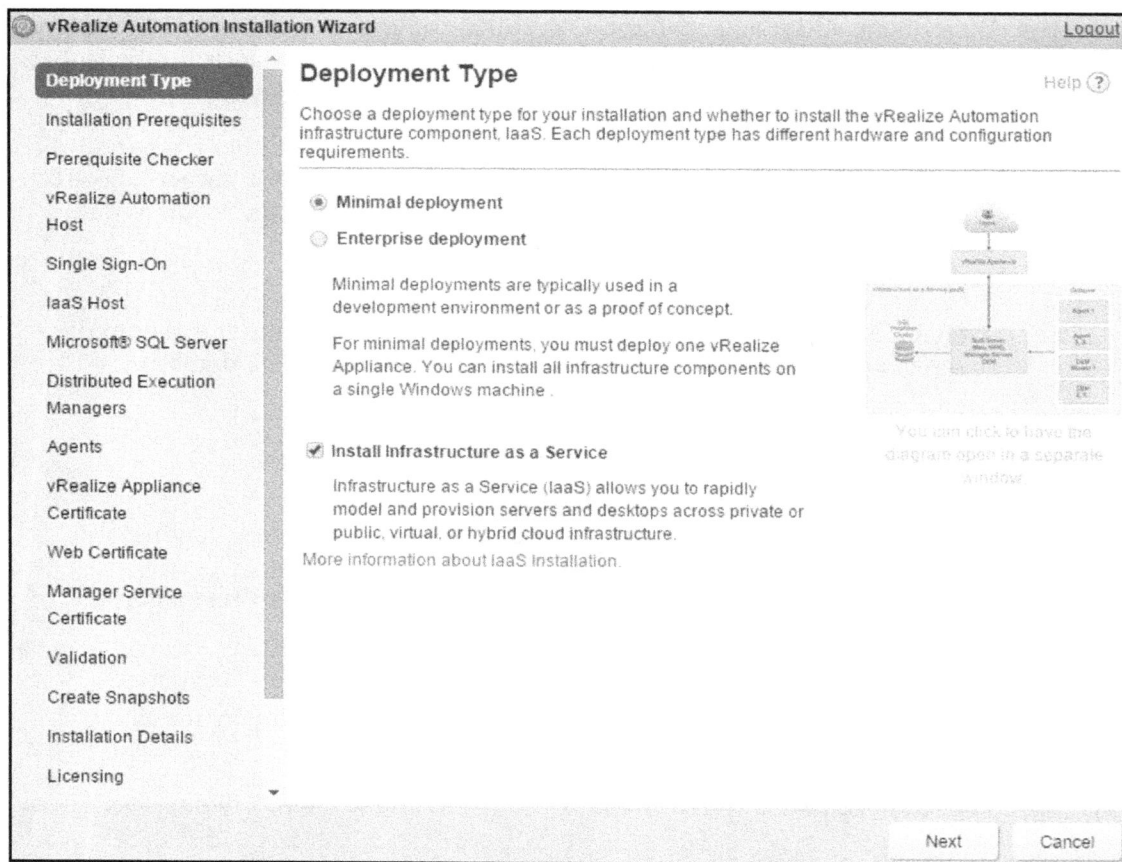

This will open the vRA appliance web configuration, which will start guiding you through the further installation. In order to assist with the configuration of the Windows VMs/components, the agent needs to be downloaded from the vRA vApp and it needs to be installed on all participating vRA Windows VMs. This ensures that vRA can configure and install missing products using the agent right at the moment of setting up the portal, pretty neat.

Take note of all names and configurations provided during the setup. Some of them will be required afterward to set up vRA correctly. One important name to write down is the vCenter endpoint name. It will be set up at the DEM worker config. The DEM will have a text field to enter the name (the default is `vCenter`). This name is required to add the endpoint later to vRA. It cannot be retrieved from the DEM once it has been set. If this name is wrong, vRA cannot successfully add the endpoint!

If vRA finds missing configuration and pieces on the Windows VMs, it will provide an option to *fix* these. This is a very handy function to prevent connecting to each Windows VM and doing it manually. Mostly, it works fine and adds the missing configuration/roles/tools directly to the Windows VMs:

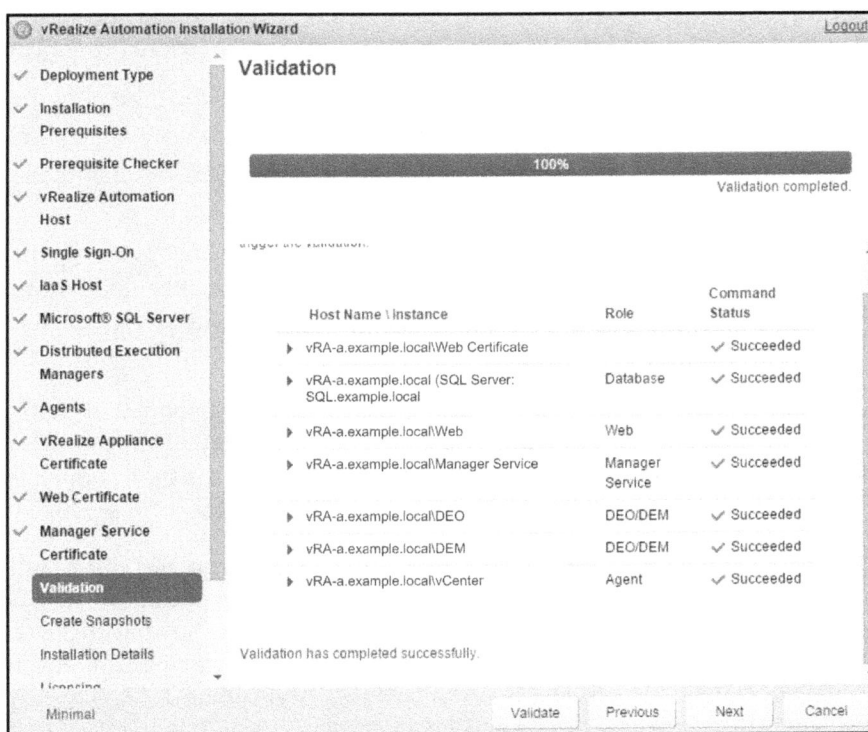

Once all this is settled and solved, the setup will suggest making a snapshot of all components (vRA appliance(s) as well as all involved Windows VMs). It is highly recommended to follow this instruction for all components. The snapshot will be used as a rollback option in case something has gone wrong with the setup. If this is not done at this point, the entire setup has to be revisited.

Advanced installation configuration

Once all components have been successfully set up, it is time to create the other necessary configuration for the components. In the case of a simple lab deployment, nothing else has to be done here. In the case of an enterprise deployment, the load balancer for the DEMs, IaaS, and for the vRA appliance VMs has to be configured properly.

This is required, since the user should only have one unified URL to use, no matter whether vRA-*a* or vRA-*b* is serving its request. The application itself is cluster-aware, so no OS cluster has to be created; this includes the Windows components as well. However, the SQL database required for vRA should also be clustered using Microsoft best practices. Refer to your SQL database admins or the Microsoft documentation for more info on SQL clusters.

The configuration of the load balancer is well documented by VMware and would be too much to be described in detail here. The actual documentation for vRA 7, including the load balancer configuration, can be found at the VMware support site.

> **TIP**
>
> Load balancer white paper: `http://pubs.vmware.com/vra-70/topic/com.vmware.ICbase/PDF/vrealize-automation-70-load-balancing.pdf`

After everything has been set up and controlled, be sure to remove the snapshots from the VMs. At this stage, vRA will be fully functional from a portal point of view and is ready to be configured for the first time.

Once the setup is complete, the system will tell you that there is a special user to log on to vRA named `configurationadmin`, using the password provided earlier in the installation wizard. This user will be the first step of configuring vRA; even for that, there is an automation VMware is offering right in the freshly installed portal.

Logging on to the system with that user will bring up a vRA portal and there will be one service under **Catalog** which will automate the setup and configuration of the first or default tenant of vRA. Even this step can now be done with a few simple clicks if desired. It is as simple as running the service, putting in all the necessary information, and waiting for vRA to complete configuring itself. However, albeit this is very handy, it is highly recommended to first understand the principles in case anything has to be altered or added manually.

vRA concepts

If this is the first encounter with the tool, it will throw a lot of new terms at administrators, yet to be understood. While it follows VMware's methodology and naming conventions, there are a couple of things which are not used by any other tool in the VMware ecosystem.

vRA's little helper

Besides the portal itself, vRA requires some helper services to actually get things done in the underlying environment. During the setup, those are configured and aligned to work together with vRA to be able to automate the underlying infrastructure.

DEM

DEM is sometimes also referred to as the *manager service*. Basically, this component is connecting vRA to possible deployment targets for VMs. This can be vCenter (as suggested during the wizard-driven installation for vRA) but it can also be other hypervisor targets such as Hyper-V or KVM. Besides that, vRA will also be able to connect to external clouds such as **Amazon Web Services** (**AWS**), vCloud Air (VMware), and Microsoft Azure, as well as OpenStack installations. Most of these targets need to have a DEM worker configured to access those. This configuration can either be added to an existing DEM or a new DEM for these targets to be deployed.

> There are also so-called *DEM workers* which should always be installed on separate VMs. Use at least two DEM workers for a production-grade environment.

The IaaS server

Basically, this is the web server component of vRA, which provides the portal as well as its basic functionality. In small environments, it can be installed together with the DEM on the same VM/OS. In enterprise environments, it is typically installed as a separate VM. The IIS configuration is done by the vRA setup routine, which takes care that all required functions for the portal are available.

vRealize Orchestrator

vRealize Orchestrator is one of the most important components in a vRA setup. The vRA self-configuration service is basically a vRO workflow, which is added as a so-called XaaS service to the freshly installed vRA. **Anything as a Service (XaaS)** basically means that anything which can be automated can be a requestable service in vRA. vRO is included in the vRA appliance or can be run separately as its own vApp. In large environments, it makes sense to separate vRO from vRA to share the load of the tools. vRO can also be installed in an HA setup and sync its content to multiple vRO tiers.

The Infrastructure tab

Under this tab, vRA offers the infrastructure options and configurations. Depending on the user role, it will display more or fewer options to be configured. The **Infrastructure** tab will cover everything which has to do with the available resources, whether they are physical or cloud resources.

Endpoints

An endpoint is an infrastructure target on which vRA can deploy VMs. The first and most important endpoint will be vCenter. The endpoint name has to be exactly the same as the one provided to the DEM during its setup. This means the name will also be case-sensitive. vRA can have multiple endpoints including clouds as well as other hypervisors. Endpoints will actually form the so-called *infrastructure fabric* from which resources can be cut out in the form of reservations and offered to portal users.

Compute Resources

Either by highlighting an endpoint and hovering over the arrow symbol or by clicking on the **Resources** menu at the left-hand pan, the portal will display all currently discovered resources. In terms of vCenter, these will be vSphere clusters, including their storage configuration such as data stores or even data store clusters. In this menu, resources from an endpoint can also be excluded.

This especially makes sense if the management cluster is part of the same vCenter, but should never show up as a resource available to end users in vRA. In this case, it can be simply *unelected* by un-ticking the box:

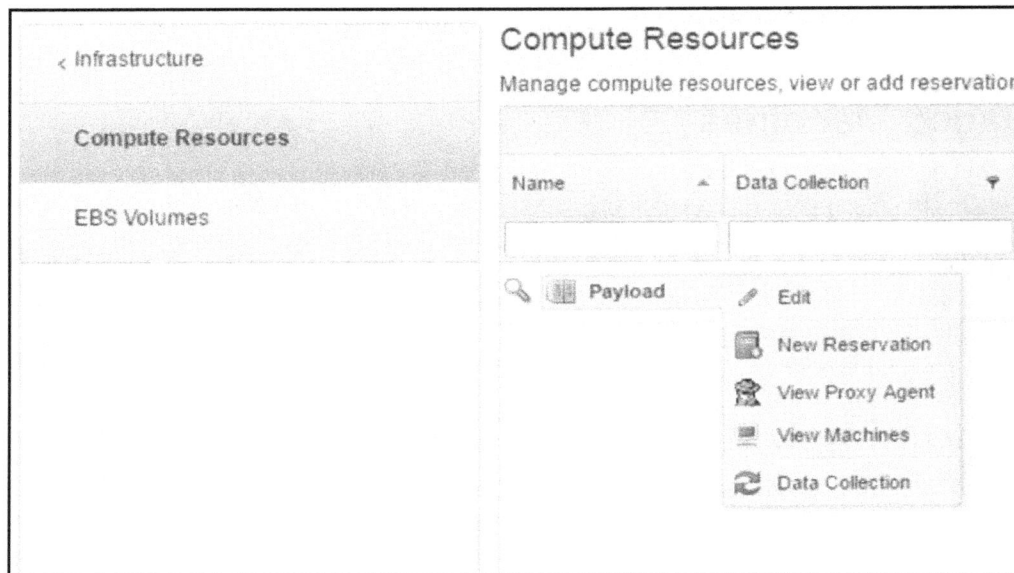

Reservations

This handles the reserved capacity for a tenant/business group based on the actual available resources. For example, not all resources from the cluster might be made available for a given audience:

- Resources: Cluster has 4 TB of memory, 20 TB of data stores, and 120 GHz of CPU available
- Reservation: Cluster has 2 TB of memory, 5 TB of data stores, and 70 GHz of CPU available

This reservation will be enforced by vRA and is unknown to vSphere or vCenter. Also, it has nothing to do with resource pool reservations. However, a vSphere resource pool can also be chosen as a provider instead of an entire cluster. The idea of a reservation is to guarantee a select part of the infrastructure fabric without exposing all of its capabilities. Reservations can be dynamically increased and shrunk.

Managed Machines

Under this option, vRA will list all current managed VMs deployed using the portal (or imported). This is especially useful since not all users will see all VMs deployed, they will only see their own VMs. If there is an incident to analyze, an administrator with the appropriate role assigned could use this to trace whether vRA is able to reach the VM. Besides that, it will also list the owner and the state of all deployed and currently managed VMs for quick identification.

The Administration tab

Under this tab, vRA provides global and/or tenant-related administration options depending on the user's role. These options control the global configuration of a tenant. This includes connecting to an AD, defining default hostnames, and configuring business groups, as well as other settings.

Approval Policies

Approvals are important to keep an automated data center clean and structured. If everything was free and instant to deploy without approvals, users would keep creating machines until the data center eventually ran out of space. There are also process and regulatory reasons to have approval policies. This menu will allow approvals to be defined based on various different conditions.

Approvers can be defined by username or group; additionally, vRA can try to fetch the manager of a requesting user right from AD.

Approvals are distinguished in two major groups: preapprovals or postapprovals. **Preapprovals** are run before a request is processed. There will be no provisioning until the request has been approved.

Postapprovals are issued after the request has been processed. If the approver denies the request, all provisioned resources will be deleted instantly. Both can be used at the same time. There are scenarios where it makes sense to use both types of approval.

If the technical approver needs to ensure that a request can be fulfilled technically or capacity-wise, it will make sense to add this as a preapproval. If there is a financial decision-maker who needs to approve the use of resources, it might make sense to do this after the resource has been provisioned. By doing that, it will be instantly available to the user/group after it has been approved.

Finally, approvals can be set on many different actions and items in vRA, from creating snapshots to deploying machines, all the way to destroying a deployment. All these actions can have different approval rules as well as different approvers.

Not only can the different categories be approved, but approvals will also be able to be set based on conditions. For example:

- 2 vCPU and 4 GB RAM requires a technical preapproval
- The service has been requested two times instead of one
- The service is exceeding a certain cost limit
- The service is coming form a distinct user or group

Also, a configuration is possible where all approvers need to approve, or any approver can do this.

Directories Management

This setting ensures that vRA can be added to a user directory such as Microsoft Active Directory. It is used to browse users and grant access to certain vRA functionalities. Directory access can be set on a per-tenant basis, which means that every tenant can be connected to a different user directory. This ensures that separate organizations can use their own user directory and do not have to duplicate this data into any local portal user directory.

Here all the users and groups get matched to vRA's role-based access model. There are separate roles in the system, from a simple *user* to a *designer*, as well as a *tenant admin*. According to the role, they can accomplish different tasks in vRA:

User	Role
System administrator (Does not follow the multitenancy concept)	This role typically owns the entire configuration. It will ensure that new tenants are created as well as new users get assigned to these tenants as *tenant administrator*.
IaaS administrator (Does not follow the multitenancy concept)	This role takes care of all the attached resources such as cloud, vSphere, network, and so on, and will organize it into tenant-level *fabric groups*. These can then be pointed toward fabric administrators.
Tenant administrator (Does not follow entirely the multitenancy concept)	Typically, this role is close to the business. It is responsible for configuring the tenant, including its branding, as well as adding tenant users and group management. Also, resource usage can be tracked by the tenant administrator, who can then use this data to trigger a resource reclamation request.
Fabric administrator	Responsible for the management of physical machines and compute resources assigned to their fabric groups. They also take care of the creation and management of reservations and policies within their tenant. Additionally, they manage property groups as well as the machine prefixes and the property dictionary that are used across all tenants and business groups.
Blueprint architect (Does not follow entirely the multitenancy concept)	This role can create blueprints designed for the consumer to be requested through the service catalog. Typically, this role is assigned to IT architects within an organization.
Catalog administrator	Manages the service catalogs and also decides the new services.
Approval administrator	Manages approval policies. These can be added to catalogs and define what a requestor can order with or without an approval.
Approver	Can approve catalog requests from other users.
Business group manager	Manages one or more so-called *business groups*. As part of this, they can entitle users or groups in their tenant/business group to service catalogs. Also, they can request and manage items on behalf of the users in their business group.
Support user	They can request and manage catalog items on behalf of other users in their group. Typically fulfilled by support administrators as well as operators.

Business user	This is the typical consumer role. They can request services from a catalog and manage those provisioned resources in the portal.

Of course, these roles can be combined as well. There are some notable side effects when combining, so this feature should be used with care. One side effect is that if the *fabric administrator* role is combined with a system-wide role such as *IaaS administrator*, it can control all the fabric items for *ALL tenants* in the system. System-wide roles are commented with *Does not follow multitenancy concept* in this table for better understanding.

The *blueprint architect* role can see assets even if they are not part of the tenant it is located in. In detail, a *blueprint architect* can see all reservation policies, storage reservation policies, network profiles, machine prefixes, property dictionary as well as build profiles. Again, they cannot tamper with assets not belonging to their tenant, but they have a sort of *read all* ability. This is why this role does not follow the multitenancy concept entirely.

The *tenant administrator* role has a similar capability if a fabric group is shared among different tenants. Even though each tenant has its own reservations, the *tenant administrator* can see the reservation of the other tenants. Again, read-only, but it is revealed, though.

Catalog Management

vRA organizes Services in so-called *catalogs*. They can be seen as categories and therefore hold may services of a kind. Catalogs are useful to organize the service offerings, but also to give the right users or groups access to their services. Instead of entitling each and every service, the whole catalog can be entitled.

Categories of catalogs may be:

- **Infrastructure as a Service**: OS deployments of VMs or multiple VMs will be added to this catalog
- **Platform as a Service**: Application deployments including OS deployments will be available under this catalog
- **Directory services**: If there is any AD self-service for users, this might have been shown here

Property Dictionary

vRA maintains a dictionary of properties. Those can be used as inputs for the services. Typically, properties hold information, which are required for pre or post processing of service requests. This information can be used to run a vRO workflow once the VM is deployed, or to add a custom hostname during provisioning. Also, they can be used to instruct the vRA agent, also referred to as the *Guest Agent* to run certain scripts after the VM deployment. All usable vRA built-in properties and their meaning can be found in the vRA installation documentation from VMware. It is highly recommended to make yourself familiar with those in order to use the full potential of vRA.

Additionally, properties can also be user-defined to ask for specific settings to be used in vRealize Orchestrator workflows. It is recommended to use a unique preset to quickly identify custom properties, also, this helps to prevent using system-wide properties instead of custom ones.

Click on **Property Definitions** to define custom properties. Also, a property group needs to be defined in order to use custom properties in blueprints. This is just a logical container to which multiple custom properties can be added.

Reclamation

This is basically the functionality to reclaim so-called *wasted space* from the environment. If vRealize Operations is used, it can be connected to this service and will deliver data and suggestions on VMs which can be reclaimed. A reclamation request can be started at this menu based on the data provided. If vRealize Operations is not used, vRA will use its own algorithm to display reclaimable VMs.

Branding

For a tenant admin, this is where the look and feel of the portal can be changed to support any customer identity. Colors, logos, and text, as well as the login screen and even a logon box can be customized to fully blend into an organizational environment. These customizations can be done per tenant.

Notifications

Under this menu, mail servers for inside and outside notifications can be set up. vRA will send e-mails toward users for all kind of events. Typically, those include the expiration of a service, or if something is not going as it should. The servers and the e-mail account to use for these mailings can be set here. Also, under the **Scenarios** submenu, all the notification actions can be activated or suspended. This is especially important if approvals should also work with e-mail replies, therefore, this setting should be configured very carefully.

Events

This can be used to display event logs of vRA. In this list view, all vRA events are displayed plus additional content. It can be seen as the audit trail of the entire cloud portal. It is useful to analyze or troubleshoot user requests.

The second menu is called **Subscriptions** and contains a very powerful option of vRA 7. In previous versions, VM provisioning could be tweaked by adding so-called *workflow stubs*. These stubs are bound to specific VM deployment states such as preapproval, postapproval, provisioning, or deleting. These workflow stubs were used to add third-party system functionality such as IPAM functionality or implementing a backup workflow.

However, in vRA 7, these workflow stubs have been replaced with so-called *subscriptions*. These are more flexible and can be added easier than workflow stubs, since vRA can decide to run them based on a series of criteria, which the user can set. These can also include custom properties, which makes it even easier to run customization workflows during a VM deployment.

vRO configuration

This is the part where the vRealize Orchestrator interface is set up. Under Server Configuration, it can be decided to use an external vRO instead of the built-in vRO server. In large environments, it is recommended to have at least one external vRO server for executing all the necessary customization workflows. Also, if vRO is already used for daily automation in an environment, it makes a lot of sense to use the same also for the cloud automation.

> The embedded vRO comes with a series of plugins pre-set-up already. These are necessary to use all features of vRA 7 integration, such as NSX. If all these plugins need to be transferred to the external vRO, there is a simple trick how to download these:
>
> 1. Open WinSCP or another SCP copy tool of your choice.
> 2. Connect to the vRA appliance using user *root* and your chosen password.
> 3. Navigate to the following directory: `/usr/lib/vco/app-server/plugins`.
> 4. All plugin `.dar` files can now be downloaded and imported into the external vRO.

vRA concepts

Some of the vRA concepts have been already addressed in `Chapter 4`, *SDDC Design Considerations*. However, there are a few concepts of vRA which are critical to understand in order to create a sound configuration of the portal and its functionalities. The most important concept is the *service* concept. It can be seen as the central point of vRA and therefore should be well understood.

vRA organizes deployments in so-called services and service catalogs. A service is far more than just one VM; it can consist of various different constructs. However, a service always starts with a blueprint.

As a Service synonyms

In the cloud space, there are many *as a Service* definitions around. Unfortunately, not all of them mean the same thing, even if they use the same acronym. This is a list of the most popular and most used acronyms and how they are *translated* into vRA.

IaaS

Infrastructure as a Service (IaaS) and is probably the most popular cloud abbreviation. Normally, if organizations refer to IaaS, they mean simple deployments such as a single VM with or without an operating system installed. Or a bare metal deployment, also with an operating system installed. It should cover all configuration and installation steps for those deployments until it can be fully used by an end user. In most of the cases, this is the simplest way to start with automation, even though there are hidden caveats with this method.

However, this is the most standard term, since it always means to provision some infrastructure-related services per a user's request.

In vRA 7, IaaS is often reflected using VM templates to clone new VMs. However, some organizations prefer to use PXE boot environments in order to deploy VMs and keep using their legacy processes. This can be important in combination with third-party application installation frameworks such as Puppet or Salt.

PaaS

Platform as a Service (PaaS). This term is probably the most misused term in regards to cloud computing. The problem is, a platform is not a well-described asset. It can be a lot of things and therefore the abbreviation is used for all different cases where vendors or organizations think it might be a good fit. Especially in the DevOps world, this term has an entirely different meaning from a technology point of view.

Here are a few examples where PaaS might be used:

- A service deployment contains the OS as well as the application layer for multiple VMs
- A service deployment creates a VM including OS and SQL-DB configuration, ready for other VMs connecting the DB
- A service deployment creates an entire Java development environment
- A platform which runs a Java environment, ready to run `.jar` packages on demand

- A platform which runs a Java environment including even No-SQL DBs and all other necessary components to run Java programs

> **TIP**
>
> To avoid a lost in translation issue with PaaS, it is always recommended to understand the expectations as well as the use case. Once these are clear, the mutual understanding of PaaS might be clear as well.

In vRA, currently, PaaS is executed as application installation on demand using application automation services.

XaaS

XaaS is basically a VMware definition. The meaning of this is to underline the advanced functionalities of vRA in conjunction with vRealize Orchestrator. Anything can basically run as a workflow on Orchestrator and therefore can be brought into vRealize as a XaaS blueprint.

vRA has its own menu section to define XaaS. The work itself is done by vRO, which means that also the workflow must be pre-existing to be included in vRA.

Everything with an API can be automated and turned into a requestable XaaS in vRA's service catalog. That can start with an AD add-on function such as adding new users, all the way to calling non-VMware hardware to start up/install an OS.

In vRA, XaaS is used to directly include and request vRO workflows in the portal.

Blueprints

In vRA, blueprints are the building plans of services. Basically, they can be seen as templates for VM deployments. However, they can contain far more than just VMs to deploy. A complex blueprint can deploy VMs, networks, security settings, and firewall rules, as well as load balancers and more.

In vRA 7, VMware has introduced a brand-new blueprint designer. This designer is also known as the **Converged Blueprint Designer** and combines a fantastic new feature of vRA 7, multiendpoint blueprints. In the past, it was not possible to have blueprints deploying machines or services in different infrastructure fabrics. Each blueprint was locked to an endpoint in vRA. In order to achieve that, there was a separate module called **application automation** where different vRA blueprints could form an application blueprint which would have that possibility.

However, in vRA IaaS, without the application automation component, that meant that if a blueprint was made for vSphere, it could not be used for AWS or Hyper-V or any other endpoint.

In vRA 7, VMware decided to work around that limitation by allowing also IaaS blueprints including multiple different targets. So even an IaaS blueprint with two VMs can now be deployed on, for example, vCloud Air and vCenter at the same time. It will be presented in the portal as single service.

However, for single VMs, the limitation still exists and users might see a portal where there are three different Windows VMs: one for vSphere, one for AWS, and one for vCloud Air, for example.

To ease the whole process, though, VMware decided to create the Converged Blueprint Designer, which can combine different endpoint targets as well as application automation tasks:

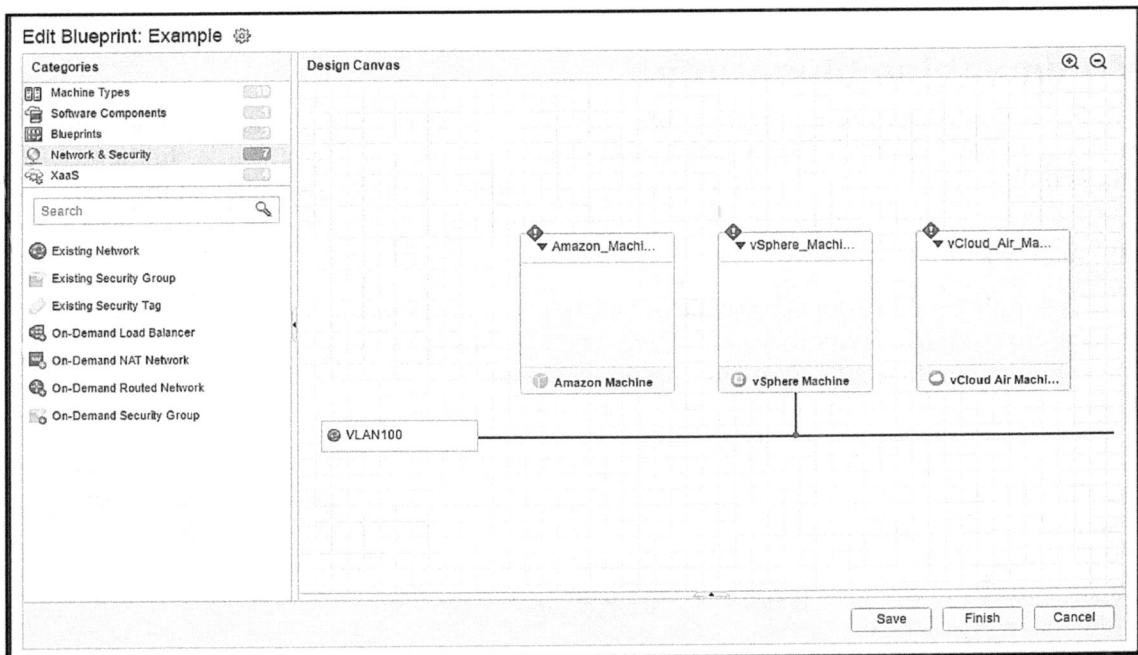

VMware typically has different categories for services or blueprints in vRA. Each of these categories refers to a very different type as well as covering different functionality and use cases.

Single machine blueprints

This is the easiest blueprint configuration. As the name implies, it refers to a single machine plus the necessary addition such as a network. The quickest way to provision a virtual machine is using vCenter templates in the blueprint. However, vRA 7 supports many other possibilities such as WMI (Windows image file) and Kickstarter, as well as using an external vRO workflow for machine provisioning. It depends on the processes and standards required to provision VMs. Whatever method may be preferred, a blueprint in vRA can be configured to use this method and automate all the steps. Even though it might be a relatively slow network installation, the added automation will still enhance the overall process.

Multimachine blueprints

Similar to single machine blueprints, they can have a different deployment method. The main difference is they can have a different deployment method per VM used in the blueprint. If some VMs might end on a cloud versus others might be deployed internally, they can and must have different deployment methods. All this can be configured in a unified blueprint by using the editor.

If VMs should be provisioned outside of vCenter, it is important to make sure that the chosen provisioning method is already working. For instance, if cloning from a template is chosen for vCloud Air, the template should be already configured and ready in vCloud Air. The same is true for vCenter and other endpoints, of course.

If the provisioning method is set, using the graphical editor can also set the order in which the VMs are going to be provisioned. This might be important if software components are installed as well on the machines. To define this, the graphical designer has a function to draw an arrow from the dependent machine to the component/machine it depends on. This can be done by clicking on the little round icon appearing in the upper-left corner of the VM.

The dependent machine will be deployed after the depending component is fully available. In the following figure, the AWS machine will be deployed after the vSphere machine is up and running:

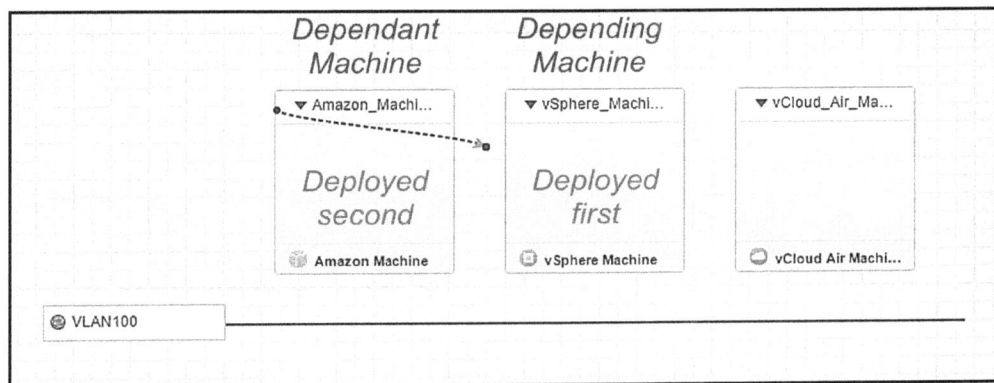

Application automation

Before vRA 7, application automation was a separate service, running on a separate virtual appliance. Blueprints had to be linked with this service, which then could use this link to provide a GUI to manage and install additional applications. This has now been merged into the general blueprint design in vRA 7.

The heading **Software Components** under **Categories** in the top-left corner contains predefined software installments, ready to be used in blueprints. Before they can be selected there, they have to be set up in vRA 7.

These are the steps to set up a software component:

1. Open the vRA portal either as `configurationadmin` or as another user with an appropriate role.
2. Click on the **Design** tab and then on **Software Components**.
3. Click on the **New** button to add a new component.
4. Give a descriptive name (ID gets auto-generated from the name).
5. Select the container type, for example, `Machine`.
6. Provide properties if necessary, for example, database name, username, password, and so on.

7. Under **3. Actions**, provide the necessary installation actions. These can be either **Install, Configure, Start**, or **Uninstall**. All of these can be using either Bash or PowerShell or CMD script, depending on the software and OS it should run on. Typically, the installation script is also downloading the software source package.

8. Prove the newly added software component and click **Finish** to save it.

9. In order to be usable by blueprint architects, it must be published. This is done by selecting it and clicking on the **Publish** button.

The container type defines what vRA will allow to be done with this application. Furthermore, it tells the GUI where and how the software component can be used. There are three different types available in vRA:

- **Machine component**: This means the software can be installed on a machine only. It is not possible to install this software on top of other software installments.

- **Software component**: In this case, the software is meant to be installed on other, already running software components, for instance, like a web server set up on top of an already installed **Apache Web Server**.

- **Named software component**: This allows one of the already defined components to be picked. This software would then be an addition/installment only for this component. This can be, for example, a Java program to be installed on top of the basic but specific Java installation.

> If there is no software component defined yet, only two options will display – **Machine Component** and **Software Component**, since the **Named Software** component needs to be present before it can be selected.

Typically, the used scripts for the actions are pre-existing for the selected software. The application team may already use these scripts to conduct unattended installations. To ease the reuse of these scripts, vRA supports the most used scripting languages, such as PowerShell, Bash, and CMD.

Sample configurations

This section will describe how to configure a blueprint, add it to a service catalog, and make it orderable for users in a given business group. It will cover the following points in greater detail:

- Creating and preparing a template in vCenter to be used for a blueprint
- Creating a network pool to be used with a pre-existing VLAN
- Creating a set of properties to be used with the blueprint
- Creating an IaaS blueprint for a VM
- Publishing the service for a given business group (entitlements)

Template preparation in vCenter

Before the blueprint can rely on the template, a few things have to be checked in vCenter in order to make it a successful and straightforward deployment. Here is a list of things which should be considered for the template:

- The most recent VMware tools should be installed in the template
- The vRA Guest Agent should be installed successfully in the template
- If it is a Windows template, it should NOT be part of a domain (only a workgroup)
- For Windows or Linux VMs, there should be a valid customization specification available in vSphere.
- The template should have a limited size, for example, 40 GB for Windows Server 2012 – with one disk. Of course, this depends also on processes, standards, and policies from the organization.
- All necessary software which can and should be pre-fitted is already installed (for example, AV scanner, backup client, and so on)

The part with the *customization specification* is possibly one of the most important. Especially for Windows VM Clones, it is important to have this ready for vRA. This will be used with every deployment and ensure that all Windows VMs are correctly activated and added to the domain if necessary.

However, also for Linux, those specification settings are important, since they take care of resetting the **interface configuration** (**ifcfg**) files to ensure the network comes up correctly. A detailed instruction on how to set up a specification setting can be found in the VMware vSphere documentation.

> Make sure to note the name of the specification; vRA will reference it by the name only, which is of course also case-sensitive.

Creating a network pool

Network pools are required to attach the deployed VM to a pre-existing LAN environment. Typically, they describe a port group on vSphere. However, it is recommended to either name them identically to the port group they attach to, or at least easily identifiable.

Network pools can additionally contain reserved IP addresses. In a sense, vRA delivers a *poor man's IPAM* where a block of IPs can be reserved for vRA and every time a VM is deployed it will get an IP out of this list. This is typically used in legacy environments without NSX possibilities.

Also, the use of an external DHCP is supported; in this case, no IPs are reserved and the VMs are just deployed relying on the external DHCP to deliver an IP address. Also, it is possible to integrate an IPAM service using vRO workflows.

In vRA 7.2, the **Infoblox** integration works out of the box:

New Network Profile - External

Create a network profile to manage ranges of static IPv4 network addresses.

General   IP Ranges

* Name:	VLAN 100
Description:	External VLAN
* Subnet mask:	255.255.255.0
Gateway:	192.168.0.1

DNS / WINS

Primary DNS:	192.168.0.254
Secondary DNS:	
DNS suffix:	example.local
DNS search suffix:	example.local
Preferred WINS:	
Alternate WINS:	

New Network Profile - External

Create a network profile to manage ranges of static IPv4 network addresses.

General   IP Ranges

IPv4 ranges: + New

	Name	Description	Start IP	End IP
✎ ✗	IPRange-Example		192.168.0.2	192.168.0.250

IP addresses:

IP Address	Machine	Last Modified	Status
			All
192.168.0.2		7/11/2016 10:44 AM UTC+02:00	Unallocated
192.168.0.3		7/11/2016 10:44 AM UTC+02:00	Unallocated
192.168.0.4		7/11/2016 10:44 AM UTC+02:00	Unallocated
192.168.0.5		7/11/2016 10:44 AM UTC+02:00	Unallocated
192.168.0.6		7/11/2016 10:44 AM UTC+02:00	Unallocated
192.168.0.7		7/11/2016 10:44 AM UTC+02:00	Unallocated
192.168.0.8		7/11/2016 10:44 AM UTC+02:00	Unallocated
192.168.0.9		7/11/2016 10:44 AM UTC+02:00	Unallocated
192.168.0.10		7/11/2016 10:44 AM UTC+02:00	Unallocated
192.168.0.11		7/11/2016 10:44 AM UTC+02:00	Unallocated
192.168.0.12		7/11/2016 10:44 AM UTC+02:00	Unallocated
192.168.0.13		7/11/2016 10:44 AM UTC+02:00	Unallocated
192.168.0.14		7/11/2016 10:44 AM UTC+02:00	Unallocated
192.168.0.15		7/11/2016 10:44 AM UTC+02:00	Unallocated
192.168.0.16		7/11/2016 10:44 AM UTC+02:00	Unallocated
192.168.0.17		7/11/2016 10:44 AM UTC+02:00	Unallocated
192.168.0.18		7/11/2016 10:44 AM UTC+02:00	Unallocated
192.168.0.19		7/11/2016 10:44 AM UTC+02:00	Unallocated
192.168.0.20		7/11/2016 10:44 AM UTC+02:00	Unallocated
192.168.0.21		7/11/2016 10:44 AM UTC+02:00	Unallocated
192.168.0.22		7/11/2016 10:44 AM UTC+02:00	Unallocated
192.168.0.23		7/11/2016 10:44 AM UTC+02:00	Unallocated
192.168.0.24		7/11/2016 10:44 AM UTC+02:00	Unallocated
192.168.0.25		7/11/2016 10:44 AM UTC+02:00	Unallocated
192.168.0.26		7/11/2016 10:44 AM UTC+02:00	Unallocated

|◄ ◄ Page 1 of 10 ► ►| Displaying 1 - 25 of 249

Upload CSV: [   ]   Browse...

Process CSV File

To create a network, please follow these steps:

1. Open vRA and log on with a privileged user (at least tenant admin).
2. Click on **Infrastructure** and then on **Network Profiles**.
3. Click the **New** button and select **External**.
4. Provide a descriptive name – best practice is to include the VLAN ID if any.
5. Provide the VLAN as well as subnet information for the pool.
6. Click on **IP Range** and enter a valid IP range for your network, for example, `192.168.0.2 - 192.168.0.250`.
7. Save the configuration.

Before continuing, ensure that the newly created network pool is associated with a vSphere port group under the **Infrastructure** | **Reservations** tab:

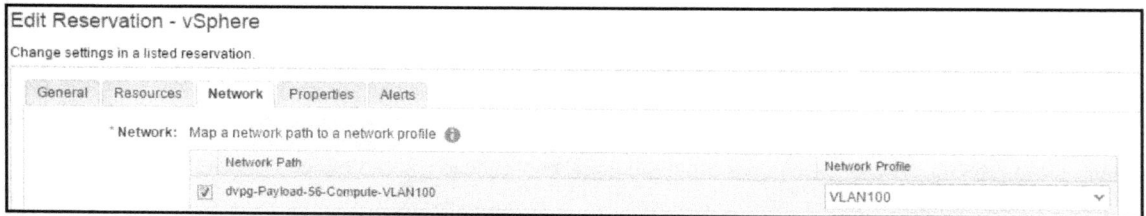

Edit Reservation - vSphere

Change settings in a listed reservation.

| General | Resources | Network | Properties | Alerts |

* Network: Map a network path to a network profile ℹ

Network Path	Network Profile
☑ dvpg-Payload-56-Compute-VLAN100	VLAN100 ⌄

8. Click on the **Infrastructure** tab.
9. Click on **Reservations** in the left-hand menu.
10. Choose the reservation regarding your tenant.
11. Click on the **Network** tab.
12. Check the network path (VDS port group) which relates to the created network profile.
13. Choose the **Network Profile** in the drop-down list.
14. Click **OK** to save the configuration.

Creating a set of properties

As described, properties will be useful to integrate third-party solutions such as backup. Let's create a retention policy property, where the user could choose how long the machine will be kept:

1. Open vRA and log on with a privileged user.
2. Click on the **Administration** tab.
3. Click on **Property Dictionary**.
4. Click on the **Property Definitions** menu on the left-hand side.

5. Click on the **New** button to add the properties.

6. Enter a descriptive property name, remember to use custom prefixes such as **Example** – note that the label can be different than the name!

7. Choose a data type, for example, `String`.

8. Define the display advice, for example, `Drop down`.

9. Choose **Pre-Defined Values**.

10. Enter the desired backup retention values, for example, `1 month, 3 months, 1 year`.

Create a properties group if not already present. This will enable the properties to be used also in blueprints by adding simply the properties group. To add a group, follow these steps:

1. Click on **Properties Group** in the left-hand menu.

2. Click on the **New** button.

3. Provide a descriptive name (maybe with the same prefix as the property). The ID gets generated automatically out of the name (needs to be unique!).

4. In the **Properties field**, click on **New** and use the selector to choose the previously created property.

5. Click on **Show in Request** so the user is able to choose from the property values.

6. Click **OK** to save the property.

7. Click **Save** to save the property group.

Creating the IaaS blueprint

Now, since we have completed all the pre-work, the design of the blueprint itself can be done using the preconfigured assets. In this case, it will be a Windows 2012 blueprint which will be added to a distinct network in a preset VLAN. For backup options, there will be a selectable amount of retention period for the user in the steps of 1 month, 3 months or 1 year:

1. Open vRA and log in with a privileged user holding at least the designer role.

2. Click on **Blueprints** in the left-hand side menu.

3. Click on the **New** button.

4. Provide a descriptive name, such as `Windows 2012`.

5. Give it a description; this will be seen by the user requesting the service.
6. Set **Archive days**.
7. Set the minimum and maximum lease time:

New Blueprint ✕

General | NSX Settings | Properties

* Name: Windows 2012

* ID: Windows2012 ❶

Assign a permanent, unique ID to this blueprint

Description: Windows 2012 Machine deployment

* Archive (days): 0 ❶

Minimum | Maximum

Lease (days): 1 | 7

OK | Cancel

TIP

Archive (days) will be the time frame during which vRA keeps the VM on a disk, even if the VM has expired its lease. It can be set to **0**, which means if a VM expires, it gets instantly deleted.

8. Under the **Properties** tab, click the **Add** button on the **Property groups** tab and select the previously set up **Properties group**.
9. Click **OK** to get to the graphical designer.
10. In the designer UI, drag a **vSphere Machine** from the left-hand side into the canvas.
11. In the top-left corner, at the **Categories** area, click on the **Network and Security** option.
12. Drag and drop an **Existing Network** into the blueprint.
13. Click on the newly added network icon to open its preferences at the bottom of the canvas.
14. Under **General**, click on the button and choose the previously created network.
15. Click on the **vSphere Machine** on the canvas to open its preferences at the bottom of the canvas.

16. In the **General** tab, provide an ID (no spaces) as well as a description.

17. Select either **Group Default** or a preset machine name prefix from the drop-down field.

18. Set the minimum and maximum count of instances allowed in the blueprint. Leaving that blank is equivalent to no limit.

After you have added all this, it is time to configure the installation method for the blueprint. There should be a template in the environment to use; this is how to configure the blueprint installation leveraging vSphere templates:

1. Click on the **Build Information** tab.

2. Select **Clone** in the **Action** drop-down menu.

3. Under **Clone from**, click on the button with the three dots to the Windows 2012 template from the vCenter endpoint.

4. Under **Customization Spec**, write exactly the name of the vCenter customization spec, including upper- and lowercase letters and possible spaces. **Tip**: Go to policies in vCenter, select it, and copy and paste the name to prevent typos!

5. Under the **Machine Resources** tab, the minimum and maximum vCPU, memory, and storage configuration can be set.

6. Under the **Storage** tab, the template disk should show up as a given. The machine cannot be smaller than the template disk size. Additional disks to add can be configured here.

7. Click on the **Network** tab and then on the **New** button.

8. Select the added network `your VLAN` - as assignment type, select **DHCP** and click **OK**. This will ensure the VM gets a VLAN from the previously created pool.

9. Click **Save** and then **Finish**.

10. The blueprint is successfully configured:

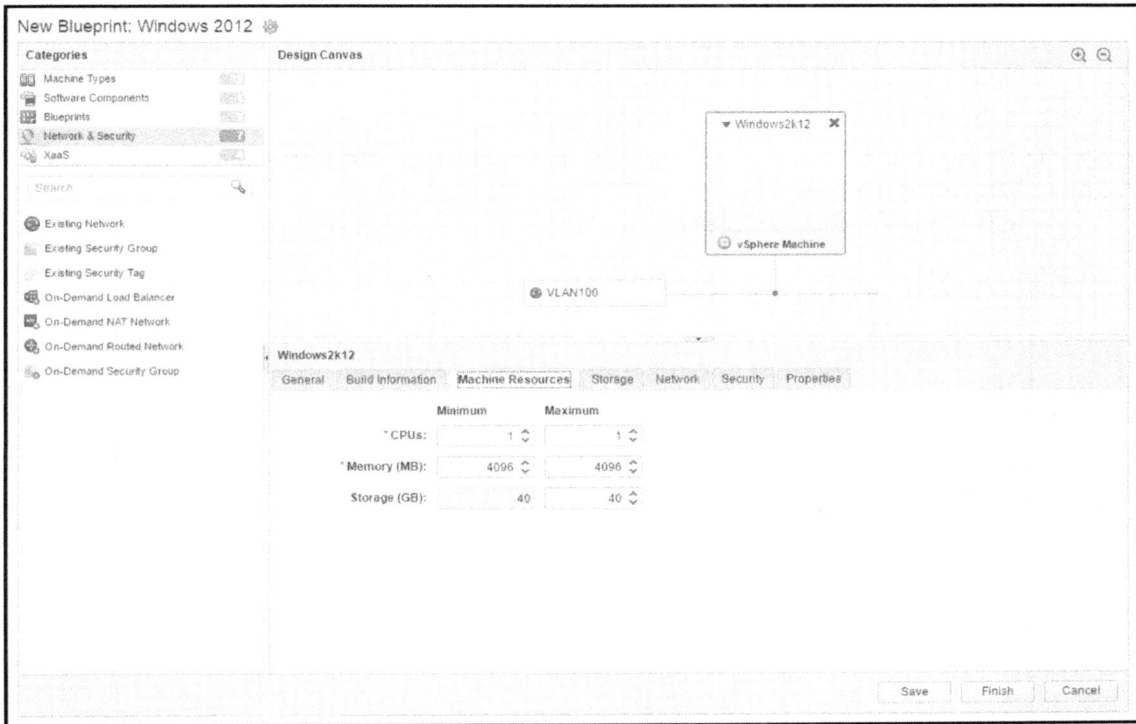

Publishing the blueprint as a service

Now, since the blueprint is configured and using all the other services, it is time to publish it. This last step will add it to the catalog and therefore it can be requested by users on demand:

1. While still logged on to vRA, in the **Design** tab, select the newly created blueprint.
2. Click on **Publish** in the heading row.
3. The blueprint status will change to **Published**.

Now, since the blueprint is published, it can be seen under **Catalog Items**. To add it to a catalog, do the following:

1. Click on the **Administration** tab.
2. Select **Catalog Items** in the left-hand menu.
3. Click on the newly added `Windows 2012` blueprint.
4. In the settings screen, pick a service (probably IaaS) and select an icon for your blueprint if applicable.
5. Click **New and noteworthy** to make the newly added service stand out:

Summary

Congratulations, this was the configuration of your first blueprint, including advanced parameters; the new service is now ready to be ordered using the catalog menu. This concludes the chapter on vRA. It was meant to provide powerful insights of what this tool can achieve with the right configuration.

Although it is impossible to describe every function in great detail in this chapter, this should be an overview of the most important functionalities. Finally, the chapter concluded in a series of sample configurations to create a first Windows service blueprint for a pre-existing catalog.

In the next chapter, the focus will be on vRealize Orchestrator. This is the powerful counterpart to vRA and will enhance the deployment of VMs by running individual workflows based on properties. Also, it can be used to create completely new services based on workflows which will be imported as XaaS services to be ordered using the vRealize portal.

6
vRealize Orchestrator

All infrastructure automation needs a central element which controls the rest of the infrastructure. In a VMware SDDC, this role is fulfilled by vRO.

But vRO does way more than controlling the virtual components of the SDDC. It can be used to control literally anything with an API and a description of how to use it. In a typical data center, there is almost never a greenfield installation possible. This means even if everything is restarted from scratch, there is almost always some service, process, or tool which requires integration. Be it for billing, for monitoring, or just for simple IP address management, integration is key.

Probably one of the best arguments for vRO is its price. VMware includes vRO in every vCenter license, without any additional charge.

> More documentation, plugins, and info about vRO can be found here:
> `http://www.vmware.com/products/vrealize-orchestrator.html`

Besides that, it is a mature and versatile orchestration platform, which offers way more integration than only the VMware ecosystem. vRO can be extended by using so-called plugins. These can be downloaded from the VMware solution exchange. Also, uploads are possible to this space. It can be considered as vRO's app store. Plugins may be free of charge or come with licensing, which depends on the vendor and the function of the plugin. Often, hardware or software vendors provide these for free with their solutions, but there are also famous examples where a partner has created a plugin for a certain tool and charges customers a license fee for using it in vRO.

This chapter will cover the following topics:

- vRealize Orchestrator principles and its basic data model
- Workflow creation 101
- Integration between vRealize Orchestrator and vRealize Automation
- Sample vRealize Orchestrator blueprint integration configuration
- vRealize Orchestrator and external services (XaaS)

vRealize Orchestrator principles

The orchestrator is installed as a virtual appliance which can be obtained from the VMware website. Once installed, it has to be connected to the VMware vCenter by using the **vSphere Identity Appliance**.

Workflow elements and design

In vRO, all automation tasks are managed in so-called workflows. A workflow is a number of actions and decisions which will be executed in a structured and preset order. Workflows can also call other workflows to accomplish tasks. The workflow calling subworkflows will always keep track of the status of all elements it has in its execution path. However, even if there are virtually no limits on how many nested workflows a workflow can call, it makes the reading and understanding of a function quite complex. This feature should be used with care in order to keep the human readability high enough for easy troubleshooting.

In vRealize Automation, it might be necessary to create custom workflows for third-party integration or to realize tasks which are required by established processes. vRealize Orchestrator makes it easy to create, manage, and update workflows. However, it comes with principles which should be known to make this an easy and straightforward task.

Therefore the data model, variable behavior, and best practices should be known before creating custom workflows.

Besides vRO's capabilities in calling workflows in a structured manner, it is also very important to develop and code these workflows in a structured and simple manner. There are various guides from VMware on how to code and ensure that not everything gets packed into a giant scripted task.

Functions should be separated in small chunks of scripted tasks (if necessary). If they get used more often, it might be worth it to create so-called *actions* which can be used in different workflows independently. The first step to successful vRO workflows is to embrace the difference from traditional scripting. By breaking complex tasks into multiple elements within a workflow, vRO can play all its strengths to make these workflows easy to maintain and to troubleshoot. The following section will discuss the elements and the creation of a simple workflow. However, it is just an example; for more detailed guidance on coding and workflow creation in vRealize Orchestrator, there is a very good VMware white paper, *vRealize Orchestrator Coding Design Guide*.

> The VMware workflow coding guide can be obtained from this web link: h
> ttp://pubs.vmware.com/orchestrator-70/topic/com.vmware.ICbase
> /PDF/vrealize_orchestrator_coding_design_guide.pdf
>
> Also, there is a very helpful web blog called the **vCOTeam** which can be found under www.vcoteam.info, it has good examples for beginners and advanced workflow coders.

Attributes, inputs, and outputs

Each workflow in vRO knows three basic variable types. These are important to pass on data between either workflow elements or subworkflows. There are major differences between those variables in how they can be used within a workflow definition.

In general, vRO has different variable data models to offer. These are based on the information the variable might store. This is quite similar to scripting languages or virtual basic script, where different variable models need to be used for the same reason.

vRO covers the obvious content types, such as text, number, and boolean. But there is also a product- and use-case-specific data types such as VC:Virtual Machine or VC:HostSystem. These types are introduced by their plugins in vRO. Other plugins can introduce new types; there is also a possibility to create dynamic types to build a data model for as yet unknown third-party systems.

Creating a custom Java plugin can either do this or by using the *Dynamic Types plugin*, which will auto generate a custom vRO plugin based on any third-party API calls.

Besides that, variables can either be a single item or an array of those things. It is important to declare the right type since otherwise vRO will error out. An array cannot be assigned to a single item variable, vice versa might be possible, but needs adapter code in JavaScript.

In general, all these parameters can be assigned to workflow elements for further processing. Input parameters can only assign on the **IN** tab of a workflow element; output parameters can only be assigned on the **OUT** tab. Attributes can be assigned on the **IN** or the **OUT** tab of an element.

Inputs

If the workflow needs information prior to running, these are declared as inputs. Inputs can also be optional to provide additional functionality. A workflow which will migrate a VM to a select host will have basically two inputs:

- VM to migrate
- Destination host system

There could also be optional inputs such as changing the VMDK format while migrating or the overall criticality to use while migrating the VM. But to run at least these two inputs must be selected by the user.

If an input reflects a plugin type variable, the selection can be based on browsing the known vRO environment. In the case of the VM, it will allow the user to browse through vCenter and select the VM by clicking on it. This comes true for the host system as well.

A nice function with this method is that the workflow will basically not allow any false entries. A VM cannot be selected as an input for the host system. This is a very important fact at vRO, the variable type can be critical to a successful workflow.

Attributes

Attributes are a form of global variables, active for storing values during the workflow runs. Same as for inputs, they will have different types, but generally, they are used to store dynamic information, as it might be needed while the workflow is running. They can be seen as the short-term memory to hold such things as arrays, text, or even type-based information.

To store and forward information, workflow elements can read attributes (**IN** tab) or store information into attributes (**OUT** tab). If an element is configured to store information into an attribute, everything which has been stored before in this attribute will be overwritten. To make sure information stays valid throughout the end of the workflow, individual attributes need to be used.

Outputs

Output parameters are important to actually return a result based on an action within a workflow. Some automation tasks need to produce outputs. An example could be a workflow which might wait for a certain event to conclude. It would produce an output to tell whoever issued the run what status that event might be currently in. Another example could be a workflow which generates a list of items based on filter criteria. The output parameter would be an array containing that list. Also, the output will be available even though the workflow has finished (hence the name) and can be used for other workflows. Mostly, this technique is used for workflows calling subworkflows. To understand the outcome, it is recommended that these subworkflows come back with an output which can then be used in the original workflow calling the sub.

Configurations

Configurations are basically preset inputs for a workflow to run. They become handy if there are a couple of workflows using similar inputs each time they run. A configuration can be used to store that information centrally.

Also, configurations exist outside of workflows, which means that inputs for workflows can be linked to the content of configurations. For example, let's assume an e-mail address stays the same for all workflows to notify an administrator. In this case, this would be an input variable with type `string`. To prevent putting that in each and every workflow, a configuration can be created to hold that data. Each workflow can then be linked with its e-mail-input parameter based on this configuration.

If at any time the e-mail address needs to be changed, only the configuration needs to be altered to hold the new e-mail. All the workflows will automatically use the new value. This is a very important feature if multiple workflows might use the same data. It can be a huge time-saver and also reduces complexity and effort a lot when working with multiple workflows in semi-complex and complex environments.

Workflow elements

Workflows contain multiple different elements. All of these elements have a different function as well as different requirements. The most helpful elements are the following:

- Action elements
- Scriptable task
- (Custom) decision
- Workflow element
- Switch

There are much more which will help to create a meaningful workflow, those are the ones maybe used most often and therefore interesting to dig deeper into.

Action elements

vRO comes with many preset and preprogrammed actions. They can be seen a preconfigured scripts performing a distinct action. Each plugin may bring its own actions to make the creation of automation tasks easier.

However, it is also possible to create your own actions in vRO to be used with custom workflows. If a third-party API does not come with a plugin but a certain functionality might be used frequently, this can become very handy. Similar to configurations, actions are only linked with workflows as an element. Therefore, if the code of the action changes and the version number of it has been increased, the updates are picked up by all the workflows using the action.

This is another reason why an action might be better as a couple of scripted tasks repeating code in a workflow. Workflows with actions will be far simpler to maintain and manage.

Updates for vendor-created plugins can also easily be introduced using actions. The workflows will pick up the new version just by accessing the latest action element.

To create your own action items, vRO has its own menu and folder structure for it. It can be found under the **Actions** menu item (vRO needs to be in the **Design** view). The icon looks like a gear with a play symbol in it.

Within this menu, a folder can be generated in reverse DNS standard `subdomain.company.function`. For instance, a certain internal function for `acme.local` might be called `local.acme.aircon`.

Within this folder, all actions for managing acme's air condition might be created. The action elements (actions) are written in JavaScript. If any outcome data should be provided by the action, the `return <value>;` command needs to be used to output variable content.

Scriptable task

A scriptable task is used in a workflow to accomplish things which cannot be covered by any of the other workflow elements. It is important to first search for what needs to be done in the library to be sure that a scripted task is needed.

Scripted tasks are the most static bits in a workflow. They can only be changed if the entire workflow is edited, which makes the workflow more difficult to manage. Only very straightforward and simple things should be covered in scripted tasks.

They use JavaScript as a scripting language and also the **IN** and **OUT** tabs to read or write into vRO variables (inputs, outputs, or attributes). Mostly, they may be used to search arrays for specific data and then pass it on into one of the workflow variables.

Sometimes they need to be created since a specific operation is not covered any actions or workflow element. They can be used to access APIs through a plugin-provided scripting class (for example, **vcPlugin**) to accomplish these tasks. If a scripted task is created, vRO will offer rich and detailed help for all available plugin-based and JavaScript-based commands. This help screen can be browsed while editing the code in the same window.

Decision

This element is used much like an if-statement in a script. Based on a criterion or action element, it can either follow up the `true` branch or the `false` branch. The term true or false branch is used to identify which way to follow. Literally, a workflow can continue successfully even though the `false` branch is taken by the decision. That highly depends on the design of the workflow and what needs to be accomplished using the decision. There are three types of decision elements:

- Decision
- Decision activity
- Custom decision

The basic decision takes a workflow variable (boolean type) as input and, based on its output, it will either continue the success branch (`true`) or the failure branch (`false`). The content of the variable has to be pre-set at some stage in the workflow (or as an input).

The decision activity is based on a to-be-selected action element. The action element must return `true` or `false` in order for the decision to work properly. It follows up the branches based on the same principle as the normal decision.

The custom decision offers a tab called **Scripting** in which JavaScript can be used to form the decision. However, it should not use extensive scripting to return `true` or `false`. Often this is used to write an `if` statement and also work with provided vRO variables. However, a decision has no **OUT** tab, therefore altered information cannot write back into a variable. If more scripting is required, it is recommended to use the simple decision and use a scripted task for the complex JavaScript elements.

Workflow element

This is used to call other workflows in the current workflow. It just needs to be dragged into the execution line and then a workflow to call can be searched for. If this workflow requires additional **IN** parameters, vRO has a function to automatically put them into the parent workflow as requirements. If this is the case, a black bar will appear, asking to add the activities parameters as input/output to the current workflow. On the far-right side, there will be a button labeled **Setup**. It can be used to control the name of the variables. If no names are applied, the original names from the selected subworkflow will be used. If the called workflow has an out parameter, this can be used for further processing in the original workflow.

Calling workflows can be very handy if multiple complex tasks need to be accomplished. Instead of creating one big and complex workflow, the task can be broken up into smaller bits and therefore each can be accomplished by a single workflow. In order to bring the big picture back together, a master workflow can be used to keep track and call all the subworkflows to accomplish the task.

This technique may also be used if a bigger team is working on automation and not all members have the same skills and functions. They can add their work as self-contained workflows for others who might require their output to fulfill their targets.

If one is familiar with an object-based programming language, this is a similar approach. The subworkflows call a basically their own objects with their own descriptors, inputs, and outputs.

Switch

This element is used to switch between different workflow branches based on variable content. It can be seen as a case statement. Based on the select variable, it delivers an easy-to-configure statement. It can do various different comparisons based on the variable type. If the variable to be checked is from type `VC:VirtualMachine`, the comparison can be the VM name, whether the variable is empty or not, the power state, the guest OS, and so on.

This means it basically understands the variable type and delivers a number of checks which can be performed on the variable. Based on their success (`true` or `false`), a distinct branch will be chosen to continue the workflow.

Workflow creation 101

Workflows in vRO typically live in a folder structure under the workflows tab. To create a new workflow, it is recommended to create a folder first, maybe with the name of a certain project or the description of the workflow types it may hold. Most vendors just use the product name as the folder name and then do subfolders to distinguish different functionalities.

Once the location is set, the workflow itself can be created in the folder by right-clicking on it and selecting **New workflow**.

Creating the workflow

Before starting to create the workflow, its purpose should be clear. Let's create one based on a simple example. Let's assume a backup system is backing up VMs based on what folder they are located in. Also, the folder is a placeholder for the applied retention policy. This is a proven practice and many backup tools could actually support such a setup with their vCenter integration using VADP. Also, this workflow might be triggered by vRealize Automation based on a user's choice.

There are three folders:

- `1month`: VMs in this folder will be available for up to 1 month after their deletion
- `3month`: VMs in this folder will be available for up to 3 months after their deletion
- `1year`: VMs in this folder will be available for up to 1 year after their deletion

When a user in vRealize Automation is ordering a VM, the blueprint will offer a parameter where the retention policies can be chosen. They are identical to the folders in vCenter. The parameters can be handed over by vRA to vRO by using so-called *custom properties*. These properties are provided by vRO when using a workflow subscription to call a vRO workflow. These concepts have been discussed in `Chapter 5`, *VMware vRealize Automation*.

The workflow should have one input: the vRA properties containing the VM name as a string and the folder name as a `string`. Based on that input, it should simply move the VM into the given folder in vCenter:

1. To create the workflow, the orchestrator client needs to be set to the **Design** mode. Under the workflow tab, the folder, which should contain can be selected/created by expanding the **Library** folder.
2. Right-click on the folder and select **New workflow**.
3. Provide a meaningful workflow name such as `VM Backup mover`.
4. The orchestrator client will now open the new workflow in editing mode. The canvas will be shown where the workflow can be constructed:

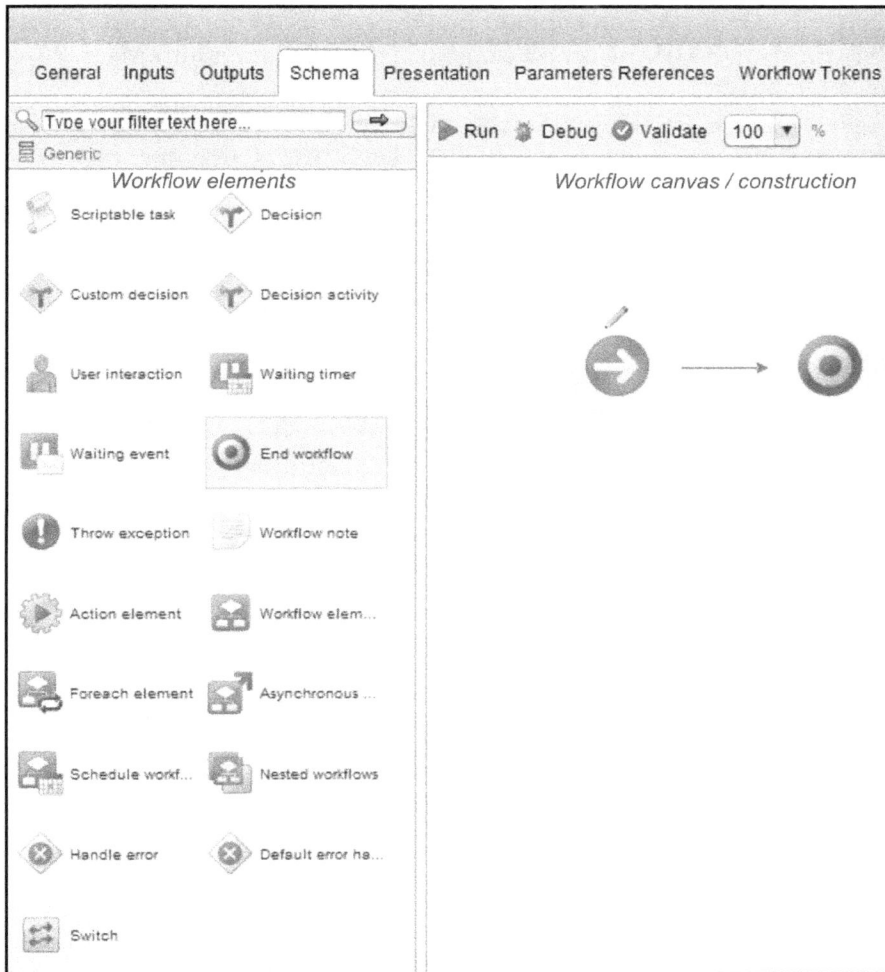

On the left-hand side of the pane, all the selectable workflow elements are shown. On the right-hand side, the canvas is shown where the overall flow and structure of the workflow can be constructed. Elements can be simply added by dragging them on the blue arrow pointing from the start to the end workflow element.

5. Drag the icon for **Action element** into the canvas. In the appearing search box, look for the **getAllVms** action element. This will gather all VMs in the connected vCenter server.

6. Hover over the action element and click on the pencil icon to edit its metadata. In the appearing window, click on the **OUT** tab. The Action item has a yet unbind `actionResult` variable. It needs to be bound to a newly created attribute in the workflow in order to be useable for other elements in it.

7. A click under **Source parameter** on **not set** will open another smaller window. In this window, an attribute can be created dynamically to store the output of the `actionResult`.

8. A click on **Create parameter/attribute in workflow** will open a window called **Create parameter** where a name needs to be provided. A description can be added, such as `Contains all vCenter VMs`. The type and array settings will be preselected based on the action elements output settings. In the **Create** section, **Create workflow ATTRIBUTE with the same name** should be selected. Once OK has been clicked, the system will bind and create a new attribute with the provided name:

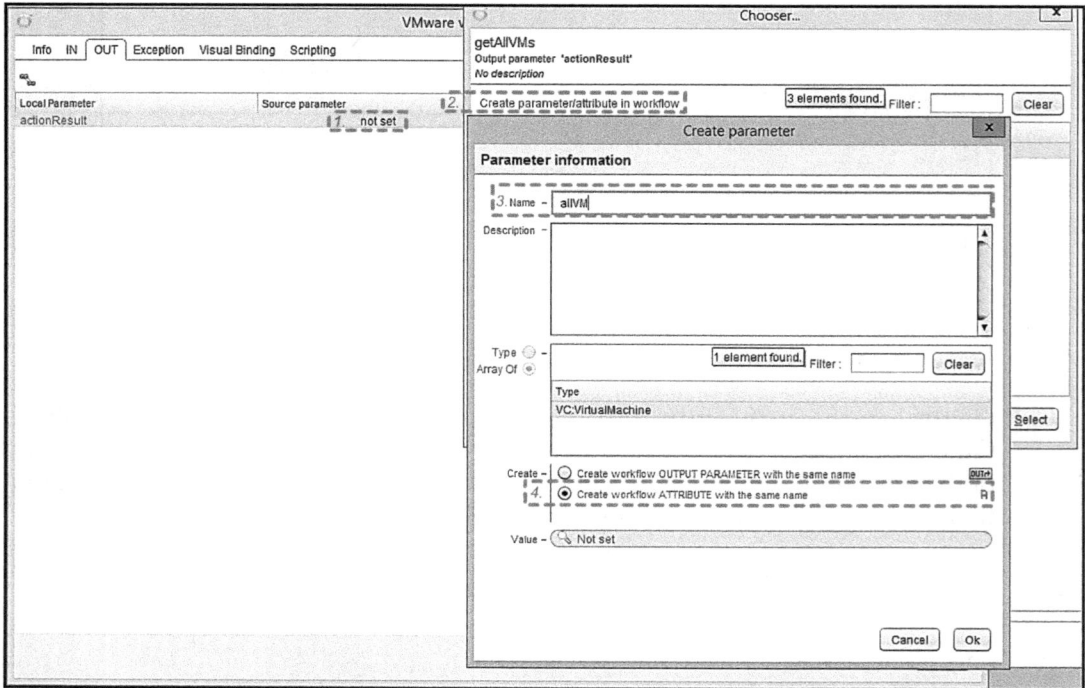

Get the properties from the service in vRA. This is done in multiple steps, for now, these are the steps in vRO to make sure the data from vRA can be processed:

1. Drag and drop a scriptable task into the workflow.
2. Click on the *pencil* icon to start editing it.
3. Click on the **Info** tab to provide a meaningful name such as `Process VM Properties`.
4. Click on the **IN** tab to define an input variable. The procedure is similar as for the action elements output. There are three icons: a line with two dots, two lines with two dots, and an **X**.
5. Click on the line with two dots (first icon) to add a variable.
6. Click on **Create parameter/attribute in workflow**.
7. Enter a name such as `machine` and select type **string**.
8. In the **Create** section, make sure **Create workflow INPUT PARAMETER with the same name** is selected.
9. Click **OK** to save and proceed:

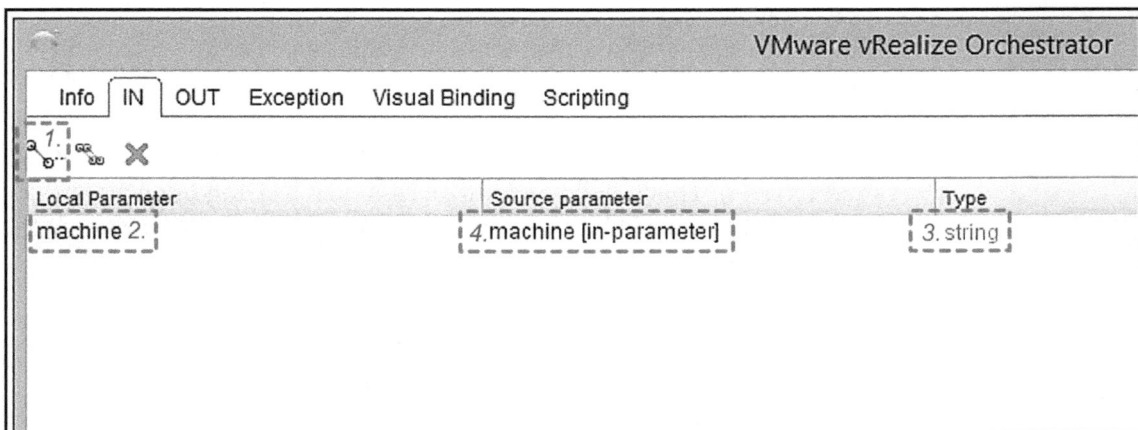

			VMware vRealize Orchestrator
Info	IN	OUT	Exception Visual Binding Scripting

Local Parameter	Source parameter	Type
machine 2.	4.machine [in-parameter]	3. string

10. Click on the **OUT** tab to define the attributes the scriptable task will store its date into:

    1. Click on the *Bind to workflow attribute icon* (far-left icon, line with two dots).
    2. Click on **Create parameter/attribute in workflow**.
    3. Provide a variable with the name `parsedMachine` with the type **any**.
    4. Select **Create workflow ATTRIBUTE with the same name**.
    5. Repeat these steps until entering the attribute name, create one called `retentionPolicy` with type `string`.

> Attributes are case-sensitive; it is important to respect the case and use exactly the spelling in all scriptable tasks. Otherwise, the attributes will not be recognized by vRO.

11. Click on the **Scripting** tab to add the following JavaScript:

```
//Get the properties from vRA
var parsedMachine = JSON.parse(machine);
retentionPolicy = parsedMachine["properties"]["Backup"];
System.log("Found backup property: "+retentionPolicy + "on VM name
"+parsedMachine["name"]");
```

The code will parse the input (`machine`) into a **JavaScript ObjectNotation (JSON)** object (`parsedMachine`). This will be easier to access than a string or an XML. This will only work if the code is JSON-compatible; vRA offers properties in JSON format, so this works well with this method.

After that, the retention policy (`retentionPolicy`) will be parsed out of the JSON object which will be the target folder name. The brackets are used to navigate through the JSON object and find the right identifier to write into the variable. Since the name of the folder is a string, the variable `retentionPolicy` is of type **string**. A JSON object type is not defined in vRO, therefore the `parsedMachine` is stored as type **any**.

The last line is to log the output for debugging in vRO.

12. Create another scriptable task and name it `Prepare folder object`:
    1. Bind the `retentionPolicy` as an IN parameter on the **IN** tab. Click on the *Bind to workflow parameter/attribute* icon at the far left.
    2. Select the `retentionPolicy` attribute from the list.
    3. Click on the **OUT** tab and click on the *Bind to workflow parameter/attribute* icon.
    4. Click on the **Create parameter/attribute in workflow** link.
    5. Enter a meaningful name such as `folder`.
    6. Select as type: `VC:VmFolder` and **Create workflow ATTRIBUTE with the same name**.
    7. Click **OK** to bind the new attribute to the scriptable task.

13. Click on **Scripting** to add the following code:

```
Var folders = VcPlugin.getAllVmFolders();
for (i in folders)
{
    if ( folders[i].name == retentionPolicy )
    {
        folder = folders[i];
    }
}
System.log("Found folder: "+folder)
```

This code will read all available folders in vCenter. Since there is no action element to accomplish this, the `VcPlugin` scripting class was used. The command provides an output as `VC:Folder` in form of an array. This array is defined in the first line. The next line will create a for loop to access all iterations of the array (all folders). For each folder, it will check whether the name fits the name of the chosen retention policy attribute. Once this is accomplished, the folder at this position gets written into the folders attribute for further processing.

The last line is for logging the output in order to easier debug the code.

14. Create another scriptable task and name it `Prepare VM object`:
    1. Bind `allVMs` and `parsedMachine` as an `IN` parameter on the **IN** tab. Click on the *Bind to workflow parameter/attribute* icon at the far left.
    2. Select the `allVMs` attribute from the list.
    3. Repeat this steps for the `parsedMachine` attribute.
    4. Click on the **OUT** tab and click on the *Bind to workflow parameter/attribute* icon.
    5. Click on the **Create parameter/attribute in workflow** link.
    6. Enter a meaningful name such as `vm`.
    7. Select as type: `VC:VirtualMachine` and **Create workflow ATTRIBUTE with the same name**.
    8. Click **OK** to bind the new attribute to the scriptable task.

15. Click on **Scripting** to add the following code:

```
//identify the vm to move
for (i in allVMs)
{
    if (allVMs[i].name == parsedMachine["name"])
    {
        vm = allVMs[i]
}
    }
    System.log("Found VM: "+vm.name)
```

This short script will loop through all found VMs to identify the one vRA has created. The name of the VM will be in the properties vRA sends when calling the workflow. The for loop will process all VMs and compare their name to the name in the vRA properties. The if clause will identify the right position in the `allVMs` array and assign it to the `vm` attribute. Now this is no longer text but a VM type attribute holding all needed information to manipulate a virtual machine.

Finally, the log will be prepared to output the found VM's name for debugging purposes.

16. Create a subworkflow by dragging in the **Workflow element** into the canvas on the blue line.
17. In the search bar, search for **Move virtual machine to folder** and select this workflow once found.
18. Click on the *pencil* icon to edit the workflow.

19. Click on the **IN** tab and add vm as well as the folder variable by using the *Bind to workflow parameter/attribute* icon.
20. Click **OK** and then close. The workflow is now ready for moving VMs into specified folders based on a user's selection in vRA.

Since there is an already running and proven workflow to move a VM into a folder, this workflow is called by the just created one.

Once all is created, the workflow should have the following attributes under the **General** tab:

- vm
- folder
- allVMs
- retentionPolicy
- parsedMachine

Under the **Input** tab the following inputs are listed:

- machine

The tab called **Outputs** will be empty for this workflow.

Once everything looks like it should, the workflow can be saved by clicking on **Save**" at the far right bottom corner of the client.

vRO saves workflows and automatically adds version numbers to them. It is highly recommended to always increase the version number if some things have been changed. If the version number would not change (forced overwrite), all other workflows calling the changed one would still work with the *old* data – hence the version that remained the same can't tell the files apart. Therefore, it is highly recommended and best practice that each change to a workflow also increases the version number of that workflow.

Integrating the workflow into vRA

A workflow event subscription can be added to a certain status of a request. For instance, they can be run every time the VM is deployed or up and running. There can be trigger and targets defined; targets are usually workflows, triggers can be based on property content or other variables. Workflow subscriptions have already been covered in Chapter 5, *VMware vRealize Automation*.

In order to make the workflow work together with vRA, the following steps have to be done in the vRA portal:

1. Open the vRA portal and log on with an administrative user.
2. Click on the **Administration** task and then on **Property Dictionary**.
3. Click on the **+ New** button to add a new property definition:
    1. Provide a meaningful name such as Backup.
    2. Provide a label (the user will only see the label) such as Backup retention.
    3. Select **String** at the **Data type** field.
    4. Set **Required** to **No** (backup is nice, but not required).
    5. On the right-hand side, select **Dropdown** at **Display advice**.
    6. At the **Values** area, select the **Predefined values** radio button.
    7. At **Predefined values**, use the green plus sign to add all three folder names. The values of these properties should be identical to the names of the folders in vCenter. This includes uppercase/lowercase names!
    8. Click OK to store the new property:

Once this is completed, a property group should also be created for easier assignment of a number of properties to a blueprint. To create a properties group in vRA, follow these steps:

1. Click on **Property Groups** while still in the **Administration | Property Dictionary** menu.
2. Click on the **+ New** button to create a new group.
3. Provide a meaningful name, such as a company name and an identifier for the group's content.
4. Select the desired visibility (all tenants or only the tenant currently managed).
5. Under **Properties**, click the **+ New** button. In the appearing row, click the drop-down arrow to select the previously created Backup properties.
6. Before clicking **OK** to add the line, the **Show in Request** tick box should be selected for the line entry.
7. By clicking **OK**, the system will store a new properties group with the Backup property as a member.

After the properties and property group have been successfully created, an event subscription needs to be configured. This is also done in the vRA **Administration** tab. The following steps will add a workflow subscription to move a VM after creation to a user-defined folder (the `Backup` creation workflow):

1. Click on **Administration** to navigate to **Events**.
2. Click on **Subscriptions** and then click the **+ New** button.
3. Select **Machine provisioning** under the **Event Topic** tab and click **Next**.
4. Select **Run based on conditions** and chose the following options:
   1. Expand **Data** using the plus sign next to it.
   2. Expand **Lifecycle state** using the plus sign next to it.
   3. Select **Lifecycle state name**.
   4. Select **Equals** in the next box.
   5. Click on the down arrow in the last box, leave **Constant** selected, at the nested drop-down box in the box, search for `WPSMasterWorkflow32.MachineProvisioned`.
   6. Click **Next**.
5. In the **Workflow** tab, open the **Library** folder and browse to the workflow earlier created to select it.
6. Click **Next**, control the summary screen and click Finish to store the newly added event subscription.
7. In the overview, select the new event subscription (click on the line) and click on **Publish**, otherwise the subscription will not be useable in any blueprints.

Adding the properties to the blueprint

After all the properties have been created successfully, they have to be added to the blueprint in order to take effect. The following steps will add the properties:

1. Log on to vRA web interface with an administrative user or a blueprint designer user role.
2. Select the `Windows` blueprint created previously in `Chapter 5`, *VMware vRealize Automation*.
3. Click on **Edit** in the top row to edit the blueprint.

4. Click on the `Windows` VM in the design canvas.

5. In the configuration menu on the far right, click on the **Properties** tab.

6. At the properties group, click on the **+ Add** button and select the previously created properties group.

7. Select the **Custom Properties** tab and click the **+ New** button.

8. Enter the following text under **Name**: `Extensibility.Lifecycle.Properties.VMPSMasterWorkflow32.Machine Provisioned`. Be very careful when writing that since the whole term is case-sensitive.

9. At the **Value** column, enter `backup*`.

> Since the `MachineProvisioned` property forwards a lot of data for the virtual machine, it is simpler to filter for the `Backup` property. This is what this entry will do. Instead of creating a complex filter on a lot of data in vRO, the filter is created at the source and makes everything more efficient.

10. Click **Finish** to save the changes in the workflow:

Design Canvas

▼ Windows2012R2✖

Windows2012R2

| General | Build Information | Machine Resources | Storage | Network | Security | Properties |

| Property Groups | Custom Properties |

✚ New   ✎ Edit   ✖ Delete

Name	Value	Encrypted	Overridable
Extensibility.Lifecycle.Properties.VMPSMasterWorkflow32.MachineProvisioned	backup*	No	Yes

Now everything is set for a vRA to vRO workflow integration based on event subscriptions. If a new VM is requested in vRA, a drop-down field will appear to select the backup retention policy.

Based on the selected policy, the workflow will move the VM in the preset folder. This is done immediately after the VM finishes provisioning. The completed workflow runs can be controlled in vRO including variable content and log output.

This can be done in the vRO client by expanding the arrow next to the workflow. By clicking on a workflow run, all the collected information will be shown in the client window:

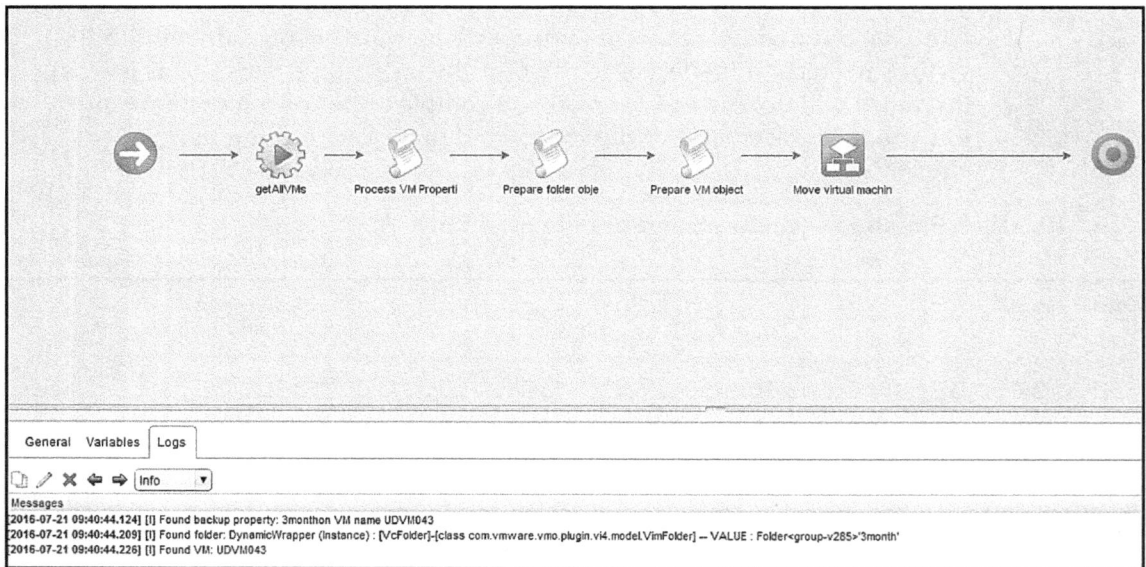

This is a good function to prove whether the workflow is running correctly and all the functions are working as expected. vRO would also list scripting errors or parsing errors if any. In this case, the workflow run will be marked as failed using a red **X** instead of a green checkmark (successful).

External services

Another use case for vRO is the creation of so-called external services or XaaS as VMware calls it. In vRA, XaaS means basically anything which can be automated and is orderable as a service.

By using vRO as a platform, a workflow can be an easy-to-create but yet powerful asset to provide third-party functionalities. Also, there are plenty of vRO plugins, which bring their own workflows for specific vendor products. By leveraging the XaaS feature, it is much easier to include those vendors and their products into the vRA portal. This means that also their offerings can be orderable as services by a given end user.

A couple of things are very helpful when using the XaaS feature of vRA with vRO:

- An item is only shown in vRA if the workflow has an output parameter which vRA can understand.
- Actions on XaaS services can be defined separately in vRA and assigned to the service. These actions are workflows on their own in vRO.
- If an item should be destroyed after the service is deleted, it needs to use vRA's *disposal* feature.
- The input mask of the XaaS workflow is basically taken from the inputs in vRO. However, the mask can be edited in vRA to be more consumer-friendly if required.
- If no output variable suits vRA, a custom set of resources can be defined in order to still assign an XaaS service to the items tab. vRO needs to understand the data type in order to forward it to vRA. To accomplish this, vRO has a feature called *dynamic types*. These can be used to create an integration plugin which is then parsing a given API to create an object/relation construct. This can then be used to advertise functionality back to vRA.

Probably vRO is used for third-party integration to a fair extent. But also to create new services and make them orderable through vRealize Automation, vRO can be used quite easily and straightforwardly. Not always do these workflows have to be created by the end user; some of them are included in the available vRO plugins. To create an *add a user to AD"* service, all necessary workflows and actions are already installed in vRO given the AD plugin is activated. This can be an easy and straightforward way to implement additional and helpful services into vRA.

Connecting vRO to vCenter

Once that is completed, the vRO service can also be registered to vCenter to run vRO workflows right out of vCenter using the right-click menu. To run workflows using the VMware API and to enable the right-click call feature, vRO has to be registered with vCenter. Actually, running a workflow in vRO does this:

1. Use a browser and put in the address of the VRO server.
2. Click either on **Start Orchestrator Client** or on **Download Orchestrator Client**.
3. If you have downloaded the client, uncompress it and open the Orchestrator Client Java executable.
4. Log on with an administrative vCenter user (since it is linked to SSO vSphere admin work).
5. Make sure the orchestrator mode is either in **Run** or in **Design,** otherwise the workflow view will not be available. The run mode is changed using the drop-down field right next to the vRealize Orchestrator logo.
6. In the top-left corner, locate the workflows icon (blue square with white rhombus in it).
7. Expand the **Library** folder and locate a subfolder called **vCenter**.
8. Expand the **Configuration** folder under vCenter.
9. Right-click on the workflow **Add a vCenter Server Instance** and click on **Start workflow...**.
10. Put in all the necessary vCenter information, select **Yes** on the question to orchestrate this instance.
11. On the second screen, it is recommended to share a session for all users to vCenter. This means selecting **No** on the first question.
12. Put in the vCenter user to connect with. Remember, if the user does not have all privileges, also the vRO workflows will have limited privileges.
13. Hit **Submit** and vRO registers with vCenter:

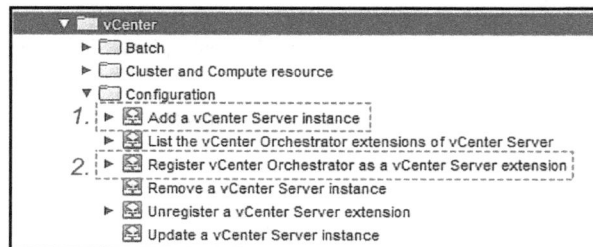

It is also possible to pass an individual user to vCenter to run the workflow. However, this means the user running the workflow must have all privileges assigned to complete all workflow steps – otherwise this will fail. Typically, one user is running the workflows like a proxy for all others.

After this has been successfully accomplished, vRO needs to register its extension with vCenter in order to connect properly. This is also done by running a configuration workflow:

1. Locate the workflow named `Register vCenter Orchestrator as a vCenter extension` workflow in the vCenter, configuration directory.
2. Right-click on it and select **Start workflow...**.
3. Click on **Not set** to browse to the vCenter instance to register with.
4. Leave the advertising address field blank.
5. The workflow will now register the vRO extension with vCenter, this is necessary to use the vCenter vRO plugin which enables admins to attach workflows to vCenter objects and run them directly by using a right-click menu.

To prove whether the extension has been successfully registered with vCenter, it is the best and most efficient way to check the extension manager. This can be accomplished best by browsing the vCenter **Managed Object Browser (MOB)** or **Managed Object Reference (MoRef)** API descriptor:

1. Open a browser and put in the following vCenter address: `https://my.vcenter.local/mob`.
2. Put in the vCenter admin credentials to open the MOB page.
3. Click on **Content**.
4. Find and click on the `ExtentionManager` link in the list (exact spelling including upper- and lowercase).
5. In the `extensionList`, locate the link called `extensionList["com.vmware.vco"]`.

6. If this link exists, the vRO server is successfully registered as an extension to vCenter Web Client:

> vCO is the old name (vCenter Orchestrator). However, it can still be found at many references in vCenter and also in vRO itself. VMware renamed the product in 2013 to vRealize Orchestrator in order to create a unified product family brand for all orchestration and automation products. If tips for workflows are needed, it is still recommended to use also "vCO" in Google in order to maximize the search results.

Home

Managed Object Type: **ManagedObjectReference:ExtensionManager**
Managed Object ID: **ExtensionManager**

Properties

NAME	TYPE	VALUE	
extensionList	Extension[]	extensionList["com.vmware.vim.inventoryservice"]	Extension
		extensionList["com.vmware.vim.ls"]	Extension
		extensionList["com.vmware.vim.sms"]	Extension
		extensionList["com.vmware.vim.sps"]	Extension
		extensionList["com.vmware.vim.stats.report"]	Extension
		extensionList["com.vmware.vim.vsm"]	Extension
		extensionList["hostdiag"]	Extension
		extensionList["VirtualCenter"]	Extension
		extensionList["com.hds.ucp"]	Extension
		extensionList["com.vmware.cl"]	Extension
		extensionList["com.vmware.rbd"]	Extension
		extensionList["com.vmware.syslog"]	Extension
		extensionList["com.vmware.vco"]	Extension
		extensionList["com.vmware.vcops"]	Extension
		extensionList["com.vmware.vdc"]	Extension
		extensionList["com.vmware.vim.eam"]	Extension
		extensionList["com.vmware.vsan.health"]	Extension
		extensionList["com.vmware.vsan.mgmt"]	Extension
		extensionList["com.vmware.vShieldManager"]	Extension
		(less...)	

If all of this completed successfully, vRO should be registered with vCenter and its workflows should also be browseable by vCenter server.

Under vCenter, it is available by clicking on the *vRealize Orchestrator* icon. Under vRO home, it should show up as connected (**Summary** tab). Now vRO workflows can be added to vCenter and can be run on so-called object-based conditions. For instance, one could create a workflow which is adding a new host to a cluster. The workflow can be only run on the cluster object.

All this can be configured using the **Management** tab. Of course, the workflows have to be already present in vRO in order to be attached to objects in vCenter.

vRO context actions in vCenter

vCenter and vRO make a powerful connection. Based on this, VMware has decided to make it even easier to run vRO workflows on vCenter objects by introducing the so-called context action. With this functionality, administrators can define a single workflow or a set of workflows which can run on a select vCenter object. Registering the vRO extension in vCenter will enable this object linkage. Also, vCenter will document and display all workflow runs under tasks, which makes them easier to monitor.

Finding and enabling context actions

This configuration is done in vCenter Web Client, which will be used to manage and enable the context actions. Looking for the orange orchestrator icon can easily identify this menu in vCenter. This icon can be found either in the **Home** screen in the **Inventories** section or by clicking on the home icon (top-left corner next to vSphere Web Client text) and selecting the menu directly.

Once in the menu, the context action can be defined by selecting **vRO Home** directly under vRealize Orchestrator in the left-hand side menu. To add or change an action, the **Manage** tab needs to be selected.

Enabling a context-based workflow

To enable a context-based workflow, perform the following steps:

1. In the vRO Home screen, select the **Manage** tab.
2. Click on the *green plus* icon to add a context-based workflow.
3. In the **Add new workflow** wizard on the left-hand side, expand the vRO Servers to select a workflow (tree view).

4. Browse to the vCenter folder and open `Virtual Machine Management/Move and Migrate`.

5. Select **Mass migrate Virtual Machines with vMotion**.

6. Click **Add** to make sure the workflow appears under **Selected workflows** in the top section of the wizard.

7. On the right-hand side, select `host`, which is the object where the workflow should be applied.

8. Click **OK** to assign the workflow as context action:

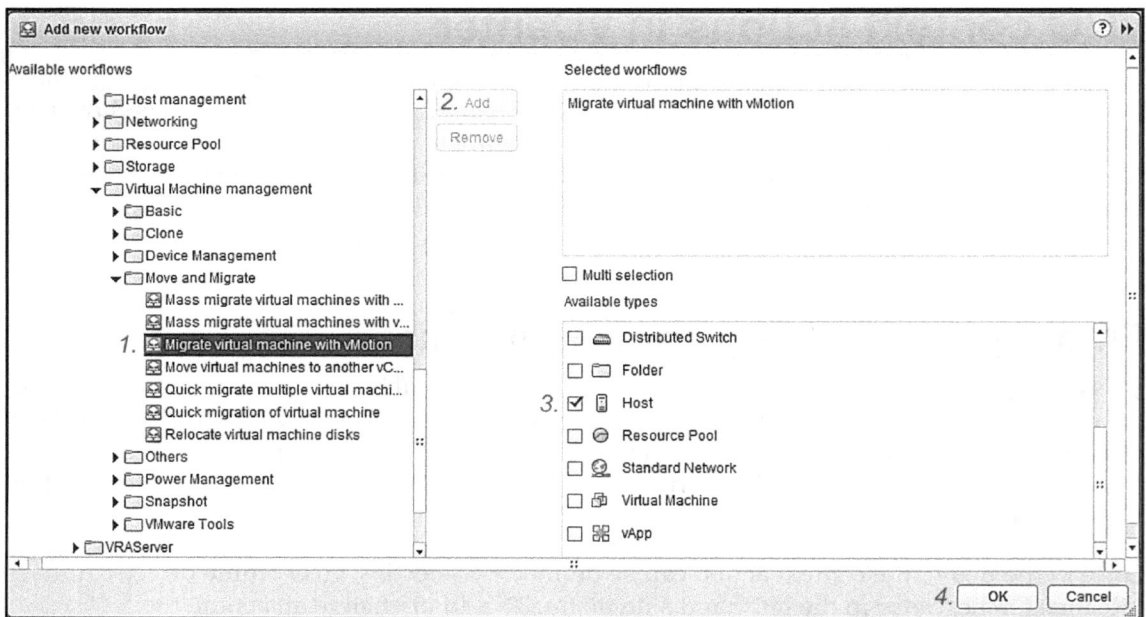

Once these steps are completed, the workflow can be executed by right-clicking on any host in the environment. There will be a menu option called **All vRealize Orchestrator Actions** and the assigned workflow will appear in this menu. Since this is a context-based action, it will not appear if a one issues a right-click on a VM or a cluster:

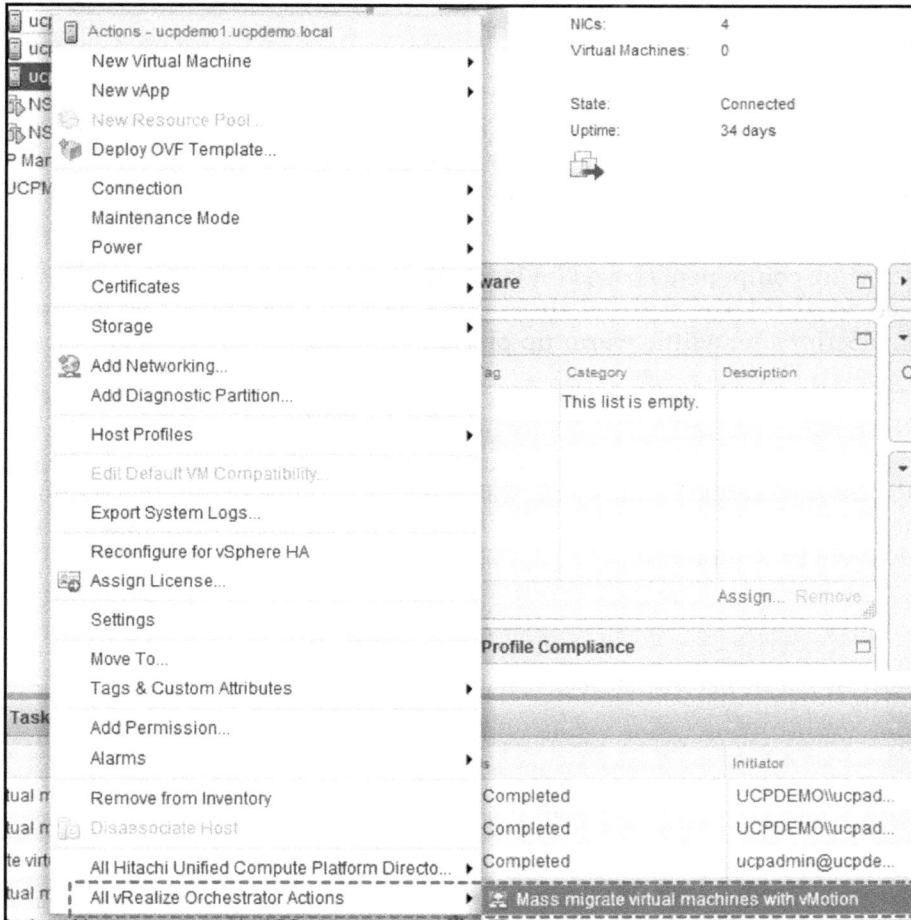

It is not necessary to set this up for vRealize Automation, but it is a very good option to introduce daily management automation tasks into vCenter. Given that vRO is configured to use a proxy user for all workflows, also admins, which might have minor privileges, could run controlled automation tasks using this option. Also, all workflows will appear in vCenter's tasks overview, which also simplifies monitoring the exit state of any run workflow.

Summary

This chapter touched on the basic data model as well as variable types of vRealize Orchestrator. Although all this is only scratching the surface of vRO, it gave a deep insight into how workflows are created as well as how they could be linked with vRA in order to enable powerful and rich third-party integration points. This is probably one of the vRO's strongest capabilities.

Also, the scripting components based on JavaScript where discussed. Given the well-implemented help for JavaScript and all scripting classes, it should be possible to get up to speed on JavaScript after a little warm-up phase.

In the next chapter, the focus will be on the creation of a rich service catalog. The service catalog is the most important functionality of the SDDC. The services have to be easy to use as well as valuable and useful to the end users based on their business case. The chapter will also discuss how services and service catalogs will be created and maintained in vRA. But not only will the catalog itself be under discussion, also the content and services which can be added will be explored.

Service Catalog Creation
7

The service catalog is the central element of each cloud environment. Based on the use cases identified it will provide the needed functionality to empower the business and speed up deployment. This will enhance the time to market significantly and enable the whole company to be able to react to market trends faster.

But to enable all these benefits, it is important to understand that this can only be accomplished if the services offered in the catalog are valid and needed by the end users.

This chapter will discuss the service catalog creation, different types of service catalogs, as well as detailed examples of simple and complex service designs.

Also, it will cover in detail how service catalogs are created in vRA and how they can be assigned to a specific business group or tenant, but also be available across different tenants. The later option is necessary if some very basic services might be worth sharing. An example for such service catalogs can be a simple OS deploy service. Even though each tenant might be a different company or division, they will all need some form of Windows or Linux deployment. So sharing a service catalog across two or more tenants for this basic service can be useful in order to lower the maintenance and operation effort for the SDDC.

This chapter will cover the following topics:

- Service definition and classes
- Service catalog creation in vRA
- Design examples using vRA
- Best practices and good practice for service catalog creation

Service catalogs

This basically reflects the shop front end of vRA. Service catalogs are categories and contain their various services. vRA does not limit the number of service catalogs, nor their name or function in any matter. There can be numerous Service catalogs be created. All the names are basically freeform text, however, there are some best practices and standards which may make sense to follow, since all cloud provider will have similar naming and functionality.

In `Chapter 5`, *VMware vRealize Automation* the three most used categories have been briefly discussed, those are basically IaaS, PaaS as well as XaaS. The latter category is a VMware introduced term and describes *Anything as a Service*.

Besides the *as a Service* ending, there are endless possibilities. There are also other categories in the market such as:

- **Software as a Service (SaaS)**
    - These are offerings like Gmail, Salesforce, Office 365
- **Backup as a Service (BaaS)**
- **Storage as a Service (STaaS)**
- **Database as a Service (DBaaS)**
    - This often means either two things (either – or – both)
        - Installing a DB on demand and making it available
        - Creating an instance/DB on an already running DB (or DB cluster)
- **Desktop as a Service (DaaS)**
    - Often in conjunction with a cloud portal where a user can order a new desktop on demand
    - Mostly referred to and used in Virtual Desktop Infrastructure environments
- **Network as a Service (NaaS)**
- **High-Performance Computing as a Service (HPCaaS)**

This list is just a fraction of possible *as a Service* categories. Each topic might be a separate service catalog. The idea behind that abbreviations was initially to introduce a common language and standard to orient to. However, there is no required naming or content of a service catalog. Sometimes services will also build upon each other.

A good example for that is the SaaS model which might be stacked on top of other categories:

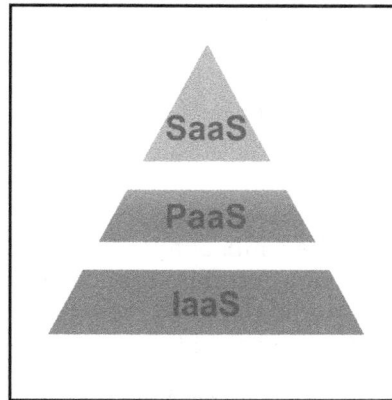

Defining a catalog

The catalog definition is based on various different factors. Its content should be easily guessed by its name. Also, the content should be sharing characteristics, which will enable to easily identify it as part of a distinct service catalog.

Here are a few examples of service catalogs and their possible contained service:

IaaS: Normally this is a catalog providing only OS installs with no further software installation or other customization. This catalog may offer a quick way to deploy an OS (with IP, domain join, security hardening, and so on) but nothing more than that.

Typical services are:

- Windows (different versions)
- Linux (different versions)
- Bare metal resources (install Windows/Linux on a blade or rack server).

Typically an IaaS service catalog is the first to start with since it delivers a fundamental functionality of every SDDC. It can easily deploy a VM containing an OS of choice including the integration into the third party management framework. Although there is currently a big hype for DevOps and **Cloud Native Apps** this can already be a huge time saver.

Directory services: This can contain additional service which may only refer to AD or LDAP actions. Since an SDDC can do more than *just* provisioning, this might enable a user to request a new user, change or reset passwords, lock or delete an existing user. This might be useful in bigger environments to speed up the onboarding of new employees. Services might be:

- Create/change/delete an AD user
- Block an AD user
- Reset AD user password

ACME business applications: This can be a mix of a PaaS and SaaS catalog and only reflecting required and necessary service to enable a certain branch of the business. Since this is a complete custom category, there is no predefined content. As mentioned the content needs to be easy to identify and should make sense in the catalogs context. Examples could be:

- Create/manage a **Customer Resource Management** (**CRM**) application
- Deploy production web server/farm (LAMP stack: Linux-Apache-MySQL-PHP)
- Other required internal business systems

Multiple catalogs

Defining one catalog might be easy and straightforward, when it comes to multiple catalogs there are a few design best practices to follow. These will not have a functional influence, but the success of the SDDC lies in its user adoption. Creating complex and difficult to operate portals (for nontechnical users) will lead to less adoption. If the portal is populating service straight from the business units.

Catalogs: As less as possible as many as required

This is a famous best practice for virtual switches in vSphere. The same principle comes true for service catalogs/services in vRA. If there are too many service catalogs created with too many services contained the user might end up rather confused than enabled. The best rule to follow here is *keep it as simple as possible*. Even if this sounds like an already known rule of thumb, keep checking your design against it. Often complex service catalog creations can be avoided by creating multipurpose blueprints or catalog items.

An example is the IaaS service catalog, VMs or Bare Metal deployments will contain an OS and are fully or partially integrated into the ecosystem after deployment. There might be no need to create a service catalog for each OS family (Windows or Linux). Also, there might only be two blueprints needed to satisfy the requirements of the users/LOBs/admins requesting this service.

Provide basic catalogs as well as specific catalogs

A basic catalog can be IaaS, given that one company has many different departments, but all need to follow the same IT processes, it might make sense to have a universal IaaS catalog, relevant for all business groups.

For a provider, the situation is similar. Basically, every customer needs to deploy either Windows or Linux VMs to get started. So a universal service catalog, providing this functionality, should be available.

By introducing a service catalog shared across tenants, a lot of maintenance effort can be saved. This ties back into the first statement as well *as less as possible*.

On the other hand, there might be application services or special XaaS offerings, which are only valid for one department, or even a group in a department. Therefore this groups can be entitled separately to a service catalog to ensure that no one else can access these catalogs.

An example for that can be super users, who might have the permission to reset another accounts password using the self-service portal. First, only these users should be entitled to such a kind of service catalog. Second, these might be very special operations per division, so also the catalog and content might be different from other departments/tenants.

Choose a descriptive and short name

It is also good to name the catalog according to its functionalities and services it contains. This is like the department in a grocery market, *Butcher and Meat* will contain exactly this, while *Bakery and Cakes* will contain different objects for the customers.

This should be one of the key principles when creating catalogs. IaaS should contain all IaaS relevant services, but nothing else. If this is mixed with some application installation service, it might become very difficult for the user to find the right catalog.

It is a good trick to imagine being a user and clicking through the available catalogs. If there is something unclear, a rethink of the catalog design might be useful. Today's users are very used to that concept, given that Amazon will always display Blu-rays by clicking on this respect category. The same user expectations will be present for an internal SDDC. If someone clicks on IaaS, the catalog should contain only infrastructure related services.

Outcome-oriented versus technology-oriented

A perfect self-service portal delivers outcome-oriented, instead of technology-oriented services. This is often difficult for very technical focused specialists since there the world is all about the OS, the application the middleware, and so on.

However, for a business user, it is all about getting the support for the business, which is needed. So the ugly truth is: They do not care the slightest about the underlying OS, they also probably do not care about the DB version or if it is using Java or PHP to display any content. For a business user, all that counts is the outcome. In this case, a ready to use application supporting them with their requirements.

Know your audience

Therefore, the service catalog should be also created with the end user group in mind. For a more tech savvy audience, an IaaS catalog might be fine.

In this case, it could probably simply be named IaaS and could contain times like:

- LAMP Stack (Linux + MySQL + Apache + PHP is usually called LAMP).
- Windows server 2012 R2
- CentOS 7.1

For administrators or a more technology-focused audience such as operators, possibly all they really need is an OS or a bit of software deployed on an OS to fulfill their requirements. In this case, such a catalog would be fine, the audience will expect this. Most of the SDDC projects are run and used by a tech-savvy audience, so often the services look like this.

For a more business-oriented audience, the service catalog might look totally different. All the tools will still be contained in the blueprint, but this time the requestor is more interested in the outcome, which is the final service to be used.

A silly example could be deploying WordPress. The user might not be interested in the version of WordPress nor in the OS or the used database. The important delivery is the application itself and that it is fully up and useable after it has been requested. Another example is the app store of a mobile device. None of the users asks themselves: Are they running a Solaris web farm to support Angry Bird?

All they care is the outcome, which is the app running on their device fulfilling its purpose.

Based on that, a catalog for business oriented users also needs to serve their needs and meet their expectations. They will expect applications like:

- External consumer portal environment
- Business application XYZ
- Customer order portal extension

The title of the service blueprints should reveal its outcome/purpose. If the business needs to extend the consumer portal environment, they might look for a service to order to do so. If they want to deploy application XYZ it might help to name the service exactly like the wanted application.

Service catalog creation in vRA

This part of the chapter will describe in detail how to create and manage a service catalog in vRealize Automation. Based on the previous descriptions it will create a sample catalog and explain how to populate it with service. Also, multimachine and PaaS service will be described in more details.

First step: Creating the catalog

In vRealize Automation, the service catalog creation is done under the **Administration** tab. This tab is only visible for either a service administrator, tenant administrator or for the vRA system administrator. To start with the catalog creation, it is important to have a user with the relevant privileges for it.

1. Open vRealize Automation in a browser, log on with a privileged user and click on the **Administration** tab.

2. In the right-hand menu select **Catalog Management**. This will open another menu where four possible selections are presented:

- **Services**: This menu contains the actual catalogs or category names in vRA. In here, new categories can be created. Also, all the items of existing services can be managed using this entry point.
- **Catalog Items**: This shows a list of possible catalog items, also called blueprints. Not all blueprints in here can be published to a service. Exceptions, which can't be published to a service, is the so-called *software service*. These are packages to be used in a blueprint to install and configure software directly onto a VM.
- **Actions**: These are elements which can be entitled to a service catalog item to execute specific functions. There are management and maintenance actions like power cycle a deployment/VM. But there are also destroy or reprovision actions, which can be assigned.

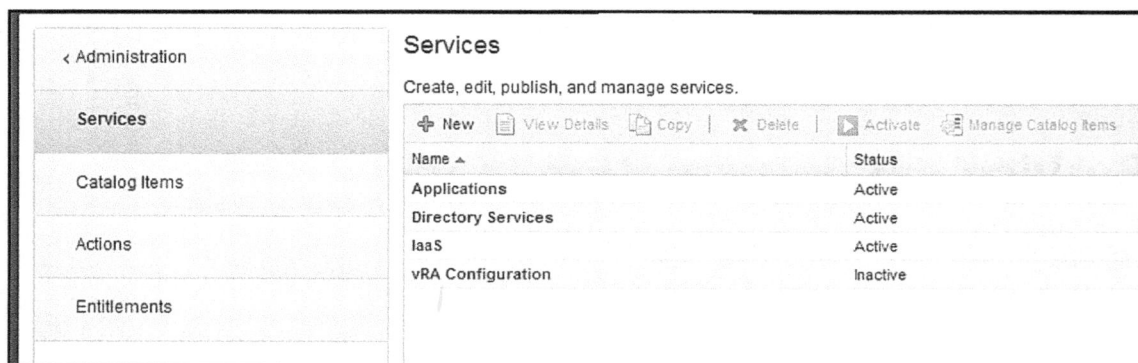

‹ Administration	Services	
Services	Create, edit, publish, and manage services.	
	✚ New 📄 View Details 📋 Copy | ✖ Delete | ▶ Activate 📑 Manage Catalog Items	
Catalog Items	Name ▲	Status
	Applications	Active
	Directory Services	Active
Actions	IaaS	Active
	vRA Configuration	Inactive
Entitlements		

3. To add a new service click on the button labeled with **New**. This will open an entry mask where the new service can be described:
    1. Provide a valid service name such as `Business Applications`.
    2. Provide an optional description.
    3. An icon can be chosen to represent the service. If there is a familiar icon available which is already used and known it is highly recommended to reuse these icons.
    4. The service status, this can be **Active, Inactive** or **Deleted**. A service can be set to inactive in order to provide maintenance or to change its content. Also, if a service is not needed any longer it can be set to **Deleted**. This will make the service unavailable to any users, but it will still remain in the service menu.

5. Also, operational hours can be provided. If this is a fully automated service, that might not be useful. However, if it requires manual intervention, operational hours can tell a user at which time the request is going to be processed.

6. **Owner**: The owner/manager/administrator of the server. It is typically a managerial role who also owns services in vRA.

7. **Support Team**: That can be a team of operational admins or designers responsible for supporting the blueprints as well as the installed components.

8. The **Change Window** will be a timeframe where the catalog is being maintained and updated. It can be predefined and is being displayed in an info box for the catalog users. Within a change window, a user cannot order catalog items.

4. If all information is correct click OK to create the service. It will then appear in the list of services. As long as there are no items entitled to this service, it will not show up in the user's catalog.

Second step: Publishing catalog items

In Chapter 5, *VMware vRealize Automation*, the creation of a blueprint was described in some detail. At the end of the chapter, it also covered briefly how to deploy a blueprint to an already created catalog. Basically, all published blueprints will show up as potential catalog items. The following steps will describe how to add a blueprint to a service.

1. While still in the administration menu with **Catalog Management** selected click on
    Catalog Items in the left-hand side menu pane.
2. Select either a line of a catalog item or click on its name to configure it.
3. In the opened configuration screen, provide the following details:

    -   **Icon**: same principle as with the service catalog.
    -   **Status**: It can either be **Active** or **Inactive**. Catalog items can be set to inactive while developers might add some work or test a new configuration. If set to inactive, it will disappear from the user's service catalog until it is set to active again.
    -   **Quota**: This can limit the number of deployments per user or group. Typically quotas are also set at the reservation level. If there is a need for a quota, it is recommended to set it at one level.

    There are many parameters in vRA, which can be set on different access levels. Sometimes it is wise to set it at the lowest level (individual) – sometimes it is required to set it at a higher level, to ensure every deployment follows the same rules. However, be aware that setting different parameters for the same configuration is also possible in vRA. The system will try to join these settings to avoid conflicts.

4. At the very bottom, the **Service** can be selected. This will then add the catalog item to the select service. Also, once the service contains items it will appear eventually in a users catalog overview. However, before a user can see a catalog to choose from, this needs to be entitled to the user or the group.
5. New and noteworthy will mark a new service catalog item for users and make it appear on their home screen in vRA.

6. Click **OK** to save and add the item to the selected catalog.

7. Once the service has been created and items have been published to the service it is time for the next step to make all available to a select business group (or multiple business groups).

Third step: Entitling a service

In vRA, service needs to be entitled to a business group in order to be visible for the users of this business group or tenant. An entitlement contains more than just the mapping of service to a user. It can also be used to define the required approval policies for a service, as well as the available actions a user could perform on a published resource out of this service catalog.

To add or edit an entitlement follow these steps:

1. While still in the administration menu with **Catalog Managment** selected click on **Entitlements** in the left-hand side menu pane.
2. Either choose an existing one or click on the button labeled **New** at the top of the list to create a new entitlement.

> Entitlements are bound to a business group. While a service can be part of many different entitlements simultaneously, an entitlement is always set to one single business groups. However, the same business group can have multiple different entitlements. This can be used to provide users of one business group different services with different security access profiles.

3. Start providing a descriptive name and a description.
4. Entitlements can have an expiration date. If this is set, the entitlement will change its state from active to inactive automatically. If an entitlement is inactive, the user access to contained services is revoked.
5. Set the status to **Active**.

An entitlement can have three state values:

- **Active**: The entitlement is useable and users can request its contained services.
- **Inactive**: The entitlement is not usable, users can't request its contained services. The entitlement was once active before it was set to inactive either by a user or an expiration date.
- **Draft**: The entitlement is in draft state. Users cannot request services used in this entitlement. The entitlement was never active before. Once an entitlement has been set to active it cannot be set back into the draft status.

6. Select the business group, which should be added to the entitlement. This selection cannot be changed afterward.

7. On the right side of this menu, the users of the business group can be added. Use the search field to look for specific users or groups. Also, be aware that only users who are members of the select business group should be added.
8. Once the users and the business group are set, click on **Next** at the right bottom corner of the screen.
9. This opens the **Items and Approvals** tab where the services or specific service items can be added to the entitlement.
10. Under **Entitled Services** chose the services, which should be part of this entitlement. Also, an appropriate approval policy can be chosen for the entire service. If a separate approval policy is required for a distinct item, use the plus sign at **Entitled Items** to add the item and chose a different approval policy.

If only the service is selected, the select approval policy is relevant for all its items. If special items require additional approval policies, they can be added at the **Entitled Items** sections. If any item is added, it will over-rule the services **Approval Policy** setting. Often users *double-entitle* and chose the service plus chose all its items. In this case, if no approval policy is select at the items, the approval policy selected at the entitled service will not be used for the additionally selected items.

11. The **Entitled Actions** section at the far right can also add additional approval policies for separate actions. This might be necessary for the destroy action, in order to prevent a user from accidently deleting a deployment. But also other actions can be configured with an approval. This depends on the use case and how the SDDC is operated.

12. Once all is set click on **Finish** to save the entitlement. If all settings are correct, the users for the select user group should now be able to order services using the service catalog under their **Catalog** tab.

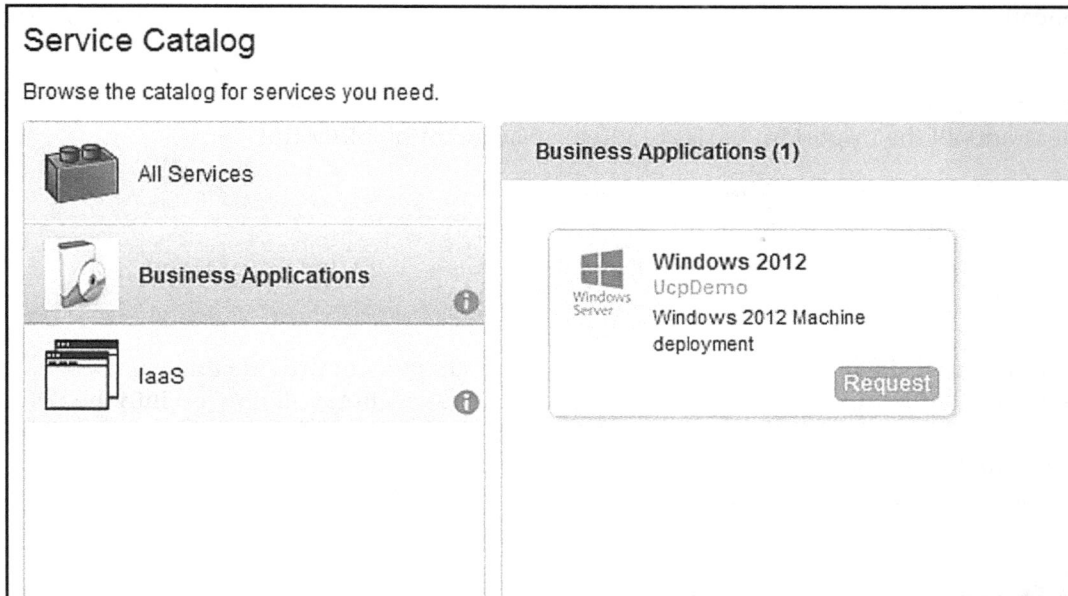

13. This is the final result, the user can see the catalog named `Business Applications` and can order a service. In this case, it is not really a business application, it is more IaaS only. In order to change that, the next section will describe how to set up an example LAMP stack which reflects a basic DB web server application stack.

Multimachine blueprint design example

Creating a blueprint for a single VM containing just the OS is one thing. But the real value comes with blueprints containing multiple VMs and also preinstalling a complete application landscape, all on demand. These are the high-value services in a catalog since the user can request an outcome, a ready to use application. Typically fully integrated into the environment.

However, these are also the complex designs and configurations. They need multiple networks (possibly also NSX), also they require user settable parameters which might be provided from one software tool to another. If there is a client-server connection involved like in a DB-App server relationship, the IP or hostname needs to be configured in the application VM, otherwise, it can't access the DB. Users and software configs need to be set as well as OS security settings need to be changed.

Before a valid multimachine blueprint design might be started, it is important to understand all the important basics of vRealize automation blueprinting:

- How to use templates
- How to use workflow subscriptions (if any)
- How to use network integration
- How to work with properties.

All those aspects have been discussed in the former chapters to provide this valid background for a multimachine blueprint creation. This section will now go into the details and discuss how to build a basic LAMP stack with a working APP to DB connection. It will be an example setup but provides all the necessary steps required to design a real application with a client-server relationship.

Software components

vRA software can be organized into so-called software components. They basically represent software components useable in blueprints. Typically, the software is installed using industry standard scripts. Also, the software might be downloaded from a central repository instead of copied onto any of the vRealize components.

vRA allows to manage three categories, also called **Container**, of software components:

- **Machine**: This type can be installed on top of VMs. It should be used for base software, which does not require any other software to be installed prior its installation. An example in the Linux world is Apache (httpd), MySQL, PostgreDB, or other standalone components.
- **Software Component**: This means that this component can only be installed on top of other software components. It cannot natively run on a naked system without any other software component installed. Basic examples for this might be PHP (makes more sense if httpd is already installed), SQL scripts to set up a DB, Java programs which require Java to be installed, and so on.

- **Specific Component**: This is a special container. In this case, one can choose an individual software component. The new component can then only be installed on top of that specific component. An example for this might be:
    - A PHP script to set up `.php` pages. It makes sense to let this only install if PHP is installed first (not just any software component)
    - A specific SQL Script for MySQL or PostgreSQL
    - Any tool which specifically requires other named components

Besides this three container versions, a **Software Component** also contains **Properties**. These can be either user settable during the request, or static in order to standardize the installation. The use of this, properties in a smart way will reduce the amount of maintenance a software component needs. A good example is variable values, for instance, if a certain username is used for accessing the DB and the user changes over time. Instead of changing the **Actions** all a designer needs to change is the **Properties** and that's it. Much like script variables used in huge batch scripts. Instead of searching the whole script for data, all which needs to change is the variable at the beginning.

However, these properties also have a second much more important role. They can also receive information from other components, like an IP Address from another VM in the blueprint, or a string like a username or a password. This is called *parameter binding*. It will be used in multimachine blueprints to convey information from one component to the other.

Finally, **Software Component** has **Actions**. These are basically scripting block. Each component will have four different types:

- **Install**: Used to do the primary install of the component
- **Configure**: Used as configuring the component after the first install
- **Start**: Brings the application up for the first time.
- **Uninstall**: Removes the application from the system

While it does make sense to follow this guide, it is not required. A software component can also have only an install **Action** set, without the other three and either work. However, it has to have at least the **Install** type set.

To actually install and setup the software, scripts are used. vRA supports the three industry standards for Windows and Linux: Bash, CMD, and PowerShell.

However, vRA will not be aware where the component is being used and using bash for installing a windows component will obviously fail. The scripting language has to be available on the target system. However, vRA will prevent designers from using CMD or PowerShell items on Linux systems and vice versa.

The support of this standards is actually good news. Since a lot of organizations might have already used scripting to some extent to automate their software deployment, these scripts can now be reused for the SDDC.

The scripts will be run using the Guest agent, this agent should be installed on every Windows and Linux template and it should be able to reach the DEM (IaaS server).

The IaaS server reach is very important when deploying a template in an external network. If the IaaS server cannot reach the VM/its Guest agent, the software component cannot be installed.

A trick might be to put the VM in an installation network and move it after the install was successful. Another is to make sure that the DEM worker can be reached from all VM networks through secure routing. But this can be tricky in a DMZ environment. The Guest and the IaaS server use port 443 (SSL) to communicate with each other.

Sample application design

Based on all this information a sample application design can be created. The scenario is a simple LAMP stack based on CentOS. It will have two VMs, one in a different network than the other. However, the VMs can reach each other through secure routing.

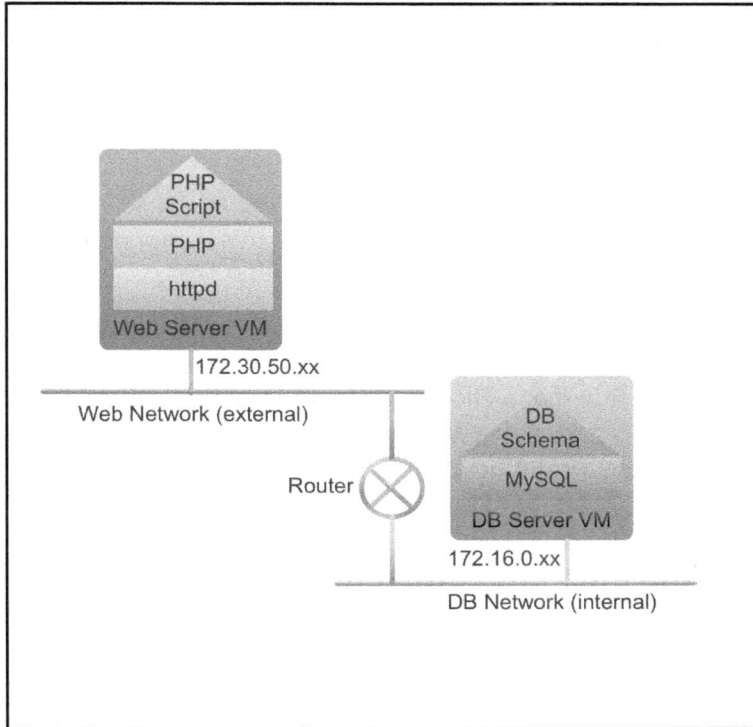

One VM will be a MySQL DB server with a database scheme to be installed containing the installation timestamp. The other VM will be a web/app server with Apache and PHP installed. It will run a PHP script, which will query the DB server and display the installation timestamp from the DB server, as well as its current time.

The application will be created for an example organization called *Flexible Software Tools Industries*. This organization will be called FST Industries from now on.

While this might sound super simple, it will require a lot of techniques used for much more complex deployments. The main difference in this scenario is the easy scripts and the light setup. But all the steps will be similar for other applications.

Defining the components

To start with the application all the software components have to be designed and created. In order to create the software components follow these steps.

Apache web server

The first software component to create is Apache. Since this component will not need any parameter to install successfully, it is rather quick to define.

1. Open vRealize Automation in a browser, log on with a privileged user and click on the **Design** tab.
2. In the left-hand side menu click on **Software Components**.
   1. Put in `Apache` as name, the ID will be created automatically.
   2. Provide a valid description such as: `Installs Apache on a Red Hat based Linux machine`.

> It is helpful to disclose the OS type. Since all works using scripts, there might be differences in Linux distributions. A Red Hat-oriented script will not work on Ubuntu and vice versa.

3. Chose a container. In this case, the container should be of the type **Machine**.
4. Click **Next** at the bottom right corner to get to the **Properties** screen.

   This application is installing plain Apache (`httpd`) on top of Linux. For this task, no properties will be needed.

5. Click **Next** at the bottom right corner to access the **Actions** screen.
6. At the **Install** stage, select **Bash** and click on **Click here to edit**.
   1. In the **Editor** window, put in the following bash script:

```
#!/bin/bash
Log=/tmp/httpd-install.log
#Install the server bits
/bin/echo/echo "Start Installation of httpd"  >> $Log 2>&1
/usr/bin/yum -y install httpd >> $Log 2>&1
#Mark the server to start in the select runlevels
echo "Setting the run level..."  >> $Log 2>&1
/sbin/chkconfig --levels 235 httpd on  >> $Log 2>&1
echo "Apache installation is complete now." >> $Log 2>&1
/sbin/service httpd start
```

This requires a functional YUM server to be reachable, either through the internet or from a local repository. Typically, organizations do have local YUM repository servers to manager their CentOS/Red Hat farm.

2. Since this is just a small Linux package, the start command will be used within the install script.

7. Click on **OK** and then on **Next** to continue to the Ready to complete screen.
8. Review the information and click **Finish** to create the software component.
9. In the list overview, select the line of the new Apache component and click on **Publish** in the head row. Otherwise, the component can't be selected within a blueprint.
10. If all that was successful, the new software component will be available.

PHP web component

The next software component to create is PHP. This will require Apache to be present in order to work properly, so the container setting will become much more relevant for PHP.

1. Repeat all steps from the Apache component for PHP until step 3.
2. For **Container** click the drop down and select Apache.

   PHP can now only installed if Apache is also used within the VM.

3. Click **Next** to get to the properties screen.

   No properties are required for this component.

4. Click **Next** at the bottom right corner to access the **Actions** screen.
5. At the **Install** stage, select **Bash** and click on **Click here to edit**.

   In the **Editor** window, put in the following Bash script:

```
#!/bin/bash
Log=/tmp/php-install.log
#Install the php bits
/bin/echo "Start Installation of php"  >> $Log 2>&1
/usr/bin/yum -y install php-mysql php-devel php-gd php-pecl-memcache
php-pspell
php-snmp php-xmlrpc php-xml >> $Log 2>&1
echo "Setting the run level..."  >> $Log 2>&1
echo "PhP installation is complete now." >> $Log 2>&1
```

6. At the `Configure` stage, select `Bash` and click on `Click here to edit`.

   In the **Editor** window, put in the following Bash script:

   ```
   #!/bin/bash
   Log=/tmp/php-config.log
   #Config the php bits
   /bin/echo "Restart Webserver"  >> $Log 2>&1
   /sbin/service httpd restart >> $Log 2>&1
   echo "PhP configuration is complete now." >> $Log 2>&1
   ```

7. Beginning from step 7 as described in the Apache install, complete those for this component too. Don't forget to *publish*!

MySQL web component

The next software component to create is MySQL. This will require no other components to be present in order to work properly, so the container setting will be **Machine** again. It is recommended to use MySQL as name and give the same description as with the former components.

1. Repeat all steps from the Apache component for MySQL until step 6.
2. At the **Install** stage, select **Bash** and click on **Click here to edit.**

   In the **Editor** window, put in the following bash script:

   ```
   #!/bin/bash
   #Update the system prior to perform installation
   Log=/tmp/mysql-install.log
   echo "Start update"  > $Log 2>&1
   #Install the server bits
   /bin/echo "Start Installation of mysql"  >> $Log 2>&1
   /usr/bin/yum -y install mysql-server >> $Log 2>&1
   #Mark the server to start in the select runlevels
   echo "Setting the run level..."  >> $Log 2>&1
   /sbin/chkconfig --levels 235 mysqld on  >> $Log 2>&1
   echo "MySQL installation is complete now." >> $Log 2>&1
   /sbin/service mysqld start
   ```

   Since this is similar to the Apache install, the start command will be used within the install script.

3. Beginning from step 7 as described in the Apache install, complete all those for this component too. Don't forget to *publish*!

FST Industries web component

The next software component to create is the FST Industries web component. This will require PHP to be present in order to work properly, so the container setting will be PHP again. It is recommended to use FST Industries_WebComponent as name and give the same description as with the former components. This component will install/create a .php script to access the DB and query the table containing the timestamp:

1. Open vRealize Automation in a browser, log on with a privileged user and click on the **Design** tab.
2. In the left-hand side, menu clicks on **Software Components**.
    1. Put in FST Industries_WebComponent as name, the ID will be created automatically.
    2. Provide a valid description such as: Installs on a Red Hat based Linux machine with PHP already present.
3. Choose a container. In this case, the container must be of the type **PHP**.
4. Click **Next** at the bottom right corner to get to the **Properties** screen.

    This component requires properties to run. In order to query the DB a couple of variables need to be present:

    1. Click on **New** and create a property called DB_Username with a type of **String**. **Override** and **Required** should be ticked.
    2. Click on **New** and create a property called DB_Address with a type of **String**. **Override** and **Required** should be ticked.
    3. Click on **New** and create a property called DB_Password with a type of **SecureString**. **Encrypted**, **Override**, and **Required** should be ticked.
    4. Click on **New** and create a property called DB_Name with a type of **String**. **Override** and **Required** should be ticked.
    5. Do not put values in these variables.
5. Click **Next** at the bottom right corner to access the **Actions** screen.
6. At the **Install** stage, select **Bash** and click on **Click here to edit**.

    In the **Editor** window, put in the following Bash script:

```
#!/bin/bash
#Create the php File on demand
touch /var/www/html/index.php
FILE=/var/www/html/index.php
cat > $FILE <<- EOM
<?php
```

```
\$dbhost = "$DB_Address";
\$dbuser = "$DB_Username";
\$dbpass = "$DB_Password";
\$dbname = "$DB_Name";
    \$conn = mysql_connect(\$dbhost, \$dbuser, \$dbpass);
    if(! \$conn ) {
        die('Could not connect: ' . mysql_error());
    }
    \$sql = 'SELECT * FROM FST_Install';
    @mysql_select_db($DB_Name) or die ("Unable to select database");
    \$retval = mysql_query( \$sql, \$conn );
    if(! \$retval ) {
        die('Could not get data: ' . mysql_error());
    }
    while(\$row = mysql_fetch_array(\$retval, MYSQL_NUM)) {
        echo "ID :{\$row[0]}  <br> ".
            "Data : {\$row[1]} <br> ".
            "Setup Timestamp : {\$row[2]} <br> ".
            "-----------------------------<br>";
    }
    mysql_free_result(\$retval);
    echo "Fetched data successfully\\n";
    echo "\\n Current time: " . date('l jS \\of F Y h:i:s A');
    mysql_close(\$conn);
?>
EOM
```

7. At the **Configure** stage, select **Bash** and click on **Click** here to edit.

   In the **Editor** window, put in the following Bash script:

```
#!/bin/bash
#Turn off firewall to enable webserver access
echo "Configuring firewall to allow HTTPD access"
/sbin/service iptables stop
#Set SELinux to allow httpd db connects
echo "Setting SELinux to allow DB connects"
/usr/sbin/setsebool -P httpd_can_network_connect_db=1
```

> This is for test/demo purposes only. In a production environment, it is strongly recommended to set the right firewall rule using `iptables` command!

8. Beginning from step 7 as described in the Apache install complete all those for this component too. Don't forget to *publish*!

FST Industries DB component

The next software component to create is the FST Industries DB component. This will require MySQL to be present in order to work properly, so the container setting will be MySQL. It is recommended to use FST Industries_DBComponent as name and give the same description as with the former components. This component will install/create a SQL script to create a DB and a table containing the installation timestamp information:

1. Open vRealize Automation in a browser, log on with a privileged user and click on the **Design** tab.
2. In the left-hand side menu click on **Software Components**.
    1. Put in FST Industries_DBComponent as name, the ID will be created automatically.
    2. Provide a valid description such as: Installs on a Red Hat based Linux machine with PHP already present.
3. Choose a container. In this case, the container must be of the type **MySQL**.
4. Click **Next** at the bottom right corner to get to the **Properties** screen.

    This component requires properties to run. In order to query the DB a couple of variables need to be present:

    1. Click on **New** and create a property called DB_Username with a type of **String**. **Override** and **Required** should be ticked.
    2. Click on **New** and create a property called DB_Password with a type of **SecureString**. **Encrypted**, **Override**, and **Required** should be ticked.
    3. Click on **New** and create a property called DB_Name with a type of **String**. **Override** and **Required** should be ticked.
    4. In this case, default values can be put in such as: dbadmin (**USER**), dbadmin (**PWD**), FST_DB (**DB Name**).

    It is not recommended to use the same password as the username in a production environment, this is just for test purposes!

5. Click **Next** at the bottom right corner to access the **Actions** screen.
6. At the **Install** stage, select **Bash** and click on **Click here to edit**.

In the **Editor** window, put in the following Bash script:

```
#!/bin/bash
Log=/tmp/FST-configure.log
MYSQL=/usr/bin/mysql
/bin/echo "Creating DB with the name $DB_Name with user $DB_Username
accessing it" >> $Log 2>&1
$MYSQL -u root -e "CREATE DATABASE IF NOT EXISTS $DB_Name;"
#$MYSQL -u root -e "CREATE USER '$DB_Username'@'%' IDENTIFIED BY
'$DB_Password';"
$MYSQL -u root -e "GRANT ALL ON $DB_Name.* TO '$DB_Username'@'%'
IDENTIFIED BY '$DB_Password';"
$MYSQL -u root -e "FLUSH PRIVILEGES;"
#create the sql content file
/bin/touch /tmp/sqlcommand.sql
T1=/tmp/sqlcommand.sql
/bin/cat > $T1 <<- EOM
use $DB_Name;
CREATE TABLE FST_Install (id INT NOT NULL AUTO_INCREMENT PRIMARY
KEY,
data  VARCHAR(100), created_at TIMESTAMP(8));
INSERT INTO FST_Install (data)
        VALUES ('The time of creation is:')
EOM
/bin/echo "Creating Timestamp table using sql file stored ad $T1" >>
$Log 2>&1
$MYSQL -u root < $T1
/bin/echo "Finished configuring FST $DB_Name with $DB_Username
accessing it"
>> $Log 2>&1
#/bin/rm $T1
```

7. At the **Configure** stage, select **Bash** and click on **Click here to edit**.

In the **Editor** window, put in the following Bash script:

```
#!/bin/bash
#Turn off iptables for app server access
/sbin/service iptables stop
```

This is for test/demo purposes only. In a production environment, it is strongly recommended to set the right firewall rule using iptables command!

8. Beginning from step 7 as described in the Apache install complete all those for this component too. Don't forget to *publish*!

If all the components are defined the **Software Components** screen should look like this:

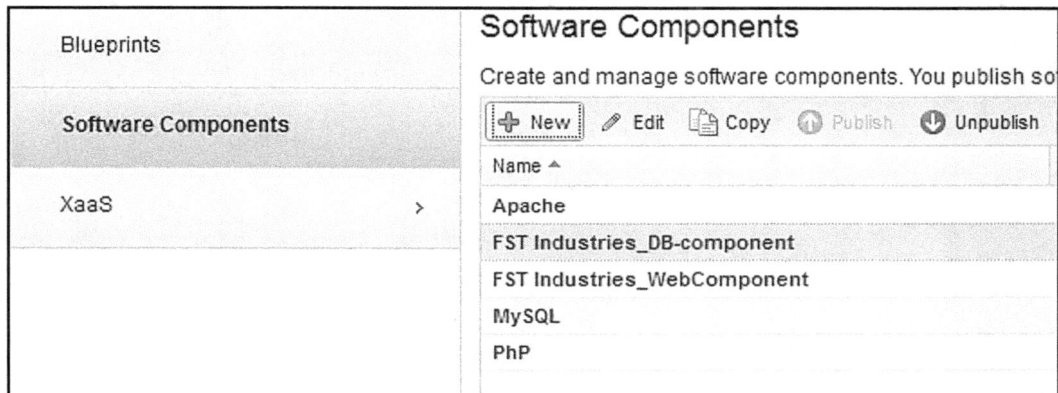

Blueprints	**Software Components**
Software Components	Create and manage software components. You publish so
	⊕ New ✎ Edit 📋 Copy ⊕ Publish ⊕ Unpublish
	Name ▲
XaaS >	Apache
	FST Industries_DB-component
	FST Industries_WebComponent
	MySQL
	PhP

Defining the blueprint

After all the components are created and defined, the multi-machine blueprint can be created. This is done similar to the blueprint creation described in Chapter 5, *VMware vRealize Automation*, under *Create the IaaS blueprint*.

Follow the same steps as in the IaaS example. The only difference is that this blueprint will have two virtual machines. Also, it will require two different networks. These networks should have a network profile attached and should be preset.

Once all this is done, the software components need be included in the blueprint. These are the steps required to complete this:

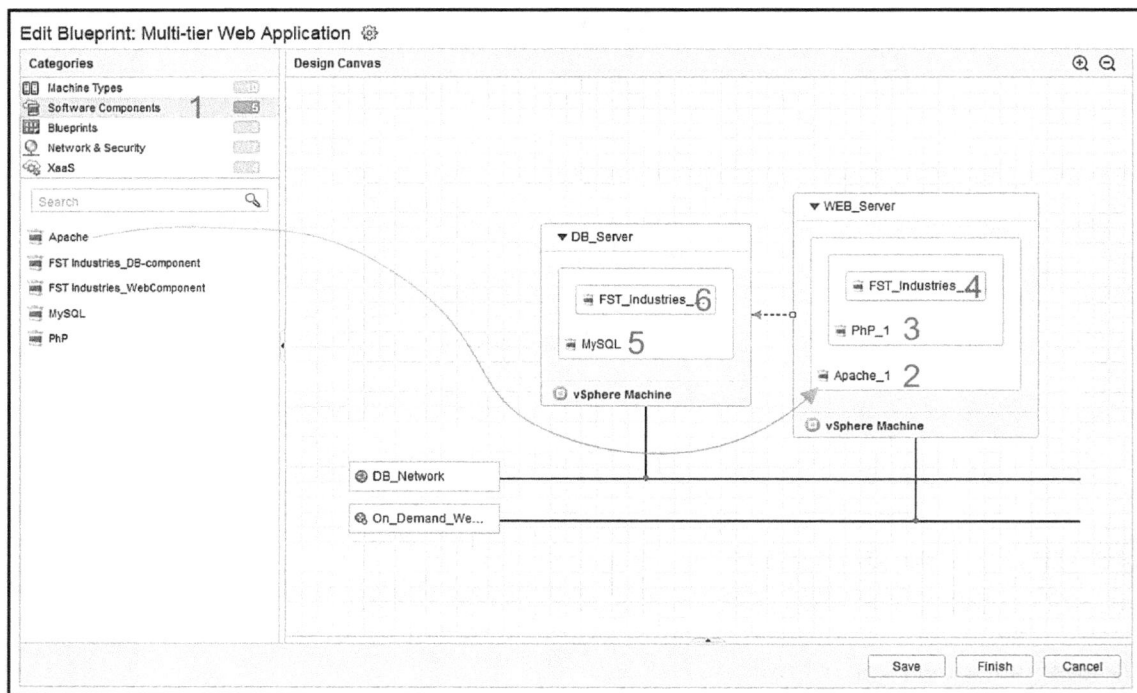

```
Edit Blueprint: Multi-tier Web Application  ⚙

Categories                              Design Canvas                                              ⊕ ⊖
  ▣▣ Machine Types                                                             ▼ WEB_Server
  🗄 Software Components   1
  ▦ Blueprints
  🔍 Network & Security                                      ▼ DB_Server
  ⚙ XaaS

  [Search          🔍]                                                              ⊞ FST_Industries_4

  🗄 Apache                                          ⊞ FST_Industries_6            ⊞ PhP_1  3
  🗄 FST Industries_DB-component                                      ◄----○
  🗄 FST Industries_WebComponent
  🗄 MySQL                                           ⊞ MySQL  5               ⊞ Apache_1  2
  🗄 PhP
                                                    ▢ vSphere Machine          ▢ vSphere Machine


                           ▢ DB_Network
                           ▢ On_Demand_We...


                                                                           Save    Finish    Cancel
```

1. In the design canvas, select **Software Components**. This will bring up the list of defined and published components to be installed.
2. Drag and drop Apache on the web server VM. Make sure to name the VMs accordingly to be able to distinguish between DB_Server and WEB_Server.
3. Drag and drop PHP on top of Apache (it will not work on other components, given the container type is Apache).
4. Drag and drop FST Industries web component on top of PHP.
5. Assign MySQL to the database server.
6. Finally, chose the FST DB component and drop it on top of MySQL on the DB server.
7. There is only one minor step left to complete the blueprint. Somehow the web server should be aware of the IP and access rights of the DB server. This is where the property binding kicks in.

8. When creating the FST components, properties have been created. The DB component has username, DB name, and password with preset values. These will show up as default values once a user orders the service. The WEB component has the same properties without default values.

9. In vRA there is a function called *binding* in order to get information from one component property and link it to a property of another.

In order to activate the binding for the web component, click on the component in the canvas. At the component overview, click on the **Properties** tab.

This will bring up the list of the previously defined properties. Next to the **Value** column there is a column called **Binding**.

1. Select the **Username** line and then click on the **Edit** button.
2. In the value, field use the *down arrow* key to get a list of available components.
3. Select the FST DB component.
4. Use the ~ sine to access the properties of the selected component.
5. Select DB_Username and click **OK**.
6. Repeat this for the DB_Password and DB_Name line.
7. At the DB_Address line, select _resource~DB_Server~ip_address. This will add the new IP address from the created DB server as value into the property for the FST web component.
8. After all, components are set to the appropriate server VM. Use the relationship handle (little dot icon at the top left of the VM) to draw it from the web Server to the DB server. That will ensure that the DB server is setup prior to the web server.
9. If all this was successful the blueprint can be published to a catalog like described earlier in this chapter. The user can now request this application and even set DB name, DB admin, and DB password.

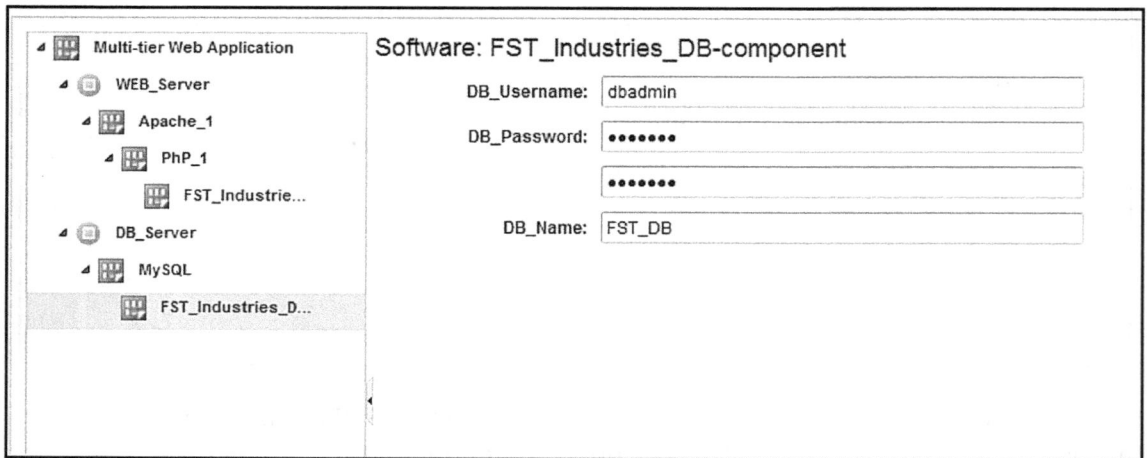

This is the screen a user will see when ordering this service. Once the user clicks **Submit** the system will set up the two VMs using the VM templates and install all the software components using the scripts provided. The application will come up and running, just waiting for the user to explore it.

Summary

This chapter described the basic catalog design as well as the different catalog types. The business case and the expectations are main drivers for filling a catalog with the right services. Also, the difference between technology-focused and outcome focused catalogs has been described. The main part was also to describe how to setup and create an outcome focused blueprint in vRA which will provide a fully running service on demand.

In the next chapter, the focus will be on network virtualization. This is a huge topic in an SDDC since it can enhance flexibility and security aspects of a data center. Nevertheless, it will also increase complexity since it adds another layer to take care of. The chapter will discuss NSX basics and describe its main functions and features. Furthermore, it will describe how to include NSX networks in blueprints and how to create on demand networks while provisioning VM resources.

8
Network Virtualization using NSX

This chapter will focus on the network virtualization technologies available for the VMware SDDC. Network virtualization is a new topic that has become important for the agile and flexible data center. When deploying services, the network part is often crucial since there are various security requirements that need to be met with an application. Also, there might be pre-existing network requirements that need to be fulfilled when porting the application to the environment. Finally, it will harm the overall agility if the whole OS deployment and storage deployment can be done automatically, but the network part might actually require human interaction. A true end-to-end automation is not quite possible without network virtualization. If it is not in place, it may cause delays and even roadblocks in SDDC projects.

This chapter will require basic network knowledge since some medium to advanced network configuration will be discussed in here. It will not provide basic training about network techniques. It is highly recommended to be familiar with the most common network terms and functions before introducing NSX into a data center. Also, VMware offers own certifications and trainings for NSX in order to be able to deploy and manage it. It is highly recommended to take such a class before starting with an NSX production deployment.

Furthermore, the chapter will discus network virtualization principles and its main use cases. Also, it will explain how a virtualized network works and what benefits it has to offer for the SDDC. Furthermore, there will be example configurations to explain how to combine NSX with vRealize and create on-demand blueprints using some of NSX's advanced features to create yet complex but easy to order blueprints, providing advanced network security and availability.

However, this is a basic introduction to NSX and its capabilities. There are some advanced functionalities such as security profiles, security tags, and the integration of third-party vendors directly into NSX, which would be simply too much to cover in this chapter. For more information about these functionalities, please make sure to visit VMware's website for the advanced NSX documentation.

The following topics will be discussed in greater detail:

- Network virtualization 101
- NSX functions and principles
- Terminology and best practices
- Basic NSX installation and configuration
- Connecting NSX with vRealize Automation
- Using NSX in vRealize blueprints
- Using vRA for network creation on-demand

Network Virtualization 101

Maybe, network virtualization is the newest member in the data center virtualization family. After compute virtualization (VMware vSphere) and storage virtualization (from various storage vendors such as IBM, Hitachi Data Systems and Data Core to name a few) it is adding additional functions and features to the network segment. NSX enables similar things for networking as ESX / vSphere has enabled for compute. It creates an abstraction layer that enables various network functions to run on top of any physical switch hardware/vendor. This is a highly disruptive technology, which changes the entire networking sector. Just as much as compute virtualization once was when VMware introduced it in the early 2000s.

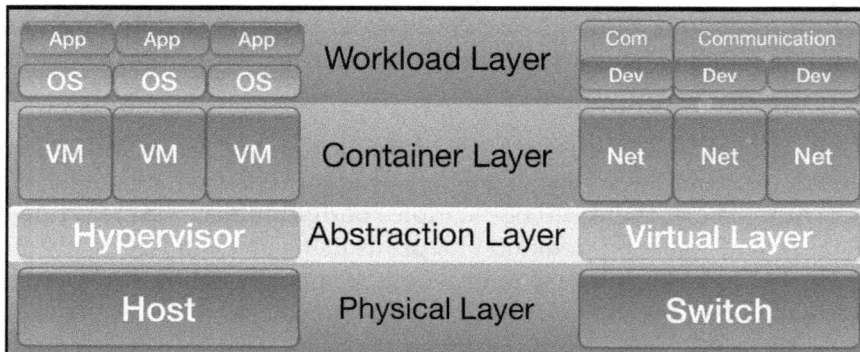

The image displays a comparison between compute virtualization and network virtualization. Although these concepts are quite different, they share some common sense, which might be beneficial to highlight to understand the technology.

Both concepts introduce different layers of abstraction. At the bottom, there is the physical infrastructure, which becomes interchangeable due to virtualization. VMware's vSphere can run on virtually any supported hardware. NSX can run on any vendor's physical network switches.

The abstraction layer is the software component. For compute that is what vSphere is, for network this is what NSX delivers.

In the compute world, the container layer is where VMs are created to act as virtual infrastructure for operation systems. In the NSX world, this would be VXLAN to act as virtual infrastructure for virtual networks. So, VXLAN can be seen as the container for the virtual networks created. It is also referred to as the overlay network.

The workload layer is in compute above the container and is the space where the OS and applications rung. In the virtual network world, this is the advanced functionality NSX brings to the table such as microsegmentation, advanced access control, and other features only available in network virtualization. It is another layer of granularity to control network flow and security aspects.

In fact it might be a bit simplistic to compare it directly to compute virtualization, but its basic deliverables tend to be similar:

- Decouple advanced functionality from hardware vendors.
    - Comparison: VM can run on any hypervisor on any supported vendors hardware.
- Move network configurations between network devices seamlessly and transparent.
    - Comparison: A VM can be vMotioned from one supported server vendor to the other (given the architecture is similar).
- Make a migration easy by bridging virtual to physical networks.
    - Comparison: A physical server can be virtualized by using P2V (physical to virtual) converter.

- Additional functions, only possible on virtual networks (VM security policies, VM-to-VM firewall rules, VM-to-VM routing and access, high availability, and so on).
  - Comparison: VM Cloning, vMotion, Snapshots, HA, and so on. Functions that have been introduced by vSphere and have enhanced the way to run servers and application ever since.
- A big advantage is also microsegmentation, which is a way to secure two workloads even if they reside in the same network within the same subnet.
  - Comparison: Many VMs can run on the same ESXi host, but they are truly isolated from each other.

This list is by far not complete and should help to understand the basic offerings compared with compute virtualization. Naturally, there are features provided by network virtualization, which lack a compute counterpart.

Besides the nice and new features network virtualization adds, it is actually required to build a truly automated and agile data center. Without network virtualization, things can get so complex that they are pretty hard to handle. So, it is more than just a nice to have, it can be a requirement for a successful SDDC. Before we can explore why network virtualization is such a game changer, it might be worth recapping traditional networking.

Current networking infrastructures

First of all, it is important to basically understand how networking works today. There is a basic model to distinguish different traffic types and their functionalities. This model is called the OSI 7 layer model and explains the various different protocols and traffic types used in networking. Since a fair share of this chapter will mention these layers, it is worthwhile recapping what each layer stands for in networking:

Layer	Protocol data unit	Function/examples
Layer 1	Bit	Physical connection, Cable/NIC/DSL/ISDN
Layer 2	Frame	Transmission layers MAC, LLTP, L2TP, PPP, MPLS, and so on
Layer 3	Packet	Multinode network structure IPv4, IPv6, ICMP, IPSec,CLNP, and DDP
Layer 4	Segment TCP/datagram UDP	Transmission of segments TCP, UDP, and NBF
Layer 5	Data	Session management RPC, SCP, and PAP

| Layer 6 | Data | Presentation/Translation between network and application S/MIME, TLS |
| Layer 7 | Data | High-level APIs HTTP, HTTPS, NFS, FTP, Telnet, SMTP, SSH, and so on |

> Network admins often refer to these layers when it comes to certain functionalities. If not already familiar, it is recommended to read more about the OSI model though to better understand how networking works and what the different layers provide.

Typically, a data center today has one of the two possible network architectures applied:

Central L2 design using a network core switches that route all network traffic through the entire data center (typically 2 HA-enabled core switches)

This means that all networks and traffic are routed through the core switch, making it the most important component in the entire organization. If the core switch goes down for some reason the entire company will be cut of the network and possibly any external access as well.

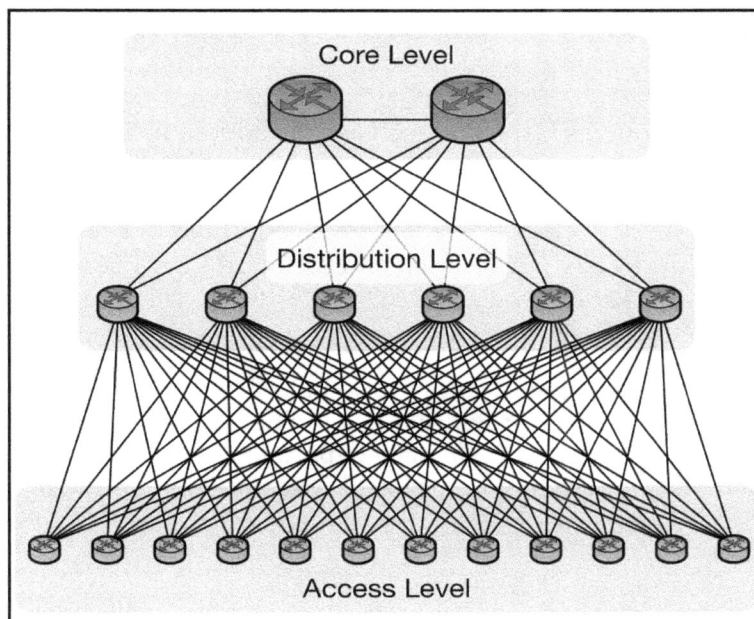

However, it also means that networks can be stretched across many different switches and endpoints. Stretched L2 networking is used to have the same IP subnet in two different data centers, to enable applications to run on either side without re-IPing them. In Europe, this flexibility became almost standard for the last years when it came to VMware deployments using shared storage between two data centers (*Storage Metro Cluster*). To enable VMs to roam freely between these two sides, the IP segment has to be the same. An IP change after a vMotion would break most of the applications, making the benefit of vMotion disappear.

This is why, most organizations started to create huge L2 network installations. However, such an L2 installation has not only benefits, but there are also drawbacks and risks, especially with large L2 architectures, making the network somewhat weak and fragile.

One of the most dangerous things is possibly a broadcast storm affecting more and more networks through the core switch. Broadcast storms can happen due to various reasons, there are technologies in place which should prevent them from happening, but sometimes, it is as simple as a wrong command on the wrong CLI and the network goes all black. Since an L2 installation is sharing all connects through a core switch, a broadcast storm affecting the core switch can bring down an entire network of an organization.

VLAN: Network virtualization known for almost 30 years

Virtual logical area network (**VLAN**) and has been introduced in 1984. It is a method to separate a physical network/switch in multiple virtual networks. Each VLAN is separated from each other through so-called VLAN IDs (also called *tags*), which uniquely identify the segment. There are 4096 VLAN tags available. However, VLAN 0 is reserved and is used as simple priority tag while VLAN 4095 is used as a wild card VLAN search/address. In VMware vSphere, VLAN 4095 is used as a `trunk all VLAN IDs` option. Given these reservations, total 4094 VLANs can be used.

> Although this sounds a lot in the first place, it might be easy to reach its limits if applied at a provider scale or in big organizations. Given that they can have hundreds of customers/ departments, and each can have hundreds (or even thousands) of VLANs, this limit will be reached fast.

VLANs are basically just virtual network containers and are able to carry any network subnets. They can also be used for multiple subnets having the same VLAN tag, making it possible to divide a VLAN in smaller segments. However, all this requires extensive routing and also limits the number of devices a segment/VLAN can support.

Since a network segment always needs to have a broadcast address as well as a network address, these two addresses can't be used for clients. If a network is separated in multiple segments, each segment requires two addresses for these functions, limiting the overall usable addresses.

Example:

Subnet mask: `255.255.255.0` or referred to as `/24`

Network address: `192.168.0.0`

Network broadcast: `192.168.0.255`

This means that 254 addresses can be used for this network. If the network would be split in four segments, the number of usable addresses would decrease by eight instead of two addresses:

Subnet mask	Network address	Network broadcast
255.255.255.192 or /26	192.168.0.0	192.168.0.63
	192.168.0.64	192.168.0.127
	192.168.0.128	192.168.0.191
	192.168.0.192	192.168.0.255

In the preceding table, only 62 addresses are usable per subnet making total 248 addresses available. This means using the subnet method to split networks can become fairly complex and reduces the amount of usable IP addresses per network drastically.

Traditional routing and security

Another big topic in networking is obviously routing and the security aspect (firewalls, packet inspection, and so on).

Each deployed workload will require some routes to reach other services as well as possible security settings like firewall rules to enable communication into protected areas. A good example for such a configuration is a LAMP stack. The web server will require access to the DB server in order to display information. Normally, the DB server will be located somewhere within the internal data center networks. A web server typically is located in a DMZ outside of the internal organizational network. The communication between both servers will happen through a firewall. But to make that work a rule has to be added for each web server communicating with its DB pendant. This means that each pair will have their own firewall rules, and this is just a simple example, to be created based on their IP address and the ports used to communicate.

> Most organizations have already so many firewall rules that it is nearly impossible to tidy them up. Also, often rules do not get deleted since the risk of breaking some important applications is much higher than the benefit a clean rules table would provide.

In an automated environment, where also application deployments are planned, it is required that these tasks be also completed once the service has been deployed.

Modern network approach

Since complexity in a data center has increased and also the amount of servers or VMs has increased, the requirements to a data center network have changed tremendously.

The server virtualization has changed the way networking and security needs to work. Since VMs can migrate from one physical host to another, the network has to provide this functionality as well in order to prevent re-IPing of VMs. Also, firewalls and security rules need to be configured dynamically or IP based in order to support this behavior. Static port-based rules or security solutions did no longer work for the virtual environment.

The new SDDC capabilities create new requirements to networking and security. Given that services and servers will not be created on demand and also deleted on demand the network has to grow and shrink with them. Preprovisioning of VLANs is an option, but requires huge pools of VLANs waiting to be used in the future. This might work for VLANs and IP segments, but firewall rules can hardly be preset and assigned as needed. New services may be deployed on demand, but then IT security kicks in and the whole process might slow down since a handover happens to manually create DMZ and security rules for new services.

Also, as described earlier in this chapter, a big L2 network has its downsides as well, for example, a broadcast storm, a core switch outage, and so on. All this can affect the connectivity and by this also the production capability of an organization. A big networking outage can be seen as production outage endangering the whole business of an organization.

L3 Networking – the new architecture

Compared with layer two networks, the new favorite design is a layer three leaf, spine architecture. Each access zone (single or multiple racks) will have its own L3 domain and connects to a leaf. These leaves then connect up to multiple spines to get connectivity to the other leaves. This means that there is no core switch anymore where all the traffic goes through.

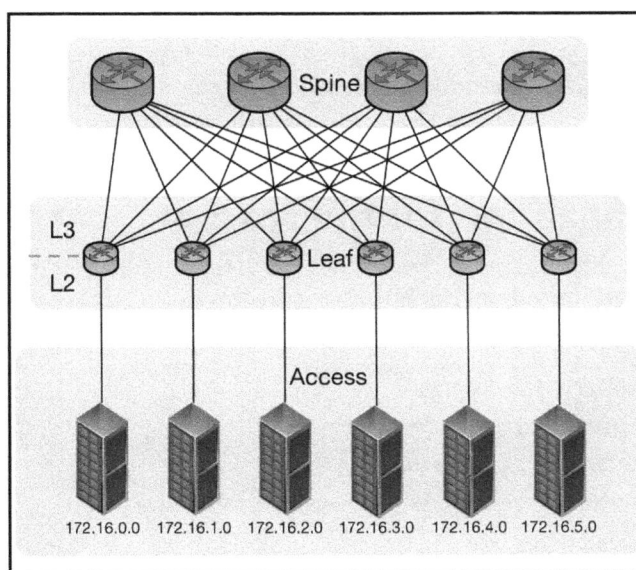

There are a couple of benefits in L3 network architectures:

- It will prevent global broadcast storms, since each access zone has its own broadcast domain/can't broadcast across all leaves (given there is no broadcast/multicast routing).
- It is enhancing the network availability while easing the configuration needed since growing the network does not require a reconfiguration of the core switch.

- Maintenance gets easier since each leaf connects to multiple spines, those can put offline for patching and the network stays still online. If a core switch needs to be updated, it generates risk since there is only one other core left; if this core fails the network goes dark.
- Security is enhanced since each access pod is required to pass a router or even firewall to connect to another access pod (optional but practical to connect leaves).
- Each access pod has its own L2 net segment, which is not stretched to other, leaves or access zones (as shown in the picture using exemplary network addresses).
- The L2 bridge is at the leaf level, whereas the L2 bridge in a core switching environment is typically at the spine level.

However, the downside of this networking design is that if a VM would now travel from one rack to another, or one access pod to another, it has to change its IP address since this represents another L2 segment. This is why, this setup is fairly complex with traditional VLAN-based networking. It eliminates the freedom of roaming VMs between racks (access pods) or even sites.

Network virtualization for the rescue

This is where network virtualization comes into play. Given that the physical L3/L2 architecture provides all these benefits but also introduces the access pod dilemma, network virtualization can add many more to this design:

- On-demand network creation
- Networks spread across access pods
- Stretched networks across sites
- Networks within access pods (no north-south traffic)
- On-demand security rules
- VM-to-VM communication limits within same network (microsegmentation)

Just to name a few, a setup with an L3/L2 network design plus network virtualization would look somewhat similar to the following picture.

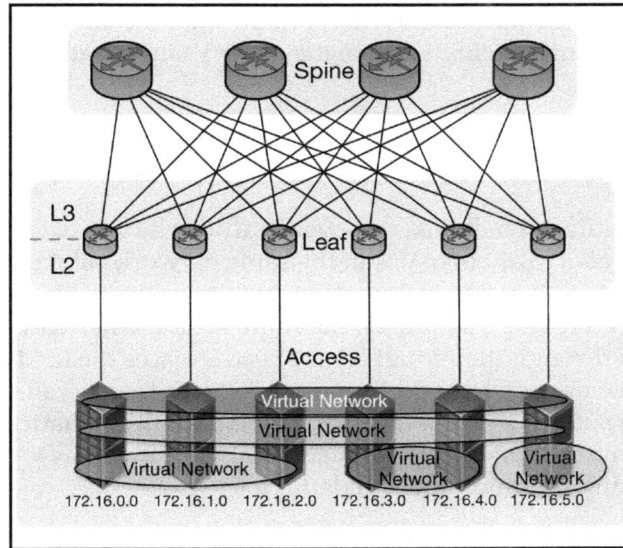

In this case, the physical L2 domain is still per access pod, but virtual networks can be spread across each pods. This works since network virtualization like NSX uses a so-called *transport zone*. This transport layer uses packet encapsulation to put a new header around a network packet and send it to its destination. The destination will be a VTEP of a NSX (VXLAN)-enabled ESXi host. This is the key functionality of NSX and enables great flexibility in creating networks. Even networks with the same IP subnet can be created and connected to different virtual routers yet existent on the same ESXi host or in the same access pod.

The graphic shows several virtual networks either spanning all pods or just existent within a single pod. However, with NSX, all these networks can have external access to the physical network or to each other over the integrated virtual router existent on every ESXi host. This opens a world of possibilities to not only put VMs into virtual networks and provide them just enough access to function but also enhance the overall security.

Also, configurations as well as the setup can be easily backed up and restored on any physical network; since all of this is virtual, it is absolutely independent from the vendor as well as the underlying hardware.

Another benefit of network virtualization is the decrease of north-south traffic for routed networks. In a traditional network with a core switch, ESXi hosts have to send the traffic through an external router if one VM wants to communicate with another VM in another subnet on the same host. The packets have to pass through the ESXi network interface through the router, back into the ESXi and to the other VM. This adds a lot of so-called north-south traffic.

This refers to network traffic, which leaves a pod northbound and returns southbound in order to reach a network client contained in the same pod but in a different network.

Besides north-south traffic, there is also east-west traffic, which is everything which stays within a pod. If a VM talks to another VM in the same network subnet but on a different ESXi host. The two hosts will communicate directly with each other without sending the traffic through a router. If these VMs are on the same host, the network packets are not even leaving the ESXi hosts through the virtual NIC. This decreases the load on more expensive network hardware such as switches and in general reduces the overall network traffic sprawl. The following picture shows examples how NSX will dramatically reduce the amount of north-south traffic and help to enhance network traffic as well as overall network performance by reducing the amount of needed hops.

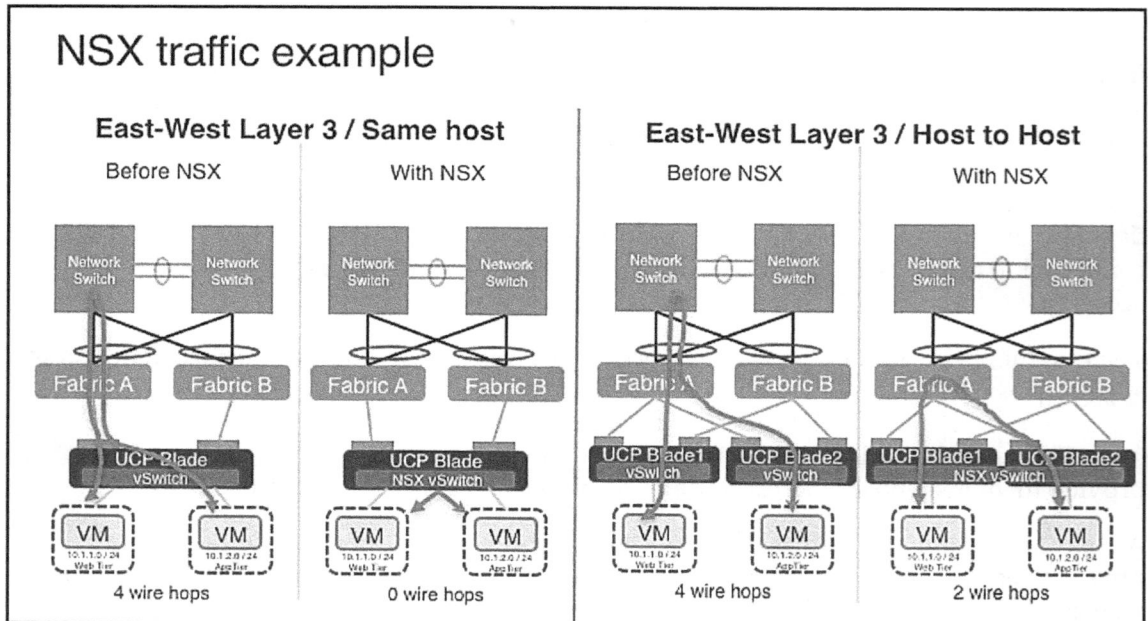

NSX terminology

NSX comes with its own terminology. It might be good to get familiar with these terms in advance to better understand their meaning and functionality if referenced later in this chapter.

VXLAN

The VXLAN IEEE standard is used as the transport network for all virtual networks created in NSX. In NSX, it is also referred to as transport zone. It carries the network packets containing the virtual network information from one NSX-enabled ESXi host to another using the specially created kernel port in ESXi. The VXLAN encapsulation is shown in the following image:

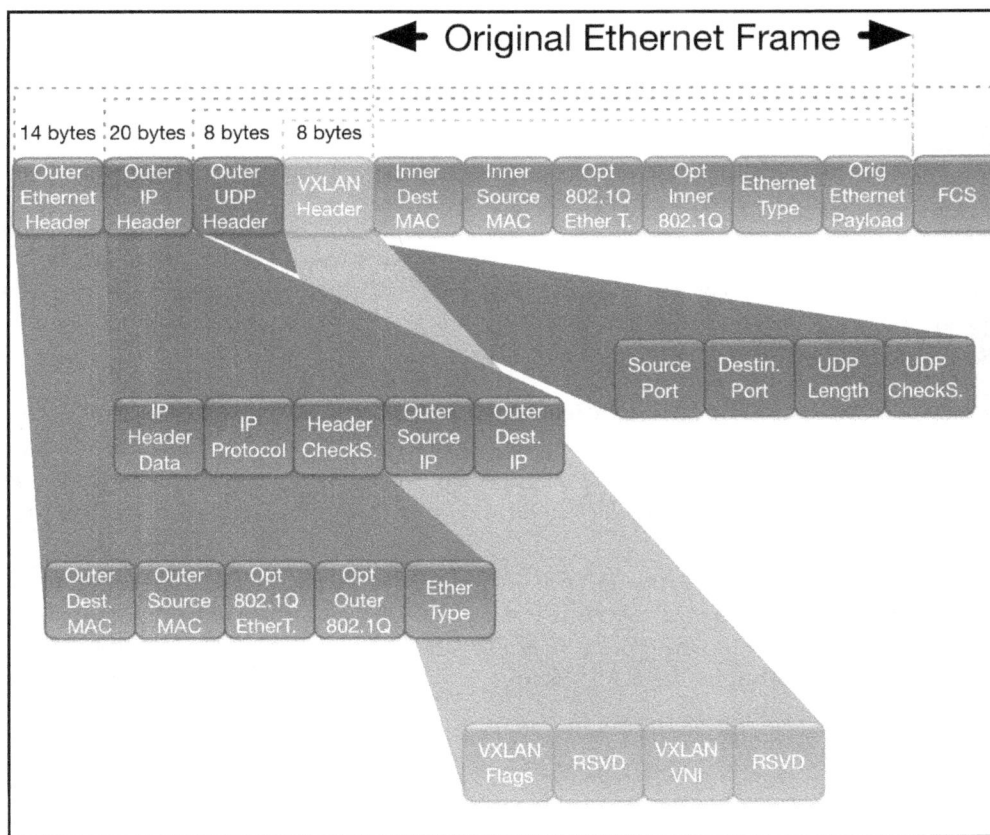

The added information is the following:

- VXLAN-specific content like **VXLAN Network Identifier (VNI)**.
- Outer UDP and IP header (coming from the encapsulating host).
- Full outer ethernet header containing all information from the sending host to the receiving host. The receiving host is either determined due to multicast requests or by the VTEP table.
- In total a VXLAN encapsulation adds another 50 bytes to a default network packet. Given this, the MTU default has to be changed from 1500 to at least 1550 or higher. This MTU change is a must since the network frames will be larger than in a traditional LAN. This needs to be confirmed with the physical switch configuration as well since otherwise they will drop these larger frames if they do not fit their set MTU.

> **TIP**
>
> Generally, it is the best practice to enable jumbo frames for the VTEPs and the transport zone. It is extremely important to ensure that the physical switches can handle the higher MTU size; otherwise, NSX will not work!

EDGE

An Edge is typically a gateway into another network. Most of the time the EDGE is the gateway from the virtual networks in a physical, external network. It can be seen as the access point into and out of the virtual world. There are following two types of EDGE devices available in NSX:

- The **Distributed Logical Router (DLR)** in NSX is a router that is installed on each participating ESXi host. It will take care of routing traffic of VMs between virtual networks even inside an ESXi or between different ESXi hosts. Although it is also a VM deployed in the EDGE cluster, it syncs its config with all participating ESXi hosts.
- The **EDGE Service Gateway (ESG)** is typically the connection between the physical and the virtual networking world. An ESG is normally connected to a DLR to enable it to route outside of NSX. However, it also offers other functions such as a load balancer, NAT (Source NAT and Destination NAT), as well as VPN connections.

Logical Switches

A Logical Switch in NSX is a virtual network where VMs can be connected. Logical switches are also often referred to as *virtual wire*.

In vSphere, they will show up as portgroups with unique ID names (number combination). However, NSX manages and maintains these vSphere portgroups. Admins should not temper with them outside of NSX.

Each switch gets a segment ID as identifier (similar to VLAN tags in traditional networking). The segment range can be customized; the maximum number of segments (switches) is **16,777,216**.

VTEP

Virtual tunnel endpoint (**VTEP**) and represents basically one of the ESXi kernel ports in the transport zone exchanging NSX traffic. The VTEP learns which VM sits on which ESXi host and creates a forwarding table. In order to find the VMs NSX uses one of the three methods to ask where VMs are:

- **UNICAST**: Each ESXi host with a VM wanting to talk to another VM asks each other host in a transport zone if the peer knows this other VM. This typically generates a lot of traffic until the VTEP learns where VMs are (if they move, the procedure begins again). The NSX controllers are used to coordinate this and to maintain the VTEP table. A benefit of this method is that ARP suppression can be enabled.
- **MULTICAST**: Each ESXi host with a VM wanting to talk to another VM sends a multicast to all hosts in a transport zone. If one of the other ESXi hosts runs the requested VM it simply responds to the multicast request. This does not require an NSX controller. However, the network needs to support multicast as well as multicast routing needs to be enabled. This is typically more effort as well as more complex to physically configure than the UNICAST method.
- **HYBRID**: This is the best of both worlds. It uses the NSX controllers to build and maintain a VTEP table and works with ARP suppression. Since it can make use of the controllers, multicast routing is not required, which makes the physical switch configuration much easier. All, which is required, is an igmp querier address and multicast IP addresses. If the peer host is not in the same multicast domain (can't be reached without routing), NSX will revert back to unicast and the controller will add the discovered connection to the VTEP table.

NSX controller

This is one of three VMs (three are required as a minimum) to run control commands and sync configurations between and with ESXi hosts. The controllers also maintain the VTEP table (in **UNICAST** or **HYBRID** mode)/BUM traffic. The controllers will always deploy in a controller cluster.

> The NSX controllers need to do Layer 2 communication. If spread across cluster nodes in different racks, this has to be taken into account. To learn more about the VTEP table, BUM traffic, and ARP suppression, you can visit the VMware blog about advanced NSX functionalities at `http ://blogs.vmware.com/vsphere/2013/05/vxlan-series-how-vtep-lear ns-and-creates-forwarding-table-part-5.html`.

NSX setup and preparation

To connect NSX to vRA and work with it in the SDDC, it needs to be set up and installed first. This part gives an overview about basic considerations and tasks to successfully install NSX in a vSphere environment. It is strongly recommended to check the required settings for HYBRID (Multicast needs to be enabled on the switches, an igmp querier needs to be set up, and so on) with the networking department. If these settings are incorrect, NSX might not work correctly. If these settings are unclear or impossible to configure, UNICAST mode needs to be used.

> VMware demands that certified consultants from either a partner or VMware's PSO must install NSX in a production environment. The installation method provided in this chapter will work, but may not be best practice for every environment. Also, before installing NSX, a design needs to be created with assumptions, risks, and constraints to make sure that it fits the purpose.

ESXi prerequisites for VXLAN / NSX

Before NSX can be installed in the environment, some steps have to be concluded in order to comply with all prerequisites. First of all, the transport zone requires its own VLAN including an IP address scheme for the VTEP kernel ports. It is important to have these IP addresses before the NSX installation since those are required to complete the setup and make each ESXi host work with NSX.

The VTEPs can be in a VLAN using a traditional L2 network. However, they can also be in different networks as in an L3 setup. Whatever method is chosen, all VTEPs are required to reach each other either over routed networks or within the L2 network.

The number of IP addresses obviously depends on the number of hosts. But there is also the chance to have multiple VTEPs per host for high availability and load balancing reasons. Based on the number of ESXi hosts and the number of VTEPs to use, it can quickly exceed a typical /24 network. It is recommended to plan ahead since this is not easily changeable after NSX has been deployed.

For example, 128 ESXi hosts with 2 VTEPs will require 256 IP addresses. A class C net with a /24 netmask will provide only 254 addresses. In order to satisfy the requirement a bigger network segment needs to be used for providing the VTEP IPs.

In this case, a /23 class C net will be required, providing 510 IP addresses in total.

Network prerequisites for NSX

A VLAN has to be prepared in order to put the VTEPs into it. However, it is not required to create a VDS portgroup, this will be done by NSX once the transport zone gets set up. Also, NSX does require the virtual distributed switch to be available. If the vSphere Licensing does not cover the use of the VDS, the NSX license automatically will.

Once the VLAN ID is prepared and also the VLAN is configured on all physical switches in order to enable successful communication between all the ESXi hosts (VTEPs), the NSX setup can begin.

Step 1: Installing NSX manager

The NSX manager comes as OVA and can simply be deployed in a vCenter management cluster. As described in `Chapter 4`, *SDDC Design Considerations*, it is a good practice to have a separate NSX EDGE cluster ready. This is important when it comes to the NSX networking component deployment. However, in small or medium environments, those components can also be deployed in the payload cluster to maximize efficiency.

The EDGE cluster typically contains ESGs and DLRs. Also the NSX controller can run in the EDGE cluster. It is important to understand that all network traffic to non-NSX networks (external networks) will flow through these edge devices/ESXi hosts. This means that the hosts in the EDGE cluster are mainly forwarding and receiving network traffic.

IMPORTANT: It is possible to have multiple EDGE clusters and add them over time. Also, the use of vMotion for ESGs is possible as long as they are on a Layer 2 network. It is not possible to migrate ESGs on Layer 3 from one EDGE cluster to the other using vMotion. In this case, any migration of an ESG will cause downtime for all its connected virtual networks. Also, this is a manual task and is not recommended.

Once the NSX manager is deployed, it needs to be registered with vCenter in order to enable NSX. This registration is done using the NSX manager web interface:

1. Login using admin and the provided password during the OVA deploy.
2. Click on **Manage vCenter Registration**.
3. At vCenter server click on **Edit** to enter the connection details and the credentials. It is important to consider using an NSX admin account with the correct roles assigned. Also, make sure that its password is not expiring!

It is important to configure NTP and the DNS network settings for the NSX manager appliance. Especially, the NTP configuration is very important in order to ensure that all connected components are having the same date and time. Otherwise errors may occur and the communication between components might be disrupted.

4. Once NTP, the DNS settings, the certificates (if required), and the backup has been set /changed, the rest of the configuration will be done using the vCenter client.

The backup setting requires a TFTP server in order to save the configuration automatically to this share. It is highly recommended to use and configure the NSX Backup service!

Step 2: Setting up the components

If the manager is installed correctly and the registration with vCenter was successful, the required components can be installed by using the vCenter web client.

> There is no NSX integration in the legacy C-Sharp client (desktop client). The only way to configure NSX is using the web client, besides its API.

To configure NSX, open the vCenter web client using a privileged administrative user and navigate to the **Networking & Security** item on the home screen:

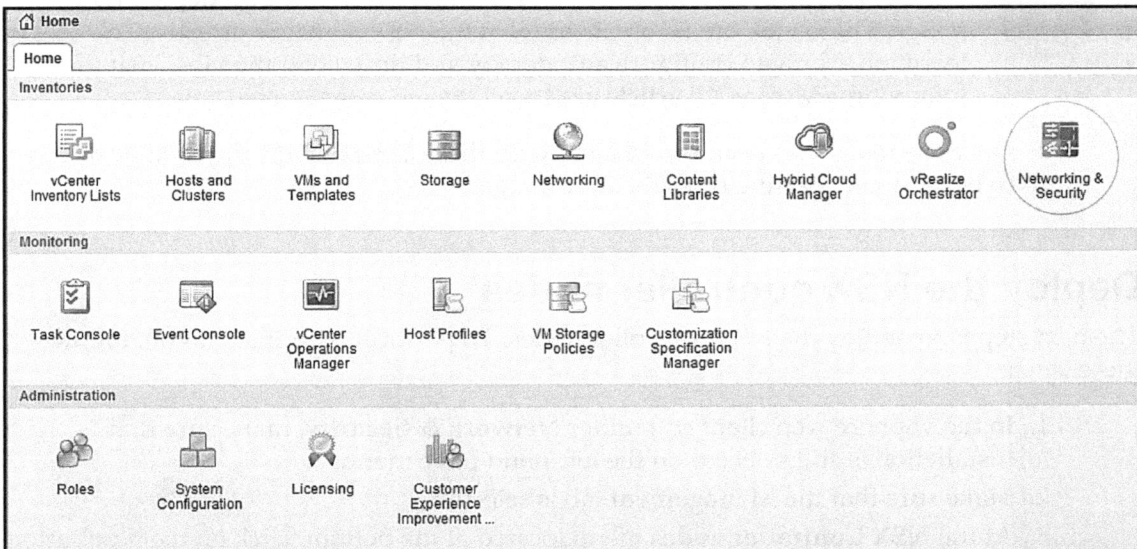

Once the **Networking & Security** screen opens, click on **Installation** in the left-hand menu pane and perform the following tasks.

Prepare the ESXi hosts

1. Make sure that the **Host Preparation** tab is selected.
2. For each cluster where NSX is needed, select **Install** in the **Installation Status** column.
3. Once the installation is completed, the NSX version number is displayed in the **Installation Status** column and the **Firewall** column displays enabled. A *green check* mark will also be shown.

> If vSphere autodeploy is used, this installation method will not work. In order to enable NSX with autodeploy, it is required to include the `esx-vxlan.vib`, and the `esx-vsip.vib` are included in the autodeploy ESXi image. These vibs can be obtained from the NSX manager directly. To learn more how to configure autodeploy and download the vibs, visit the following VMware KB article at `http://kb.vmware.com/kb/2092871`.

4. Once the image has been repackaged with these components, the ESXi hosts have to be rebooted starting from the new images.

Deploy the NSX controller nodes

The next step is to deploy the NSX controller nodes. To perform their installation, follow these steps:

1. In the vSphere web client still under **Network & Security**, make sure that Installation is still selected on the left-hand pane menu.
2. Make sure that the **Management** tab is selected.
3. At the **NSX Controller nodes** menu located at the bottom, click on the *plus* button to add a new controller.
4. Provide all necessary information in order to deploy the first controller:
   1. Choose a valid data center.
   2. Choose the EDGE or management cluster.
   3. Provide a data store (a dedicated EDGE data store is not needed, but recommended).
   4. Provide a host, make sure that each controller is deployed on a different host.
   5. Provide a VM folder (choose **Discovered virtual machine** or create a separate EDGE folder if desired).
   6. Choose a portgroup to connect the controller to. It is important that the

controller needs to be to reach the NSX manager. This might be either through a routed network or the controller is located in the same network segment as the NSX manager (recommended).

7. Select an IP-Pool to provide and address to the controller. If no pool has been created, the wizard allows to create a pool without leaving the window.

5. Repeat step 3 until three NSX controllers have been deployed. Remember to choose three different ESXi hosts to deploy the controllers onto.

Defining the segment ID

After the hosts have been prepared and the controllers have been set up, the segment ID needs to be defined. As described earlier, each logical NSX switch gets its own segment ID. So, the segment range will describe how many Logical Switches will be possible. To set up the segment ID range, perform the following steps:

1. In the vSphere web client still under **Network & Security** make sure Installation is still selected on the-left hand pane menu.
2. Make sure that the **Logical Network Preparation** tab is selected.
3. Select the **Segment ID** button and click on **Edit**.
4. In the window, provide a segment ID and a multicast address range if **MULTICAST** or **HYBRID** mode is used.
    1. Provide a valid segment ID pool , for example, 5000-10000.
    2. Check **Enable Multicast addressing** and provide valid multicast addresses, for example, 239.40.0.0-239.41.255.255.
5. Click on **OK** to save the segment ID and multicast addresses.

Configuring the transport parameters

In order to send traffic across ESXi hosts and different L3 network segments, a transport zone has to be configured. In order to do that, follow these steps:

1. In the vSphere web client still under **Network & Security**, make sure that installation is still selected on the left-hand pane menu.
2. Make sure that the **Host Preparation** tab is selected.

3. For each cluster where NSX is needed, click on **Configure** in the **VXLAN** column.

4. In the configuration window, select the switch to which the cluster should be mapped.

5. Enter the transport **VLAN ID** (as described in the preparation section).

6. Enter a valid MTU, at least 1550 or higher, for the VDS.

7. In the **VMKNic IP Addressing**, the IP pool for the management and Edge cluster needs to be defined/selected.

8. The IP Pool can be created within this wizard to be selected for the IP addresses. These are the VTEP IPs, as discussed earlier in this chapter. Ensure that there is enough IPs available for all desired VMKNics.

9. Edit the VTEP number. If this is set to 2, there will be two VTEPs per ESXi host installed (for redundancy and scalability).

10. Click on **OK** to save the changes.

After that, the VMKNics (VTEPS) will be configured and get the IPs assigned as defined in the IP pool.

> It is recommended to consider NIC teaming in order to enhance the resiliency as well as the performance of the VTEPs. Make sure that the right teaming policy is selected in order to fulfill these requirements.

Set up the transport zone

1. In the vSphere web client still under **Network & Security**, make sure that Installation is still selected on the left-hand pane menu.

2. Make sure that the **Logical Network Preparation** tab is selected.

3. Click on **Transport Zones** and then click on the *plus* button.

4. Provide the following information in the configuration window:
    1. Zone name, for example, MyOrgTransport.
    2. Meaningful description.
    3. Replication mode (**MULTICAST**, **UNICAST**, or **HYBIRD**), for example, Hybrid.
    4. Select all participating cluster for that transport zone.

5. Click on **OK** to save the configuration.
6. After the transport zone has been configured, NSX is ready for payload traffic and to create virtual wires.

Step 3: Virtual networking 101

If all the settings from step two have been applied successfully NSX is ready to be configured for the SDDC. The basics of this configuration are:

- Setting up a Logical Switch
- Setting up a Distributed Logical Router
- Setting up an Edge Service Gateway

Each Logical Switch can be seen as a network or at least a segment of a network. VMs connected to the same logical switch can communicate with each other without any routing required (except there is a security policy configured).

If VMs run on different Logical Switches with different IP address settings, a Distributed Logical Router is required in order to let the VMs communicate to each other. The Logical router connects different Logical Switches with each other in order to enable advanced network communication.

If an external access to the network is required, an EDGE also referred to as ESG, will provide this functionality. It basically has a connection to the external network as well as a connection to the virtual wires using the Distributed Logical Router. This way, it can be configured which virtual networks can access the physical networks using the Distributed Logical Router as well as the ESG as a gateway.

The following image is an example of this configuration and should help for a better understanding of the configuration:

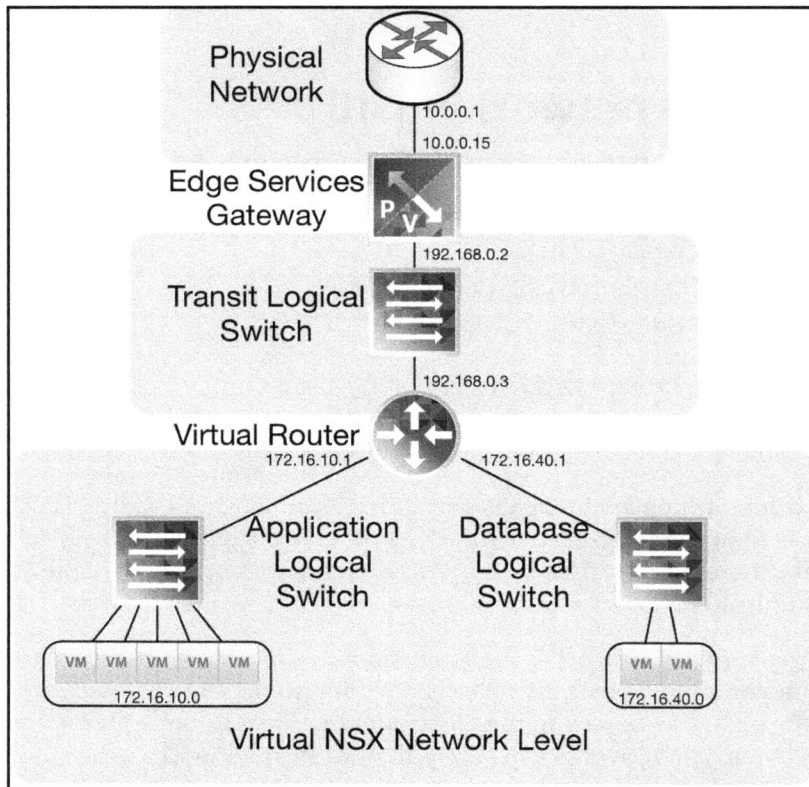

The Application Logical Switch and the Database Logical Switch will be internal Link types configured at the DLR. While the Edge Service Gateway will be a uplink type configured at the DLR. This enables access for both virtual wires to the external physical network.

Add a Logical Switch

Before we can add advanced network functions such as a router and a ESG we need to have logical switches present. Follow these steps to add a logical switch to the NSX environment:

1. In the vSphere web client still under Network & Security, make sure that **Logical Switches** is selected on the left-hand pane menu.
2. Click on the *plus* button to add a new Logical Switch.
3. Provide the following information in the creation wizard:
    1. Switch name, for example, `Application`.
    2. Meaningful description, for example, `Switch for the application server environment`.
    3. Select a transport zone by clicking on **Change**.
    4. Select an appropriate replication mode (best practice is to select the same as for the transport zone).
    5. Enable **IP Discovery** and/or **MAC Learning**. MAC Learning will introduce ARP suppression.
4. Click on **OK** to create the logical switch.

Repeat this step until all desired logical switches have been created. It is a good test to start with two, since then the distributed logical router can be tested as well to validate its functionality.

Also, it might be necessary to create the transport switch from the DLR to the ESG. This is a special virtual wire, which will only be valid for ESG and DLR interfaces.

Add a Distributed Logical Router

In order to route between the virtual wires, a distributed logical router is necessary. This is an EDGE device which will have interfaces in all logical switches where routing is desired. These are the steps to add a distributed logical router:

1. In the vSphere web client still under Network & Security, make sure that **NSX Edges** is selected on the left-hand pane menu.
2. Click on the *plus* button to add a new Logical Switch.
3. Select **Logical (Distributed) Router** and provide the following information:
    1. A name, for example, `Example-DLR`.
    2. A meaningful description.
    3. Deploy **Edge Appliance** (leave default. An Edge appliance is needed

for dynamic routing. Without it, the DLR is only capable of static routing).

4. Select **Enable** for **High Availability** if required.

5. Click on **Next** to continue.

4. Provide a valid user name (leave default) and an admin password. Make sure that **SSH access** is checked.

5. Select the data center to deploy to. If HA has been selected, choose **Compact**, **Large**, **X-Large**, or **Quard Large**. Under **NSX Edge Appliance**, click on the *plus* icon to add the ESG. Provide the following information:

   1. Cluster to deploy to (select EDGE Cluster).

   2. Data store to choose.

   3. Optional: Host to deploy to.

   4. Optional: vSphere Folder to put the DRL into.

6. At the **Configure interfaces of this NSX Edge**, add the logical switches, which needs to be connected (routed):

   1. Click on the *plus* sign to add an interface.

   2. Provide a name, for example, `Application_IF` for the Application Logical Switch.

   3. At **Connected To**, click on **change** and select the **Application** logical switch (the switch created in the prior step).

   4. At **Type** select **Internal**.

   5. Under **Configure subnets**, click on the *plus* sign and provide a LIF IP and Subnet prefix length, for example, `172.16.10.1` and `24`. This will be the virtual gateway IP for the Application network.

7. At the fifth step, choose the vNIC for the default gateway and provide the default gateway IP address.

8. At the ready-to-complete step, review the settings. If all looks correct, click on **Finish** to create the DLR.

Add a EDGE services Gateway

Once that completed successfully, the first DLR should be appearing under **NSX Edges**. The next step might be to create an ESG gateway for external access. This is similar to the DLR configuration. However, in order to connect the DLR to the ESG, the transport virtual wire is required (not to be confused with the transport zone!).

Follow these steps to add an ESG and connect a DLR to it:

1. Follow all the same steps as described in the *Add a Distributed Logical Router* section until step 3.

   Select **Edge Services Gateway**.

2. Follow steps 4 – 6 from the *Add a Distributed Logical Router* section.
3. Click on the *plus* sign to configure EDGE interfaces.
   1. Provide a valid name, for example, *Transport_IF*.
   2. At **Type** select **Internal**.
   3. Under **Connect To** click on **Change** to select the **Transport** Logical Switch (or similar name created for the ESG to DLR transport net).
   4. Provide a valid IP address and subnet prefix in the transport network, for example, 192.168.0.2 and 29.
   5. Leave the defaults and click on **OK**.
4. Add an uplink to the external network. This means the ESG needs to connect to a VLAN-backed vSphere portgroup. Also, an IP address should be available in the physical network to connect to (two if HA is required).
   1. Follow step 3, provide a valid name (include the portgroup name, for example, Uplink-IF-VLAN100.
   2. At **Type** select **uplink**.
   3. Under **Connect To** click on **Change** to select the VLAN-backed physical/external portgroup to connect to. Click on **Distributed Portgroup** in order to see those.
   4. Provide a valid IP address and subnet prefix in the selected network.
   5. Leave the defaults and click on **OK** to save the configuration.
5. Finish the steps as described in the *Add a Distributed Logical Router* section.
6. Now the ESG has been deployed successfully and should be connected to the DLR. All Logical switches connected to the same DLR will now be able to make use of the services of the ESG such as Load Balancing, NATing (Source and Destination NAT), the static VPN functionality and many more.
7. This concludes the basic NSX setup. It is now ready for workloads to use the virtual wires. Also, with this basic setup, vRA can be connected to NSX to make use of advanced networking.

Dynamic routing between virtual and physical

In order to be able to perform dynamic routing, NSX supports various protocols such as OSPF or BGP. In order to have a fully functional dynamic routing, it is required to configure those correctly and correlate them with the external virtual gateways. Otherwise, each and every route from NSX to physical and vice versa had to be added statically. Since this is not practical, the dynamic routing protocols are a must to configure correctly.

Since profound routing knowledge is required to configure OSPF or BGP, this chapter will not go into details about these configuration steps. However, if more information regarding these configurations are required, please refer to VMware's NSX installation and configuration guides under http://www.vmware.com.

Connecting vRealize Automation

Since NSX is installed and configured for basic functionality, vRA can be connected to the NSX manager in order to make usage of some advanced NSX functionalities.

In order to connect vRA to NSX, it is required to log on using a user with the tenant administrator role active.

> If the integrated vRO is used, nothing else is required. If the external vRO is used, make sure that all necessary plugins are installed, such as the NSX plugin for vRA. Otherwise, the connection will not work.

Follow these steps in order to enable NSX for vRA:

1. Login to the vRA portal using the tenant administrator role.
2. Click on **Infrastructure** and then on **Endpoints**.
3. Hover over the vCenter endpoint and select **Edit**. In the configuration window, add the following information.
    1. Select **Specify manager for network and security platform**.
    2. Put in the NSX manager address, for example, `https://nsx.example.com`.
    3. Provide valid NSX credentials, if not already existent use the **New** icon to create those.
4. Click on **OK** to save the changes.

5. Once that has been completed, verify that the NSX data collection is working. In order to do that, hover over the vCenter endpoint again and select **Compute Resources**.

6. In the Compute Resources overview, hover over the appropriate resources and select **Data Collection**. Look for **Network and Security Inventory** and make sure that the **Status** states: **Succeeded**. It can take a couple of minutes until the status is displayed. Click on **Request now** to run a new collection task if necessary.

Network reservations

Once vRA is successfully connected to NSX, some configuration change needs to be done under **Reservations**. Under **Advanced settings**, the transport zone needs to be set as well as possible security groups and routed gateways (a created DLR).

In order to do this, follow these steps:

1. Login to the vRA portal using the tenant administrator role.
2. Click on **Infrastructure** and then on **Reservations**.
3. Select the **Network** tab and check the following settings.
    1. Under **Advanced Settings** and **Transport zone**, make sure that the previously created NSX transport zone is selected.
    2. At **Security groups**, select possible security groups to use if any.
    3. At **Routed gateways**, make sure to select any DLR to include, at least the one previously created.
4. Click on **OK** to save the changes.

If all this succeeded successfully the system is ready to create network profiles containing the new functions and features.

Setting up NSX network profiles

With NSX a new form of network profiles can be used. The naming of those profiles in vRA is unfortunately somewhat confusing. Here is a short description of the three types of profiles to be used.

The external profile

Under this name, all networks with a pre-existing portgroup or virtual wire are referred to. For vRA, everything, which has been preprovisioned, is an external network. The Logical Switches created earlier in this chapter can be added to vRA by defining a network profile of this type and adding it to the NSX portgroup under reservations. This profile will be used to add VMs to already defined networks such as internal DB networks or application-specific networks.

The NAT profile

This creates a NAT network on demand using an NSX EDGE to define the NAT rules. The NAT can be created as one-to-one or one-to-many. This is set with the profile and will then be valid for any blueprint using this profile. This will be used to add VMs into a NAT profile on demand.

The routed profile

This is the most confusing type at first glance since its function is not self-explanatory such as with the other two. The routed profile will create a separate virtual wire based on the added information. VMs using this profile will be put into that virtual wire, which then is connected to a DLR to access NSX external networks. The creation of this network happens on demand. However, each VM will create its own virtual wire. This means that two services requested with the routed profile set will not land in the same network.

To create these networks, the routed profile has a different setup mask asking for a *subnet mask* and a *range subnet mask*. The subnet mask will define the size of the created pool. The range subnet mask will define the size of the segments within the pool. Here is an example of subnet mask and range subnet mask:

- Subnet mask: `255.255.192.0`
- Range subnet mask: `255.255.255.240`
- Base IP: `172.30.50.0`

This means that this profile will generate around **3306 IPs** in **224 networks** with **15 IPs each**. The IPs will start with `172.30.50.1` and end with `172.30.63.254`.

This means that it can be used in blueprints to fit up to 15 VM NICs in one of these on demand networks connected to a DLR. The network will be created with the service deployment and deleted when the service gets destroyed. It is also possible to create larger networks in order to fit more VMs into it. That is all a matter of the Subnet mask and the Range subnet mask.

In this case, the used subnet is a /18 and the used range to split it is a /28. But it can also be a combination of a /18 and a /24 resulting in fewer networks with more space for VMs.

Such a setup can be used to create DMZ networks on demand, or to crate lab networks for to be deployed right with the service/blueprint.

Using NSX network profiles in blueprint

In order to use NSX network profiles in blueprints, all required is drag and dropping the network type (nat, routed, and external) into the blueprint designer and selecting the right network profile to use.

Also, at the creation or the settings tab of the blueprint under the **NSX** tab, the transport zone has to be selected in order to use NSX within the blueprint. That is all required after NSX has been set up properly and vRA has been connected correctly.

Summary

This chapter described basic network principles and compared traditional networking approaches with the new SDN approach. Also, it touched NSX basics as well as descriptions how NSX works and what network virtualization can deliver to a SDDC. Furthermore, it touched the basic installation and configuration to get quickly up and running with the first virtual network including routing and access to the external physical network through a DLR and ESG.

In the next chapter, the focus will be on DevOps and its possibilities and opportunities. It will start with a definition what DevOps typically means and what use cases will be fulfilled by a DevOps platform. Also, it will discuss possible installations fitting in the SDDC and possibilities for developers and companies using this new approach in developing and running applications.

9
DevOps Considerations

This chapter will discuss general DevOps topics such as what can be understood as DevOps and why this might be a game changer in application development and running businesses. It will describe the basic functions and fundaments in regard to DevOps as well as its radical new approaches to developing and operating new applications.

It will require some familiarity with the basics of software development as well as some basics in regard to public cloud offerings and knowledge about software containers.

Based on these points, the chapter will also highlight integration points between an SDDC for legacy applications (all non-cloud-native apps) and a DevOps-ready infrastructure. It will highlight how these two different approaches can coexist and what a hybrid SDDC unlocks in terms of options and possibilities from a business as well as a technology perspective.

The following topics are covered in greater detail in this chapter:

- What is DevOps
- Radical new IT approach
- Where does DevOps apply best (benefits and risks)
- Containers: Virtualization 2.0
- PaaS as part of DevOps
- Possibilities to connect DevOps with vRA
- Examples for joint services and blueprints

What is DevOps

The term **DevOps** is an artificially created word and joins development and operations together in one term. In a traditional IT environment, two or more different teams perform those two disciplines. One team is responsible for developing the applications and their patches and fixes. The operations department is typically responsible for running the application and providing the required environment (physical or virtual infrastructure, networks, storage, and so on).

Typically, such environments are VMs with some kind of OS installed and the necessary addition to support the application. In case of Java, they would have the required binaries ready, so the developer can start using the environment to run the Java code.

Although this is working for years, it is a very static approach and can lead to some handover issues between the teams. An IT admin might not know the application in greater detail and therefore can only follow the developer's requirements in installing needed software on the OS.

On the other hand, developers sometimes care less about the hardware, OS, drivers, or needed software packages. They are fully engaged in making the application superior. This might sometimes involve further testing with different software components in the environment. Sometimes, they also just require a couple of hundred systems to realize an artificial load test or to check whether the application does scale as expected (if scaling is an option).

All this requires the two teams to work seamlessly together-the developers need to articulate their needs loud and clear and the operation team needs to follow this requirements and need to provide a stable but yet flexible and agile environment.

Also, the environment needs to follow internal IT regulations and process in order to be ready for the data centers production environment.

Agility meets policies

Because the operations department of any organization also needs to follow their policies and regulations to run services in a data center, the mix between DevOps such as agility and meeting policies and regulations often creates tension between the teams.

Because the developers sometimes feel the pressure of the business much more than the IT operations teams, they tend to push for untested and undocumented changes in the data center to run and test their latest code.

Because the operations team deals with the pressure of the security and regulations department much more than the developers, they tend to push back on untested or unstructured installation approaches for the sake of the data center security and resiliency.

Naturally, these two interests need to collide because it is hard to follow all regulations and provide extensive testing, but also deliver agility and flexibility for bleeding edge applications nobody has created before.

Also, support and troubleshooting plays a big role in modern organizations. If the most important application (from a business perspective) suddenly quits working, the two teams need to work together on a solution. In some organization, that might work quite well; in other organizations, the operations team start fiddling with their internal issues and the developers start checking their applications. Often there is little to no communication between the teams, which can lead to longer fixing times. Also, finger pointing will happen fast in such an environment, trying to identify the other party as the root cause of the issue and the long fixing times. Surely, everyone has found himself in such a situation once in his or her IT life.

However, the business could not care less if it has something to do with the developers or something with the operations team. All they want is getting back to work as quickly as possible to minimize the financial impact of the outage.

All these examples describe why DevOps was brought to live. It is a mix between operations and development and provides a platform that is ready for both.

How does DevOps work

Basically, the idea is to have a ready-to-run platform, which is available to developers through an API or even connected into their coding tools. The development team is not required to sync with the operations team on creating OS instances (or VMs) anymore because the platform provides a self-service interface for program/application deployments.

With a simple command or click on deploy, developers can install their applications into this environment. Also, updating is as simple because they will be able to redeploy or update right out of their coding tools.

The clue of DevOps is that they are also responsible for running the code inside this platform (operations). If a new version is ready, they will take care of either redeploy or update the running code. In case of an outage, they will work through the deployed application and check all necessary fix routines for the application themselves. If it turns out to be the platform, they can simply redeploy the application to a different platform in order to quickly fix the issue.

For the operations department, it is an enhancement too. All they have to provide is the platform for the developers. The platform can have its own policies and regulations. It does not require the installation of single servers or OSes to work. All the operations unit needs to take care of is that the infrastructure services are connected such as DNS, authentication, security as well as other IT basics, and work for the entire platform. This platform can be installed in a supported (by policies and regulations) environment and provide the advanced developer functions by software abstraction.

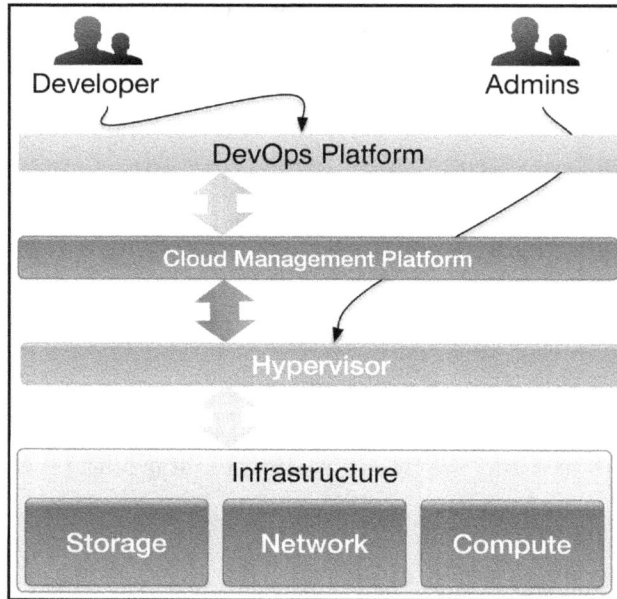

DevOps is the approach to provide agility, speed, and flexibility but in a controlled and supported manner. One of the biggest supporter and provider in the DevOps space is Amazon Web Services. Basically, two-thirds of the EC2 offerings are targeted toward DevOps and developers. Also, one of the biggest strength is that it is super quick to set up an environment end getting the first deployment going. Everyone can try it themselves just with a credit card and 10 minutes to spare.

What are containers

The DevOps movement has also introduced a new *old* player in the data center, containers. **Containers** are fundamentally different from VMs, and they serve more the purpose of a microservice architecture. Instead of installing everything that an application requires in a VM, all these components could be containers on a container host.

The best known company providing a container framework is probably Docker. However, albeit Docker is a fairly young company, container technology itself is well-known since a couple of years. Containers are based on the LxC extension in the Linux kernel, which has been around since it was developed in 2008. However, Docker created a very easy-to-use and lightweight framework around LxC, which made it much simpler to use and adopt it. With these new capabilities, it now can be easily used as an easy-to-control and flexible way of application delivery. This is the main focus of containers; they are about flexible and agile application delivery. The underlying architecture is from less interest; it is all about the applications and the capability to deliver and rebuild on demand. This approach is somewhat contrary to the traditional IT, where a lot of energy goes into the installation of an OS and the automation of application deployment.

Containers are not VMs

A broad misbelief is that a container and a VM are somewhat similar. That is by far not the case; both technologies introduce unique advantages and challenges. However, virtualization has become commodity, so it is only natural to compare it to the new additions such as containers. The following table shows some of the main differences between containers and VMs:

Virtual Machine	Container
Permanent virtual disk	Stateless
Separate OS per VM	OS shared by container host
Complete Ethernet stack	Port-based communication-network shared with container host
All applications, monolithic and Legacy	Cloud Native or third-platform apps. Not suitable for legacy apps
Require guest OS and app patching	No patching required-destroy and rebuild (respin)

VMware also introduced their entry in the container movement by announcing two different products to leverage containers on vSphere:

- **vSphere Integrated Containers (vIC)**
- **Project Photon**

vIC is shaking up the definition between a container and a VM quite heavily since VMware introduced a microcontainer OS to run in a VM. This creates tiny VMs for each single container to run on a vSphere host. The advantage of this technique is that they can use all vSphere family features and functions to run this environment. This enables not only NSX to work with containers for enhanced security, but also vRealize Operations to do advanced monitoring. Since the base is a VM, VMware can integrate this fairly well into the existing ecosystem of the SDDC. In the latest vRealize Automation version, there is even an integration into the portal to order (vSphere Integrated) containers right out of the portal.

Project Photon is different though. It is an open source project which offers photon OS, a container runtime platform. By leveraging VMware technologies, it can be used to bring up container hosts using the command line. Furthermore, it also offers advanced security functionalities such as authorizing containers to run only on also authorized hosts. Its function is very close to a container host and uses the VMware ecosystem to provide additional value in security, reliability, and availability. Furthermore, it integrates well with different container frameworks, such as Docker, rkt, and Garden from Pivotal.

Containers are a flexible way to share single host resources for microservices. This means that a container host is always the OS base for all the containers it houses. In a hypervisor, the OS is always unique to the VM. The hypervisor patch level will not affect the VM OS or vice versa. Therefore, a VM is more isolated than a container. On a container host, the OS patch and security level will also always affect the container itself.

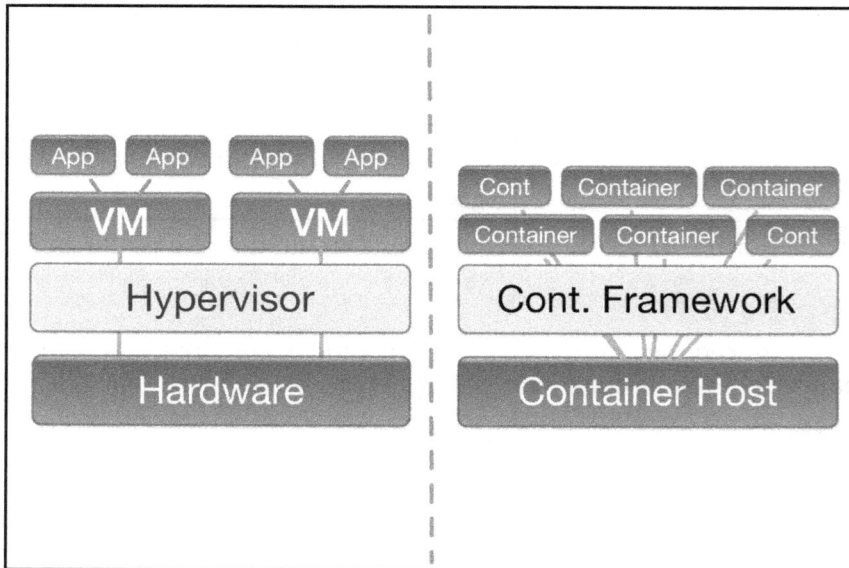

The preceding image shows the main differences between those two architectures. The containers have the ability to access the hardware of the host directly due to the fact that the OS resources are shared among all of them. Therefore, the OS (Linux) will dispatch any access to the underlying hardware such as network cards and SAN controllers (if present).

In a hypervisor, the hardware is made available through virtualization or often paravirtualization of the component. Network is a virtual NIC driver; storage is a virtual SCSI driver; and so on.

Container host: Virtual or physical

There is currently a debate where to run containers best. Some people say that hardware is the perfect choice. Since containers will use the underlying OS and the included OS abstractions to access the physical world, there is only little impact to performance. The native OS drivers can be used. Also, since containers are stateless, they do not require a state full failover in case something goes wrong. All they need is another container host where they get access to their data (if any).

But there are also challenges with this approach. The security and monitoring framework for containers is different than for virtual environments. All this would have to be recreated for container hosts. Also, the maintenance of the hosts is disruptive. Since the container cannot be migrated while they are running (like VMs) maintenance on the container host always means that the containers need to be restarted on a different container host.

To run container hosts on top of a hypervisor (in VMs) will have the advantage that it can be easily and quickly done. So if the container movement in an organization is more or less from scientific nature, virtualization is the easy choice since a container host can be easily deployed as a VM.

Container hosts on top of a hypervisor will also have benefits when it comes to enterprise requirements like uninterrupted management. In this case, container hosts could be evacuated using vMotion without any interruption. This saves time and effort also in a DevOps environment. Other functionalities like HA will help to make a container host quickly available after a hardware outage.

However, this also means that the slight overhead of the hypervisor plus the overhead of the container framework might affect the container performance in a way. Unfortunately, there are no real numbers to put against. Typically, a VMware vSphere overhead is in the one-digit range dependent on the application. The Docker or LxC overhead is also very low, but can be affected by the number of containers to run and the settings used (reservation of resources).

Like in other SDDC decisions, this decision should be taken based on the intended use of containers. If there is a well-established vSphere environment where all the monitoring and a lot of automation is already working, it might be the right thing to deploy the container host on top of the hypervisor.

DevOps and Shadow IT

Given the agility and flexibility platforms like Amazon provide, some developers get frustrated with their internal IT since they cannot deliver such an offering. This is why, in some organizations developers turn toward providers like Amazon to run their DevOps environment there. As described earlier, the setup is quick and easy, and all developers really want is developing their code quicker and deploying their assets/artifacts faster.

The problem is that they tend to bypass IT completely from that process, which also means bypassing regulations and data security policies. If an organization is identified to put customer data protected by privacy laws on the public cloud, fees can be as high as millions of dollars, not to speak from the image damage this could cause.

Other risks are that the public environment is not as protected as the internal IT, which might make it easier for hackers to steal protected data on those environments.

In general, such a bypass is called **Shadow IT** since it creates a secondary IT environment not necessarily following any policies or rules and regulations. Sometimes, these Shadow IT projects are even forced by the business to get some results quicker as usual.

Besides the regulatory issues and potential security flaws, shadow IT can also have a negative impact on an organizations budget. Although the initial start might be easy and cheap, there is a tipping point where it becomes quite expensive to run everything on an external cloud. Also, if it becomes necessary to migrate data back from the public cloud into the own data center, it might be a very costly operation. Many providers do have additional charges in place if data is leaving their premises (download).

This is why, a modern organization cannot ignore the possible need for a DevOps environment since this might lead to Shadow IT. In order to provide developers the speed and agility of such an environment, it is possible to combine it with the SDDC to enable the best of both worlds. Such a hybrid setup would be able to support legacy applications as well as the newest generation of applications, created using DevOps principals (also referred to as Cloud Native Applications or CNA).

Radical new IT approach

DevOps is a radical and disruptive way of doing IT. It focuses on applications and it tends to ignore hardware beneath the app. This sounds harsh compared to the classic IT approach where servers and the OS is in focus in order to provide a good, secure, and scalable environment for the applications.

In DevOps, applications become stateless since they store the data elsewhere; that might be an object-based storage or a NAS/SAN mount into the container. This means the container can *spin up* wherever it needs to be, given that it can access its data. There is no means in patching containers – just the container definition (the package) will be updated. To deploy this patch the old container will be destroyed and a new container will be started with the updated service/application code.

Also, containers in DevOps are not a place to install an entire legacy app. Ideally, they house just parts of an app so-called microservices. These microservices can be used to form an app modularly. This can be imagined as follows:

If an application requires a PHP component and a Java component and a web server component, all these can be their own container. They can then be working together in providing the services to the application (the Java component). If there is a need for a second or a third web server, developers can just start a new http container and include it. Also, if the Java app needs to store data, developers can either mount a volume in the Java container or directly access object-based storage through https calls.

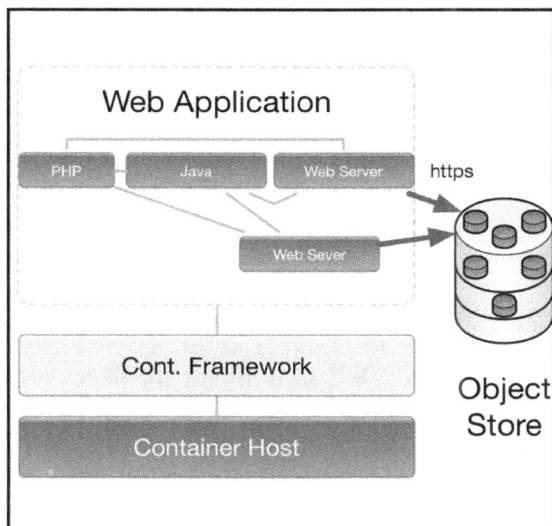

This approach is way different from a *classic application to server* model everyone in IT has been used to until today. Therefore, it changes the entire way of providing an environment. However, it also changes the entire way for processes, monitoring, security, and so on. It is a truly disruptive and innovative approach in running services and applications.

Also, since containers are not bound to hardware, they can run virtually everywhere. The development can happen on a public cloud where it is cheap and quick to spin up new containers and also mass test a thousand instances just for one day. After that is completed the whole config can be ported to an internal data center where the application than runs in production.

New versions of it can be created by cloning the production containers and introducing change in an isolated environment; once that is completed the changes can be brought into production just by redeploying the updated container definitions.

No wonder developers love all these features since they make their daily life so much easier. No more tickets to get server, no more requests for a VM needed only to put their code on.

Cattle versus pets

There is a very famous analogy for traditional IT and the new approach with DevOps. It goes like this: Traditional servers are like pets: When they are ill, we bring them to the doctor, we care about them individually and make sure they get all they need to live a happy life.

DevOps is like cattle: It is a huge herd; the individual will not receive any special treatment. Even if one cow is ill, the herd can still move on. One cares about the entire herd and not about the individual cow.

DevOps and especially containers are seen like a herd. If one container has a problem, it will not be repaired in the container. The developer will simply spin up another version of it to see if it is fixed. If required, fixes are applied to the container definition only.

Although that adds a lot of flexibility to the development and deployment lifecycle, it might also introduce tension between the traditional IT and the new DevOps teams. In traditional IT, issues get analyzed by opening a ticket, looking for the root cause to prevent a possible reoccurrence and then finally fixing the problem.

Since a DevOps environment is meant for massive scale, this procedure would not be simple. If one has thousands of containers running, it is virtually impossible to check every single incident and try to find a root cause. However, containers do also introduce new challenges to the IT team.

Changing the organizational culture

A DevOps approach is not just another tool in IT or another way of doing application development. It introduces a cultural change within an organization. From the business all the way to the developers, DevOps will change the way they are working with each other. It is meant as an agile way of developing and running business relevant applications. For that to function many established business processes are required to be revisited and rewritten. Traditional processes and structures will no longer work or be relevant. Much like in an SDDC environment, where old processes have to be refreshed and adopted to the new automation, in DevOps entirely, new processes have to be established. This can start with simple things like monitoring.

Containers can't be monitored like a standard virtual infrastructure. They need their own monitoring framework and processes. Whether it be performance or error monitoring, there are a couple of tools already available in the market. However, many of them are targeting a specific container framework. This means that the right monitoring solution has to be applied to a specific container framework. If the container framework changes, the monitoring has to change as well (or one has to have multiple monitoring instances, one per each container framework they use).

Also, performance monitoring needs to be ultimately decoupled from the underlying hardware. Since a container can run virtually anywhere, it is irrelevant if the underlying hardware can be monitored; ultimately, it is the container performance on the platform that needs to be monitored.

This also introduces new insights for developers, since the hardware has become so interchangeable, they cannot blame a specific OS, driver, or hardware implementation if an application is not performing as intended. Since it can be easily deployed on different environments, the performance of the application itself is much more transparent than in traditional environments. This adds pressure to some developer teams since it now depends on how they use the container technology to perform well. Discussions such as add more RAM or more CPU to make it faster might be soon obsolete.

On the other hand, the infrastructure becomes supertransparent as well. If an application does not perform locally, but runs fine on the cloud, the underlying infrastructure is now identified as bottleneck. Therefore, the local IT needs to react and improve the environment to perform as expected.

However, besides all this benefits, DevOps is a cultural change in an organization, which requires all departments to ultimately work together. IT gets closer to the developers. The developers will need to spend some time with security considerations. And finally, the business will spend more time in order to make sure that their cases and requirements are clear for to the developers. This will help creating the applications quicker, and it will also enhance the team work of each department in an organization.

If someone tries to enable DevOps and only talks to the developers, it might fail or create a Shadow IT with security risks. If the business is not involved in decisions, the business impact in doing DevOps might be not as big as expected and the organization might fail to compete. If IT is not involved and can't deliver the requested environment or integration, developers and the business will go elsewhere looking for an alternative.

PaaS as part of DevOps

PaaS is the most confusing term in an SDDC since different people refer to it for different descriptions and different parts of the SDDC. Basically, it can be broken down into the following two major meanings:

- Installing one or multiple VMs and putting software on top of it, ready for consumption.
- Providing a platform ready for developers to deploy applications into. This platform will provide several spaces or tenants such as development, quality assurance, and production. All the developer will need is an access and its application to upload.

This chapter is about DevOps, and this term is not set in stone and can describe different implementations or functionality of SDDC services. The first part discussed containers as cornerstone of DevOps. Often, this is also the first thought of any developer when it comes to application delivery automation. However, there are other implementations available, which will deliver even more flexibility and ease of use than a naked container host.

For containers, one has to be very Linux savvy. Even if a distribution like Docker is used, it does not work without the Linux bash command line or at least a good understanding of Linux and how it works. Container frameworks such as **Docker Swarm** or **Mesosphere** try to provide a management instance across many container hosts to make a distribution of containers or application possible. This normally adds a cloud-scale-like ability to container frameworks. However, this is still very container focused. To manage different stages or create different folders/zones or tenants these frameworks are clunky to use.

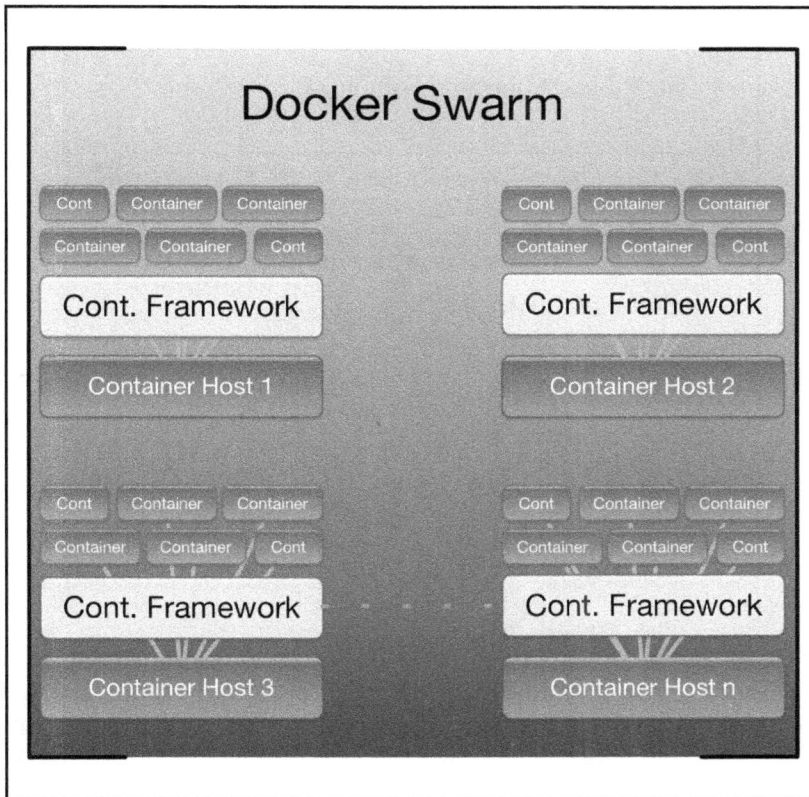

This is why there are other implementations, leveraging the container technology but hiding all its complexity from the user (the developer) plus adding other functionalities like multitenancy and staging of applications.

The Cloud Foundry framework

Cloud Foundry is a framework developed by a company named Pivotal. Pivotal was part of VMware for a while before it has been spun off into its own organization. It still is part of the EMC (Dell Technologies) family of organizations. It provides a framework for rapid and easy application development.

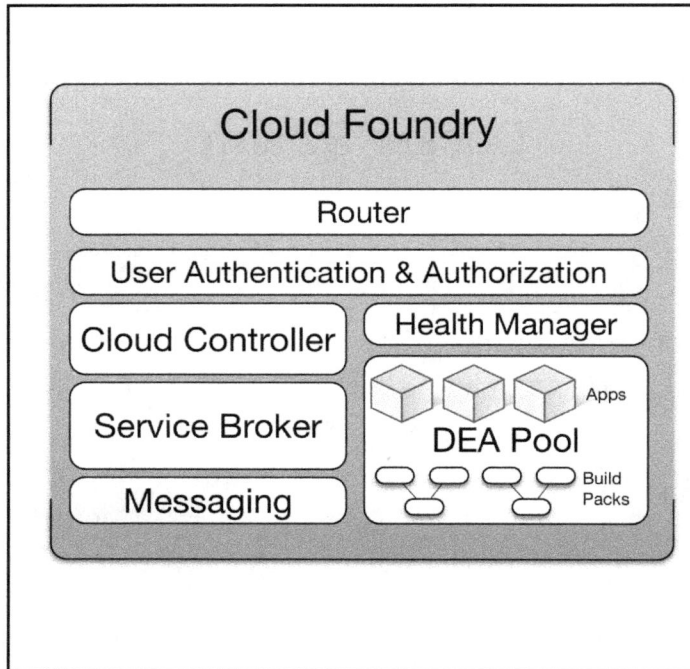

The framework is based on containers as well, but its features are ready-to-use CLI for developers as well as built-in multitenancy and so-called stages. Stages are useful for modeling the cycle of application development. Each application will be in a development stage, after that it might enter the quality assurance stage. Finally, it might get into the production stage once all other tests have passed.

The **Droplet Execution Agent (DEA)** of cloud foundry handles the staging process. Also, it performs the following key actions:

- **Managing the warden containers**: This runs applications in the containers.
- **Stage applications**: Once a new application or an updated version is pushed to Cloud Foundry, the Cloud Controller selects DEA from a pool to stage the application. DEA uses an appropriate built pack to create a droplet.
- **Run droplets**: Managed by a DEA, it reflects the lifecycle of an application. The Cloud Controller can instruct DEA to start or stop or a droplet. Also, a DEA can monitor the state of a started application for broadcasting it.

> To learn more about Cloud Foundry visit `docs.cloudfoundry.org` and read through the documentation. There is a lot of useful information in these documents, which can get any developer up and running with Cloud Foundry quite quick and easy.

However, an application might have many more stages; this is really just an example. This might be a relic from the old days, but DevOps does not mean that software doesn't need to be tested or approved anymore. It means that the cycle between these stages is a short and as automated as possible.

Besides that, it offers many other features like ready-to-use services using the built-in service broker. These services can now be simply consumed by the pushed applications. This means that a developer does not need to ask for DB to be deployed anymore; they can simply use what Cloud Foundry has to offer. And there are certainly more services available than just databases or NoSQL.

Cloud Foundry can also integrate with object storage and make it available through the service broker. Given that a developer does not have to bother with all these things, all they do is push their application into the platform and connect it to the provided services. This can be seen as a giant platform, ready for any modern application. Instead of creating a farm to host all required services by various applications, Cloud Foundry can dynamically react to whatever the developers need.

Cloud Foundry has easy-to-use tools and a complete command-line interface to migrate an application between all these three (or more) stages. Each stage can have its own data service (either DB or data storage) as well as its own network and security policies. This makes it easy for developers to ensure that the application gets the right security-level based on the selected stage.

Cloud Foundry and the SDDC

The framework can run on many public clouds as well as on the vSphere hypervisor directly. It is lightweight and relatively easy to set up. Once up and running it can be used to immediately serve new applications.

Given all this descriptions, it sounds like it supersedes the traditional SDDC with its framework, containers, and stages. However, while this might be true for cloud-native apps, legacy as well as big monolithic applications will still need a traditional environment.

Therefore, it is possible to combine both worlds and provide the best possible solution. Developers can use the PaaS framework; vRealize Automation can be used to provision supportive Cloud Foundry services such as DBs or other needed applications. Also, if developers require any additional service, which is not yet existent, this could be provisioned using a combination of Cloud Foundry command line as well as vRealize Automation REST API.

An example for this might be a MS SQL DB server, which is not included in Cloud Foundry. This SQL service could be available as a blueprint in vRA, and developers can trigger its deployment once it is needed for a given space or stage.

To accomplish this, it is possible to connect Cloud Foundry with the vRA REST API. This connection can be a new service/app within Cloud Foundry which triggers the deployment. The developer would not need to login to the vRA portal, they can stay in Cloud Foundry and still use their development toolset or the Cloud Foundry command line. This creates a nice bridge between the enterprise or legacy world and the new cloud native apps approach. However, VMware has also something to offer when it comes to an automated application development.

vRealize Code Stream: DevOps without containers

This is VMware's approach to make DevOps ready for the enterprise using a smart and developer-oriented portal named **vRealize Code Stream**. It is meant for app development in a highly automated environment. This might be the bridge between the SDDC and its automated delivery of services, as well as the requirements and needs today's developer have. The trick is that it can achieve this without a container framework, by leveraging the existing environment.

vRealize Code Stream needs vRealize Automation to be installed upon. So, it is an add-on to an existing VMware SDDC environment. Also, it integrates with many application development frameworks given that it comes prepacked with the JForg Artifactory.

Using this, it is possible to create custom repositories containing code or script artifacts for automated provisioning. For the repository service, there is also an API, which could be used using many development tools. This enables a developer to update artifacts right out of their development tool of choice. Furthermore, it means that a pipeline can automatically always use the most recent artifact out of that repository.

Since the repository and vRCS itself support so-called parameters, an artifact or code can have a distinct number; once this number is called upon execution, only the artifact matching that property will be processed.

All about the pipeline

In vRealize Code Stream, it is possible to create a so-called pipeline. The pipeline describes an application development lifecycle. Similar as in Cloud Foundry, it is possible to create stages. But instead of manually moving and application from one stage to another, it is possible to achieve this by using automated and programmable guards.

This means that if an application passes a defined test in a given stage, it will advance automatically to the next stage. This can be defined based on various different conditions from a test performed by Jenkins over a workflow output up to a manual approval.

This automates the way of quality assurance of an application in an environment. Instead of running all this tests manually and then moving a service to the next stage once successful, a simple check can perform this now automatically.

Each stage can contain various different objects. It can deploy a VM based on a vRA blueprint, it can install an application from the repository (JFrog Artifactory). It can even integrate with Jenkins or other programmer's tools and establish a direct development link to the deployed environment. Then, a developer can define the criteria of the gatekeeper to limit if and when an application can reach the next stage.

Typically, an approval is set to move an application from the QA stage into the production stage. This approval can be accomplished using the built-in vRA approval functionalities. Once the QA was successful, the app may enter the approval state. If the approval is granted, it will automatically merge into production, no human intervention required.

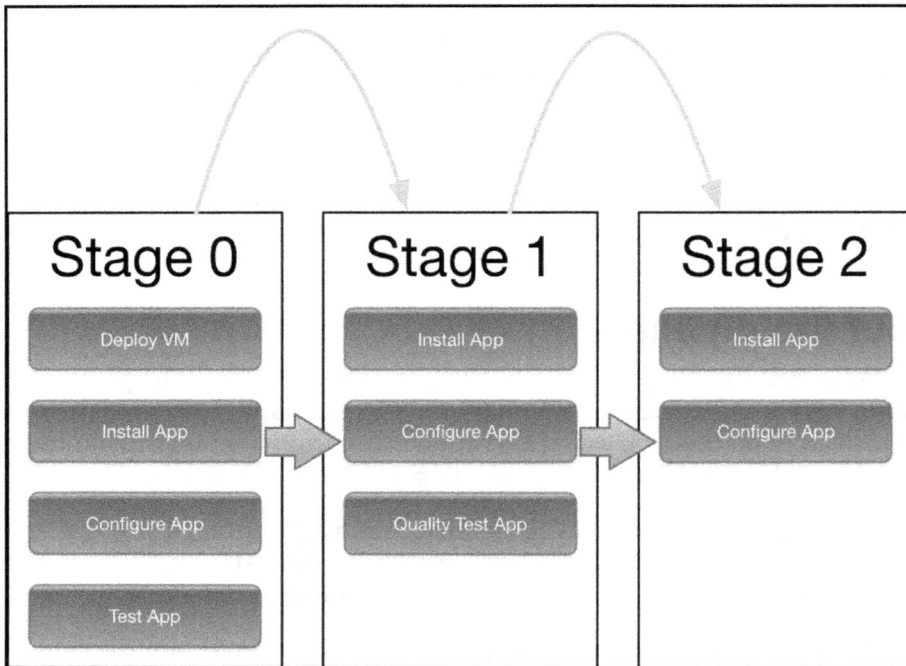

The preceding image shows the different stages. The blue arrows represent the gatekeepers. Once all criteria are met, the application can migrate automatically to the next stage. The shown pipeline works as follows:

- **Stage 0**: The test environment deploys a new VM, installs the app, configures it and runs some tests and deployments. This is repeated as often as necessary to develop the actual app.
- **Stage 1**: There is already a VM running (the running system) the app gets reinstalled, configured, and QA tests will run to ensure that the developments from **Stage 0** are stable.
- **Stage 2**: This might be the production stage. The app gets reinstalled (like a respin with containers) and configured. Now it is finally running, no more tests are necessary.

Although this is a very basic example, it shows how powerful this method of application development can be. Of course, it is also possible to model more complex application pipelines in order to automate them. There is no limit on how many stages can be used, albeit it might get very messy if there are tens or hundreds of stages in a pipeline.

However, the system does more than only automating the deployment. Each pipeline run is logged and can be reviewed. Each stage will have a status for each step. This is intended to make troubleshooting as easy and straightforward as possible. A developer can even get output from the different action all the way up to bash scripting output.

This is meant for any application development process to get fully automated. It creates a bridge between the new DevOps world and the legacy applications, which might not yet are ready to run in containers. Given this approach, any application can be made DevOps-ready.

However, as described earlier, each pipeline creates its own development environment by deploying VMs or installing additional software on already running VMs. This means that it ultimately is deploying a couple of VMs per development or QA run. If there are many developers actively using this to deploy their very own application development environment, this might put heavy load on the cloud portal as well as the virtual infrastructure beneath it. It is important to understand that factor in order to design the underlying vSphere infrastructure since the Code Stream requirement might be totally different from the enterprise SDDC requirements.

vRealize Code Stream integration

vRealize Code Stream does not only use VMware vSphere as an endpoint, it can also be integrated with many other services as well as other DevOps frameworks in order to automate the build and provisioning workflow.

As described in the Cloud Foundry section, there is the concept of stages (or spaces), but there is no gate automation available as in Code Stream. However, it might still make sense to use Cloud Foundry as a platform for developers. In order to achieve the best of both worlds, vRCS can integrate with Cloud Foundry.

This is done through the so-called Plug-In Instances. They can be registered with various endpoints. As of vRealize Code Stream version 2.1, the endpoints are:

- **A Jenkins Server endpoint**

  This enables any Jenkins test or job to run in the pipeline. It can also invoke a Jenkins build job during the modeling/execution of the release pipeline.

- **vRealize Automation Server endpoint**

  This plugins enables the modeling and deployment of vRA resources within a pipeline. Multiple vRealize instances can be provisioned in a single pipeline using this plugin.

- **vRealize Orchestrator**
  - **Workflow for a custom task**: This enables the connection to vRealize Orchestrator workflow to run within the pipeline. Also configuration as well as passing on values for parameters will be possible.
  - **Server endpoint**: This triggers any workflows on an external vRO from within the release pipeline.
  - **Workflow for a gating rule**: This can trigger a vRO workflow to act as a gating rule in order to automate the release to a new stage.

- **Microsoft Team Foundation Server**

  This enables the connection to a Team Foundation Server in order to manage build projects.

- **Cloud Foundry Server endpoint**

  This is used to deploy and manage lifecycle of an application into Cloud Foundry.

- **Bamboo Server endpoint**

  This is used to run tests and other plans as well as custom automation and scripts in Bamboo. This can also invoke a build plan during the modeling and execute this plan within the release pipeline.

- **Bugzilla Server endpoint**

  This generates or updates tasks in Bugzilla from within the release pipeline.

- **JIRA Server endpoint**

  This generates and updates GIRA tasks or issues out of a release pipeline.

Given this rich integration, it should be possible to use vRealize Code Stream in a variety of development environments. With the plugin for Cloud Foundry, it is even possible to automate the release management and use Cloud Foundry as native PaaS offering.

Also vRealize Orchestrator will be a mighty tool for release automation. Since vRO is also featuring a rich plugin availability and architecture, it will be easy to model several different easy and complex gatekeeper rules.

The Jenkins and Bamboo integration might be the most interesting one for the developers. These tools are often used for coding and the creation of artifacts. The ability to directly connect a pipeline and deployment tool is tremendously enhancing the deployment speed.

While the JIRA and Bugzilla integration is more, targeting continuous improvement and project management.

One integration that has not been mentioned yet is the integration in Socialcast. **Socialcast** is a communication tool often used for company internal purposes. It has features similar to Facebook and can be seen as a company internal social media platform.

vRealize Code Stream has the ability to post updates from a given pipeline right into a Socialcast group. While this might sound a bit awkward in the first place, it actually can provide a lot of value. Basically, it is an easy way to make pipeline executions transparent for a broader user group. This is a way of sharing progress in an easy and straightforward way.

vRealize Code Stream from VMware for the SDDC is meant to joining two different worlds: The world of DevOps with the world of enterprise IT.

By providing smart and easy integrations, it can be seen as a bridge between these two different worlds and the option to truly be able to fulfill the developer needs as well as the enterprise IT requirements.

SDDC and DevOps: A mixed world

The SDDC is perhaps one of the biggest enabler for DevOps as well as for running legacy applications more agile and dynamic. However, for most organizations, the SDDC is a way of running and deploying their well-established and often still required legacy applications.

Given all the changes a DevOps environment introduces, it will collide with established and required policies and processes in an enterprise environment. The classic approaches will not work since they possibly slow down DevOps operations and also create unnecessary overhead to such an environment.

An example for this will be an IPAM and CMDB solution. Given the short and temporary life of a development environment, it might not be necessary to track the hostname and IP address from all the VMs in the environment. Also, it might not be required to add all OS and software configuration items to the CMDB since they can change on a day-by-day basis. Therefore, all these processes have to be ignored; otherwise, the environment might become too slow for developers so that they have again to come up with a different solution.

DevOps requirements

For pure container environment such as Cloud Foundry or Docker Swarm, this is even more true. It makes no sense to register a container host in a CMDB or log its IP address using IPAM. The containers will communicate with each other using network ports. Also, containers are temporary and stateless, there is no need to track their status in a CMDB. The pure approach to make all this work together with legacy processes and tasks in any organization might as well kill the DevOps approach.

However, ITIL does not become irrelevant just because of DevOps. But it is necessary to adopt it to this new world. Changes in a production environment should still be announced, approved, and documented. Given that some of these containers run on container hosts in production, they could be treated as if they were vSphere hosts in a cluster. It maybe impossible to know exactly on which host the container runs, but maybe it makes sense to track on which swarm/cluster the container tends to run.

The resources should be easily available and flexible in its deployment. Although the container host is running on physical or on virtual servers, there should be enough flexibility available in order to quickly add resources to a given swarm or cluster.

In a Cloud Foundry world or PaaS world, there should be options in order to quickly onboard new services in order to make them available through the service broker. If it takes several weeks in order to establish a new service, this will ruin the whole case of having the platform available for developers.

Besides the technology aspect, DevOps will always introduce a change in the way of running the current IT environment. It is literally impossible to operate these new environments if all the boundaries are still to be met to integrate into the legacy processes coming from a different era of IT.

Enterprise requirements

In earlier chapters of this book, enterprise requirement of legacy applications have already been discussed briefly. An enterprise application might need to follow strict ITIL rules in order to be integrated in an existing data center. There sometimes needs to be an IPAM in place as well as a CMDB in order to store the configuration and setup of all these applications. Also a ticketing system might be required in order to keep track of possible incidents and problems in the environment.

With the use of automation, these tasks can be completed without human intervention, while the application is being deployed. A ticket can be opened and logged right out of the cloud portal. Given that these applications are quite static, it makes sense to automate the data exchange between CMDB, IPAM, and a ticketing system. The application is probably going to statically run for a longer period so the data will stay relevant as well.

Once an application is going to be archived or deleted, also the data can be automatically updated to mark the application as *archived* in the CMDB and release the IP address again in IPAM. This automation makes sure that no resources are wasted and that IP addresses could be reused once their original owner has disappeared from the data center.

> Albeit this is possible, there are organizations having rules that IP addresses and especially hostnames must not be reused with new services. This is normally done to prevent errors based on host name/IP confusion. There might be still colleagues thinking that a given IP or hostname is part of a distinct service. If the service behind the hostname/IP is a new one, this might lead to severe errors caused by human interaction.

Legacy and DevOps: Coexistence in one environment

Given all the differences between DevOps and the legacy world, one might think it is important to create a separated environment for each type.

This is typically not recommended. Separate environments lead to island solutions within a data center. Each island needs to be managed and controlled separately. They need to be monitored and run by a different team or the same team. However, given all the effort to separate two environments within a data center, it might not be efficient or agile to do this with a DevOps installation.

Also the integration from Development to Operations might be difficult if the production environment is somewhat separated from the development (remember the stages). Therefore, separating environments is not a good option since it can actually lead to a slower deployment instead of speeding up development and deployment times.

As described in the earlier sections, there is a coexistence with vRealize Automation possible. It is not only possible but should be achieved in order to minimize effort in running the environment and enabling the DevOps team to really use what the SDDC has to offer.

Even if there are a lot of things possible with containers, there are always some applications that can't be easily stuffed into this new way of running software. There might be requirements for on-demand DB creation, for object-based storage, for e-mail connectivity, or for other legacy services. These services can be deployed and automated using the traditional SDDC methods like deploying an application on top of a VM or using automation to register these services to a service broker.

Also, the SDDC is empowering DevOps. It is more a symbiotic relationship than a competitive one. There are several things that might not be as easily possible in a DevOps installation if there is no SDDC running side by side.

Use DevOps principles to manage the SDDC

Besides the pure developers view of DevOps to run application in the SDDC, there is another point of view worthwhile to cover. The SDDC itself consists of blueprints, which will deploy services. These blueprints are basically software or at least code definitions of infrastructure. In a production environment, it is very common to have a development SDDC and a production SDDC. Once new services pass all test and quality assurance criteria in the development SDDC, they can be transformed to the production environment. However, this task had to be done manually in the past or by the use of complex command-line tools without the ability to version control or roll back in case of an error.

This is quite close to what developers do in software and why DevOps is so popular. They simply want to be able to quickly reapply an updated version of their software. The same principle comes true for blueprints; it would be very handy to develop a simple blueprint and then put it in production, but fully automated with the press of a button.

This is where the vRealize Code Stream Management Pack for IT DevOps comes into play. This was formally known as project Houdini by VMware and does apply DevOps principles to managing blueprints.

It is based on vRealize Code Stream and is available as an add-on service catalog in vRealize Automation. The target audience is blueprint designers and SDDC admins who want to develop services in one vRA instance and then simply transform these into the production vRA instance, once ready.

Its Version 2.1.1 supports the following blueprint types:

- IaaS blueprints (vSphere only at the moment)
- ASD blueprints and actions
- vRO workflows and actions
- XaaS blueprints

Furthermore, it allows the teams to select a blueprint including all its dependencies and configurations and transforms it either to another tenant or even to another vRA instance. It will resolve all dependencies and ensure that these are also installed and ready in the target system. Additionally, it can run tests of that blueprint if desired by the requestor. Once all that is completed successfully, the blueprint will be available at the new vRA instance or tenant.

The big advantage is that all these operations are stored in a version controlled central database. So each update or change can easily be tracked and also be rolled back if necessary. This is a huge advantage since it eases publishing new services and tremendously reduces risks in the event of failures.

These *infrastructure as a code* packages can also be managed and will appear under the **Items** tab in vRealize Automation. All of these are able to be deployed to different tenants, vRA instances (including vRO), or even vRA instances in different data centers.

This is a very powerful way to apply the DevOps principle to infrastructure and leverage its full agility in order to create, test, and deploy service within the SDDC. The plugin is available through VMware free of charge, but requires vRealize Code Stream to be configured and installed.

So besides the application DevOps approach, it should definitely considered to also run an *infrastructure* DevOps approach using these technologies in order to have the same efficiency and agility when it comes to the development of new SDDC services.

Summary

This chapter described DevOps in general. Its purpose and what differences it might bring to an SDDC. The general meaning and purpose of DevOps was discussed in order to understand that this way of creating applications requires different approaches. It also listed several approaches to run cloud-native applications and listed ways to further automate their release and tests. Also, it listed tools to integrate in vRA in order to be able to provide the best of both worlds for DevOps as well for the classic legacy IT application. Finally, it highlighted a way of applying the DevOps principle to the SDDC service development, in order to leverage its agility and flexibility for the creation and distribution of infrastructure blueprints.

In the next chapter, the focus will be on capacity management in an SDDC. It will highlight why it is important to do predictive capacity planning as well as which tool in the VMware family can be used to further provide this functionality. Also, it will highlight how to operate vRealize Operations Manager and create so-called dashboards in order to provide a quick capacity overview of the SDDC environment.

10
Capacity Management with vRealize Operations

This chapter will dive into capacity management for the SDDC. Since requests through the cloud portal now drives the deployment and consumption of services, users expect that there are elastic or nearly limitless resources available. Similar to a public cloud provider, where resources are virtually endless and always available. The big cloud providers typically have a predictive analytics model to understand when if and how they need to provide additional resources to back the users demand.

Typically for a cloud provider, this is accomplished completely transparent in the background. It is their desire to keep the illusion of limitless and endless resources alive for their customers. In the end, this is what a lot of customers are looking for: quick and easy onboarding. No waiting time until some physical installation is going to be finished.

This implies that capacity management in a highly automated environment like the SDDC is a very important topic. Being informed about the resource consumption is not the only important aspect; the capacity planning should also be tied directly into the order management process. While the idea of a system self-ordering its resources sounds a little bit frightening in the first place, this is actually how the big providers are doing it. They have predictive algorithms to inform them that based on the current usage they will need x amount of servers in the next x weeks. This allows an order to be placed to have the servers shipped and up and running before the demand actually catches up with the available resources.

Now, arguably cloud provider will have a different business model than an organization, which is only running its own IT. However, capacity planning is also crucial for this environment. If ever a user will be hindered to provision a service because there are simply not enough resources, this will harm the trust and reputation into the local IT department. It could harm the relationship so badly, that users might actually consider provisioning their services externally instead of internally.

In this part, the following topics will be covered:

- Why capacity monitoring needs to change in an SDDC
- vRealize Operations Manager capacity management principles
- Overview of reports and dashboards for capacity management
- How to create projects to predict future capacity
- Setup of example reports and dashboards for capacity monitoring in an SDDC

Capacity monitoring in the SDDC

Most organizations do a very basic but well-established form of capacity planning. Typically resources are tied to projects or to a bigger data center initiative. Groups participating that initiative may provide a budget and growth plan. These plans are used to buy required hardware, which will be available for the entire project time phase. Sometimes, if more resources are required as expected, there will be additional servers shipped to fulfill this demand during the project run time. All this requires a proper planning and a big amount of human interaction. Also it requires being aware of what is going on in the data center and a good amount of preplanning.

Traditional monitoring and capacity planning tools might not be able to deal with the different requirements a SDDC introduces. Furthermore, using legacy capacity planning tools might increase the overhead for the workforce and in worst cases maybe even limit the way the SDDC can be consumed.

Since the SDDC environment itself is constantly changing due to the automated deployment of workloads, the tools to actually keep track of these changes should be able to automatically adapt to these environmental changes.

The legacy project approach does only partially work here, since there might be users or groups who simply got a resource pool to deploy into. Sometimes even the teams themselves do not know how much capacity they might need. However, they can track their consumption in the portal watching their resource pool filling up. But all these resources have to come from a powerful and well-managed backend. And this backend needs to be constantly checked for possible capacity constraints.

One solution for this could be to have dozens of empty servers running in case their resources are needed. But this obviously is a very expensive way of providing resources on demand. Since all these servers would need to be preinstalled and preconfigured, but in the end, if they are not needed, do not provide any value.

The other option is to have an automated resource demand management due to capacity monitoring. In order to do this, it is important to use a system, which can provide also predictive analysis. This is needed to get a capacity alert before the end user is affected. The system needs to be able to pick up a trend, interpolate that trend and then provide a forecast when the demand will be higher than the backing resources. Ideally it provides an alert way before that point in order to prepare the infrastructure team to replenish hardware upfront.

This approach is similar to what modern car manufacturers are doing today. Instead of having all parts always available in a big warehouse, they calculate with transport times and include the trucks having the parts in their preorder system. The logistic department takes care that the schedule is met and that parts arrive exactly as they are needed. This way they can significantly reduce their warehouse cost and be flexible in their manufacturing process.

An SDDC works quite similar like this example. VMs or furthermore services are deployed on demand, there can be days where more of them are needed and days where less of them are deployed. However, the backing resources need to be available as the services require them. This implies that in a fully automated deployment environment also the resource ordering and installation processes need to be automated.

This means that it would not only be helpful but required if the system is able to reorder without any human intervention. Obviously an approval will make sense for this automation.

In order to accomplish that, it is not only required to have a capacity monitoring in place which can predict demand and create trustworthy forecasts, it is also required to change the established ordering process in an organization.

So a SDDC requires a different approach to capacity monitoring than a traditional data center. It needs a powerful forecast and prediction tool. Based on that forecast it will also require a changed ordering process. Instead of modeling resources in a project, they are now ordered based on demand predictions and actual resource consumption.

vRealize Operations Manager

vRealize Operations Manager is often referred to as VMware's monitoring solution. But it provides way more than just simple resource monitoring. Not only that it has full capacity management capabilities, it is also is a learning system, which can self-adapt to a changing environment. This makes it the perfect solution for the SDDC, since it can automatically pick up changes in an environment. Additionally it can also learn the standard behavior of VMs and services. This enables the tool to recognize a change in the behavior and trigger an alert based on that behavior.

Traditional capacity management tools might only be able to work with thresholds. While this sounds perfectly acceptable in the first place, it can introduce issues in a dynamic environment such as the SDDC. Since the values constantly change it will be very hard to set valid thresholds for a capacity management tool to kick in. Also, a threshold needs to be well thought through, given that the supply management chain needs time to order and deliver the required resources.

vRealize Operations Manager is solving this dilemma by using a completely different approach. It does not necessarily look for fixed values it looks for usage patterns and creates estimated growth rates. This is a powerful way of monitoring capacity, since it can also solve these cases where traditional systems might have troubles.

For example: In a SDDC environment, there might be a new business project coming up. A given department maybe starts to add tens or hundreds of VMs. vRealize Operations will pick up this behavioral change and will issue a capacity alert if necessary. The alert will tell the operations team that if this trend continues, they have to add more resources in X amount of days.

A traditional capacity-planning tool might be triggered at 90% resource usage and send an alert, but that might be to late in order to guarantee that there is no resource constraint. The following workflow presents a typical order workflow until the gear is available in the data center:

- Order is processed and sent to the vendor/partner
- After 3-6 weeks the resources is arriving the organization
- After 2-3 weeks the kit is ready to be configured in the data center
- After 1-2 weeks the resources will be completely configured and ready to be used

That means that the capacity heads up needs to be at least 10 weeks ahead, shortest 6 weeks ahead of the actual requirements for those resources. Otherwise users will experience shortcomings and possible degraded performance while using the SDDC. This may lead to less adoption or even force users to look for alternative ways of running their workflows.

> Never underestimate the importance of capacity planning and supply chain management in order to keep the SDDC functional and resources available. Any notable disruption in the service might diminish the usability for the end-users which may lead to loss of trust in the service.

vROps 6.3 deployment workflow

The deployment of the tool is very straightforward. It is provided as a vAPP and to successfully deploy it all an administrator has to do is follow the necessary onscreen menu. Version 6.3 has major improvements over the older versions and comes as a single VM, instead of two VMs in a vAPP. This reduces the overall complexity of vROps and makes it easy to install.

The first thing to do after a successful deployment is to connect it to vCenter. This is done in the so-called **Solutions** menu:

1. Open vROps in a web browser by pointing it to `https://vrops.example.local`.
2. Logon with the given admin (local users) name and the password provided during the vROps installation.
3. Click on the *Administration* icon located at the top row of the left hand column. The icon has a little gear symbol.
4. Click on **Solutions** in the left-hand column
5. Select the **VMware vSphere** solution in the table and click on the **Configure** icon in the **Solutions** area.

6. In the **Manage Solution – VMware vSphere** window, enter the following details:
   - **Display Name**: vCenter
   - **Description**: vROPs monitored vCenter
   - **vCenter Server**: vcenter.example.local
   - **Credentials**:
     1. Click the *plus* icon to add credentials.
     2. Enter a credential name for example, vCenter.
     3. Enter a valid vCenter username.
     4. Provide the password for the selected user.
     5. Click **OK** to set the credentials.
7. Click on the **Test Connection** button and wait for a positive feedback
8. Click on **Save Settings** to store the configured configuration for the solutions adapter.

Adapter Type	Description	Instances	Version	Provided by
vCenter Adapter	Provides the connection information and credent...	1	2.0.3774211	VMware Inc.
vCenter Python Actions Adapter	Provides actions for vCenter objects using Pytho...	0	1.0.3774212	VMware Inc.

Manage Solution - VMware vSphere

✛ ✗

Instance Name ▲

vCenter

Instance Settings

Display Name: vCenter

Description: vROPs monitored vCenter

Basic Settings

vCenter Server: vcenter.ucpdemo.local

Credential: vCenter

Test Connection

▶ Advanced Settings

◁◁ ◁ | Page 1 of 1 | ▷ ▷▷ | ⟳

Manage Registrations   Save Settings

Close

vROps can also be installed in HA mode with more than one instance. This setup is also controlled during the initial installation. However, it requires more resources and some preconfiguration tasks to make that running. To learn more about this expert setup please refer to the vROps installation guide at `https://pubs.vmware.com/vrealizeoperationsman ager-63/index.jsp`.

After vROps is set up and the vCenter link is established it is ready for being used for analytics and capacity monitoring at the vCenter level.

There are many more solution adapters available for vROps to connect it also to the non-VMware world. It can be connected to various storage vendors, SAN switches as well as networking gear. But also exotic use cases such as temperature sensors or power consumption can be monitored and forecasted with vROps (if a solution provider is present, or could be customized). This might not be necessary for capacity management, but for advanced data center analytics that might become very handy.

After all considered solutions have been set up it will start collecting data. The tool needs a while to get meaningful data to provide trends and detect patterns in the data center. Usually this time is about two to three weeks. So if vROps is not showing any usable data at the second day after the installation, be patient and wait until there is enough data available for valuable output.

Also, the guesses and trends will get better over time, since the tool can learn from long-term patterns as well.

Capacity monitoring

To start with the capacity monitoring it might be helpful to understand the general structure of vROps and how it is organized. Please be aware that this structure differs between the basic/standard system and the advanced/enterprise system. The described layout refers to the advanced and enterprise version of vRealize Operations.

First of all, if a user who has admin privileges assigned accesses vROps using a web browser, it will display the environmental overview screen. This typically includes all solution adapters and all data. It tries to focus everything what is going on in the environment on one simple dashboard.

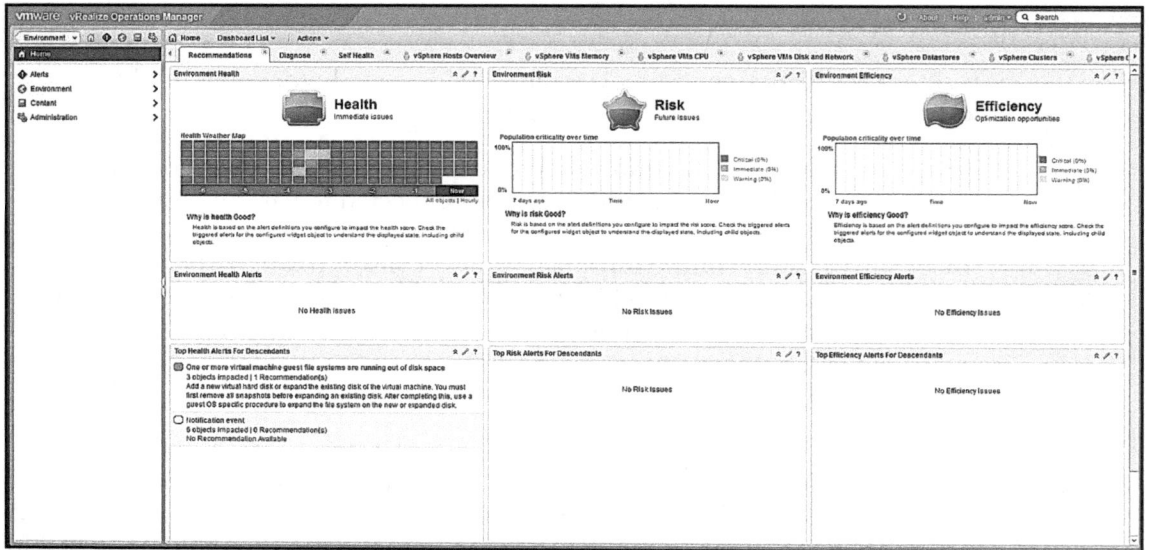

This overview contains three major badges:

- **Health**: This is mainly used for monitoring and analytics purposes.
- **Risk**: This will provide a forecast of potential issues, these will include capacity constraints. However, the data is always an estimate based on the collected raw data and trend forecasts.
- **Efficiency**: This is basically showing how efficient resources are being used. If Efficiency is low it is a good indication that resources are *overprovisioned* this means a VM might has more RAM or CPU configured than it actually needs, very common. This is used for capacity control and monitoring purposes as well. Bad efficiency rates will affect capacity as well (wasted resources).

Unfortunately these values are shown for all gathered data. While this sounds handy in the first place, it means that a lot of values will actually delude individual capacity issues. The following diagram describes this dilemma:

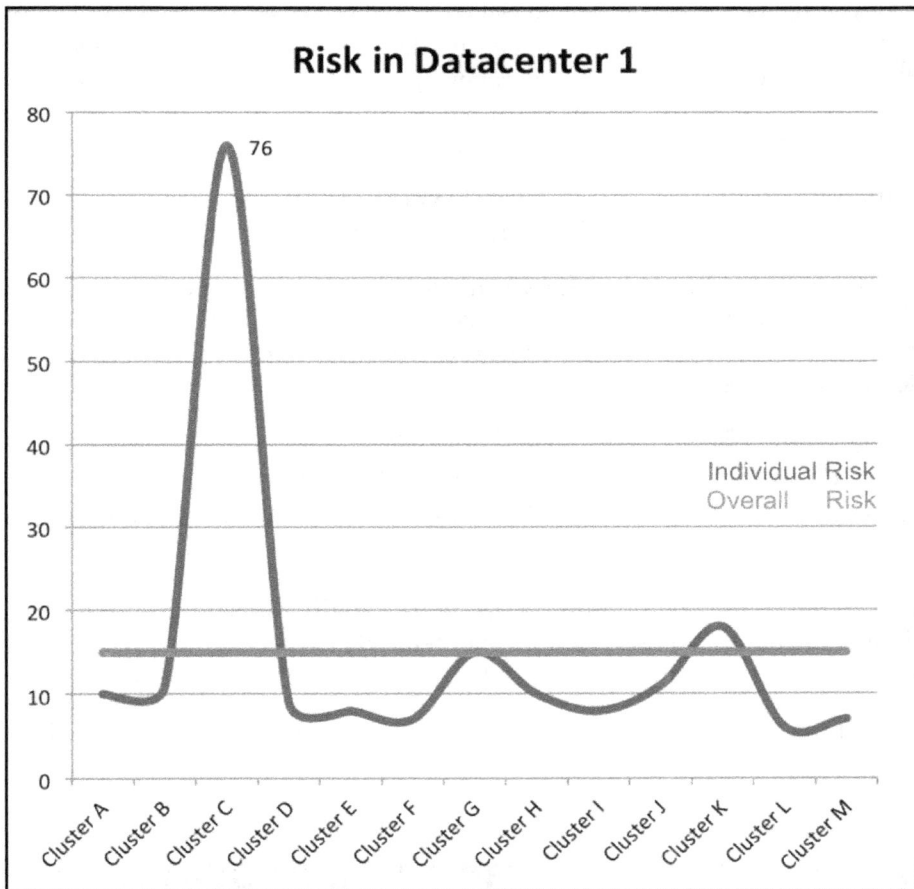

The dark red line displays the individual risk value for each cluster. By looking at the diagram it is pretty clear that **Cluster C** might have an issue of some sort. The other clusters are doing well so far. What vRealize Operations is now doing is calculating the entire risk of the data center, including all clusters. This will lead to a loss of details for the individual risk. The lighter blue line shows the overall risk calculated for the data center. Given that all other clusters are doing just fine, the overall risk is quite low, not really alarming.

So the general overview including all metrics and data cannot be seen as the ultimate data center risk/health or efficiency display. It is more a hint and tries to provide a slight insight that overall everything is doing well.

> If this view contains severe risk values (orange or red) something serious might have happened in the entire data center. Given the high level overview, things need to be severely bad to have a big influence in that view. So in that case it is helpful to identify that there might be a *global* issue going on in the data center.

The rule of thumb for vRealize Operations is: Do not judge the environment based on the 10,000 feet overview given when logging on to the system.

In earlier versions of vRealize Operations Manager, these badges did also show numbers. So the health value could be 98, risk 8 (lower is better), and efficiency 95. However, VMware decided to remove this number scores, since they confused a lot of people and the capacity planning team had to answer questions like:

- Why is our efficiency only 95 and not 100?
- Why do we have a risk of 8; is there something wrong?
- Does a health of 98 mean that 2 fractions of our environment have problems?

While the numbers where just displayed to back the colors (100-80 green, 80-60 orange, 60-45 yellow, 45-0 red) they had nothing to do with actually displaying problems. A score of 8 risk might just mean that some systems are potentially exceeding their assigned resources, but not that there is actually a real issue.

However, to get this problem solved VMware applied a simple fix to all new vROps Managers: No more numbers in badges.

Overprovisioning and resource allocation

Besides the overview dashboard, the system comes with hundreds of detailed views and reports, which can be used to get a good understanding about resource demand and resource availability. To get started, it is recommended to look at an individual group of items to examine their capacity needs. However, ultimately the system should send a warning pro-actively. Based on this warning it than might make sense to examine the mentioned resources closer. Resource warnings and related actions will be discussed later in this chapter.

In order to being able to understand what vROps is displaying it is important to be aware of how virtual resource management and provisioning works in vSphere. The following example is based on an extremely overprovisioned data store:

- It holds 10 VMDKs
- Each thin provisioned with 500 GB
- Consumed space is 0.5 TB

> In vSphere, one speaks of overprovisioning if more resources are allocated (provisioned) than actually available. While this is common practice for CPUs and even memory virtualization, for disk space it needs some extra effort. If the CPU or memory resource is constraint, the VM might operate slower. If disk space is suddenly no longer available, most OSes stop operating at all. Therefore disk space is a more critical resource than CPU or memory.

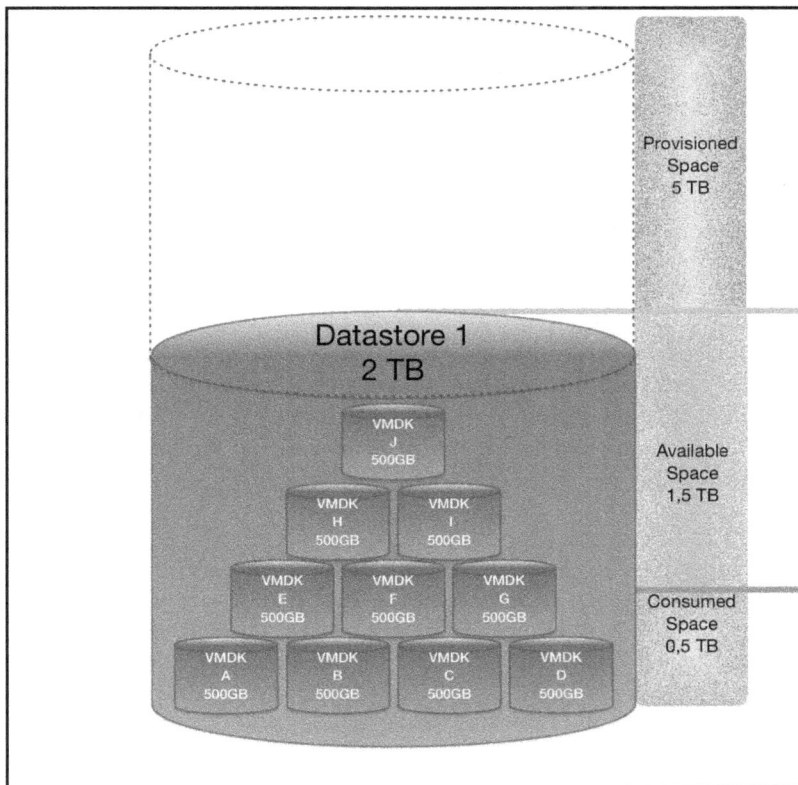

The setup in the preceding image is very risky. Some applications have high resource requirements but than they eventually never use all the allocated resources. However, there is no guarantee that an application/VM will not start using all its allocated resources.

Some prominent examples for unforeseen use of resources are quite trivial:

- OS updates can consume a lot of disk space
- Application based backup (for example, database dumps)
- Application updates
- Software maintenance (new installs)

In some environments this might take a while, but be prepared that the database admin maybe besides tomorrow to move from a simple to a full backup pattern for some reason. Or just the the additional database dump according with the backup, since there is enough disk space left in the OS, right...?

Normally, vSphere does allow setting a limit on overprovisioning. This would than prevent putting to many VMDKs onto a data store. These limits are typically set in percentage of the data store's capacity. So if a data store has 2 TB, a limit can be set to 150%, which means that it will allow an allocation of 3 TB or an overprovisioning of 50%.

In this case, such a limit has not been set. The data store happily supports every single VMDK as long as there is enough physical space left. However, the overprovisioning is a 5 TB on a 2 TB data store. This means the resource is 250% overprovisioned.

As mentioned in `Chapter 3`, *VMware vSphere: The SDDC Foundation*, vSphere will have some special abilities to protect VMs from stopping to operate due to out of storage issues by using storage DRS out of space avoidance moves (if configured and enabled). However, this function needs other available resource to bounce the VMs off to. This either requires attached empty data store, which will harm the efficiency, or an intelligent process to add resources based on the growing demand. Given this, is important to understand that with the over-allocation, there is one important metric to look after: *resource demand*.

Demand is created if the VMs start to touch more and more of their allocated resources. This means they eventually start to physically (well virtually actually) consume the allocated space. And from this demand a trend can be calculated.

vRealize Operations Manager will closely monitor the allocation and the demand and provide insights and a trend for both. While capacity trend might not change so quickly, the demand can change very quickly.

The following screenshot shows an example view in vRealize Operations how such a data store would look like. The view is provided at the **Capacity Remaining** tab on a select vSphere cluster:

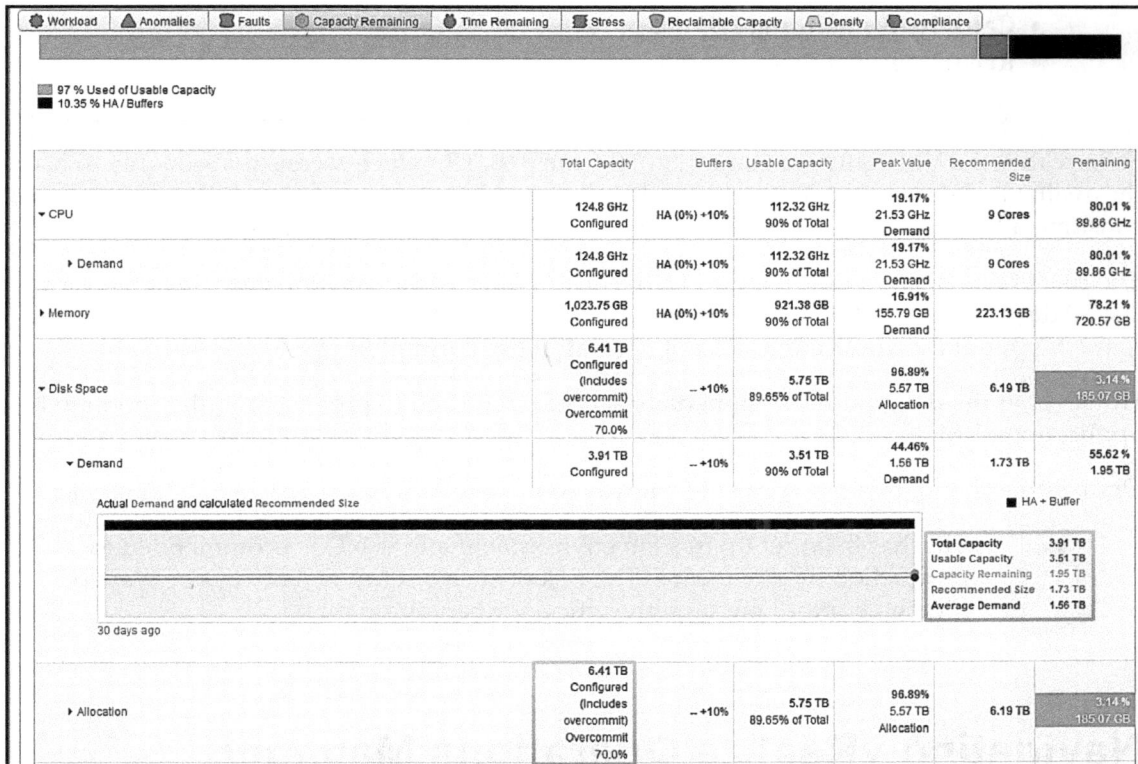

vRealize Operations has already highlighted the areas limiting the clusters capacity. In this case it is the **Disk Space**:

- The total capacity says **6.41 TB** (including 70% overcommit)
- The system detected that already **5.57 TB** (96.89%) has been allocated to VMs
- The physical available storage space is 4 TB

vROps will not only highlight the values, it will also send e-mail alert notifications to make sure that this status is not missed by anybody. However, by looking on the demand graph, it shows that the demand has been pretty flat for the last 30 days.

Also, the **Demand** row shows all the disk details:

- **Total Capacity**: 3.91 TB
- **Usable Capacity**: 3.51 TB (includes HA buffer)
- **Capacity Remaining**: 1.95 TB
- **Recommended Size**: 1.73 TB
- **Average Demand**: 1.56 TB

So in reality the VMs only consume 1.56 TB from 3.91 TB, which means that roughly 45% of the available data store space is utilized by all these VMs. However, the VMs could consume all the way up to 6.41 TB, which is 2.41 TB more than available.

The risk of this disaster occurring can currently be seen at the demand chart. It is flat for the last 30 days. Seems that this is one of the cases where a lot of resources have been provided to the VMs, but the applications do not need all those currently.

However, if the demand rises, immediate action is required to prevent any disruption to the applications/VMs.

On the other hand, this is a very efficient way to make use of resources; risky, but efficient.

This has been set up in a lab environment and is NOT recommended for production by any means. The risk of such a setup will always be way to high no matter how high the efficiency benefit might be.

Navigating vRealize Operations Manager

vRealize Operations Manager is a very mighty tool for both, capacity planning as well as data center analytics. Therefore it has a very rich user interface full of data and objects to inspect. The capacity planner will properly need different menus and dashboards than the vSphere administrator or the data center analyst. This section should provide an overview of useful functions for capacity planning and where to find them in the tool.

Capacity remaining

This has been discussed earlier, the capacity remaining dashboard is available for vSphere resources like hosts, clusters and data centers. To get to this view follow the following steps:

1. Open vRealize Operations Manager web UI in your browser.
2. In the home screen click on **Environment** in the left-hand pane.
3. At the updated view, click on **vSphere Hosts and Clusters**.
4. Expand **vSphere World** | expand the vCenter | expand the data center to finally click on to the desired cluster to view.
5. In the main dashboard click on **Analysis**.
6. Select the **Capacity Remaining** dashboard in the **Analysis** tab.

This will provide a detailed overview of the cluster and its resources as shown in the following graphic:

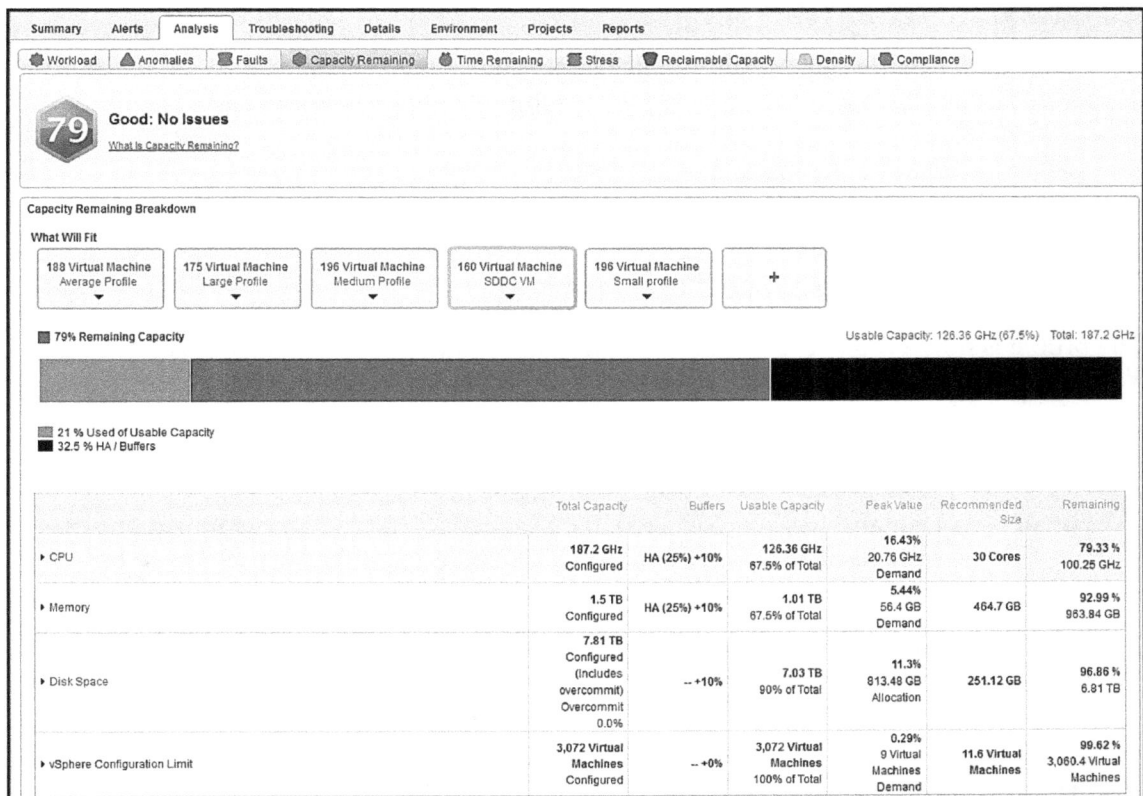

Like in the former example, this overview provides a quick an easy way to check the capacity demands and risks for the selected object. In this case, it is a payload cluster providing resources for the SDDC. There is also a very basic scenario based what-if analysis available at the **What Will Fit** top section. It shows some rectangles with VM counts in them. The numbers are based on a workload profile. Each rectangle symbolizes a separate workload profiles. However, defaults will never really fit all customers so it is also possible to create custom VM profiles based on actual workloads (VMs) running in the environment.

One of these profiles has been created and is called `SDDC VM`. This is not just some CPU, memory, and disk space profile. It takes all the workload data (including demand, performance behavior, and so on) and stores it. Than it compares it with the capacity remaining in the cluster. Given that it is using the real data from the actual deployed VMs, it is far more accurate than the default profiles.

To create one of these profiles, follow these steps:

1. Click on the rectangle with the *plus* sign.
2. In the configuration window provide a valid profile name and description.
3. Click **Enable this profile for all Policies** if desired.
4. In the **Metrics** section decide for a filter mode. Either **Allocation** or **Demand** or both.
5. Now click on **Populate metrics from…**.
6. **At Existing Virtual Machine** select a VM to act as a standard. Try to select a VM configuration describing the most used blueprint of the SDDC environment.
7. Click **OK** to save the profile configuration.

The profile is now available, however it might take a little while until it shows a number of VMs.

> If **Allocation** has been selected, the number of VMs will be calculated based on their allocated resources.
>
> If **Demand** has been selected, the number of VMs will show how many of them will fit based on their resource demand. In other words, based on their currently used resources.
>
> If both is selected, the system takes both considerations into account and try to give the best prediction

As of today these profiles cannot be edited after they are added. If you need to change the profile (for example, from **Allocation** to **Demand**) it needs to be deleted and recreated from scratch.

> These profiles are a good way to ensure that the resources are available given the specific `SDDC VM` configuration. This will rise accuracy and therefore makes it easier to react to possible resource constraints.

Right next to the **Capacity Remaining** dashboard there is also a **Time Remaining** dashboard, which will basically interpolate the time remaining until the resource will be 100% used. If this value is bigger than one year, it will simply state **>1yr**.

The resources in the table can be expanded by clicking on their down arrow. In case of **Demand**, a diagram will display current and future (interpolated) demand. Based on that future demand the remaining time will be calculated.

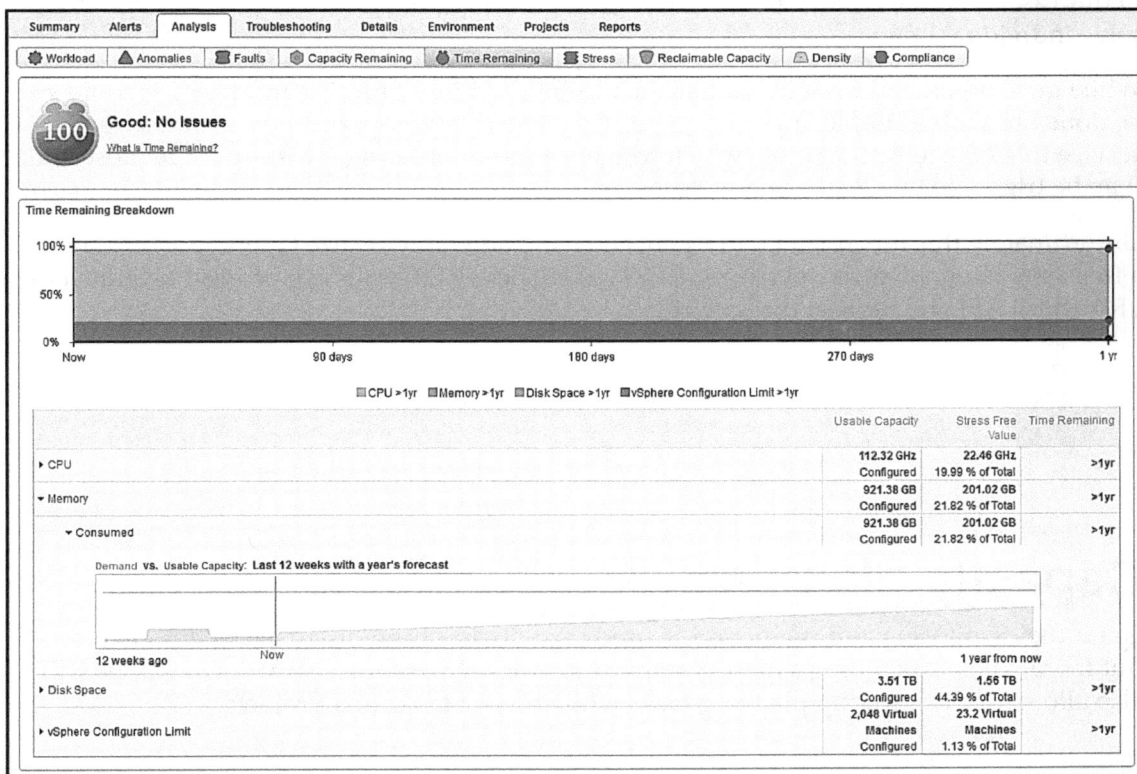

The preceding image shows a growing memory demand. Based on the last 12 weeks the system detects an ongoing trend. This trend will be added to the forecast. Given all this metrics the system can predict when the current resources will no longer be able to serve the demand. The current resources called **Usable Capacity** are shown in the graphic as purple line. The red area is the current and future demand. When the red area and the purple line is crossing this marks the time to add resources to fulfill further demand. In this case this point is further ahead than a year, so it is not shown in the graph.

These conditions can change very quickly. If a user deploys multiple VMs into this cluster the memory demand will change. This will lead to a recalculation of the time remaining estimate. Therefore alerts can be defined based on time remaining notifications. If this might drop to 3 month for example, an alert could be send to the procurement department in order to make them aware of the upcoming resource constraint.

Eventually the alert could automatically trigger a purchasing management system to order additional resources. The financial department will only be involved to approve the order. In this case system would bee configured as self-healing (or self ordering in this case) to solve individual issues.

While most organizations will not like the idea of machines ordering machines, it could still be done but with a simple approval chain. This would be an opportunity to add a XaaS service to vRealize Automation, which triggers a server ordering. This service request could than be triggered by vRealize Operations.

Unfortunately this functionality does not come included in vRealize Operations, but there is a free alert plugin, which can trigger REST calls. These REST calls can be used to launch the vRA REST API and request the service.

> Please be aware that VMware does not officially support the plugin for the custom REST action for vRealize Operations.

Capacity planning

So far the monitoring and prediction of used capacity has been discussed in this chapter. But there is also a planning aspect to prevent low or risky resource situations. vROps will also allow for this capacity planning tasks with an extra tab called **Projects**.

At the beginning of this chapter, it was explained that resources where often added or bought based on projects and that this is no longer accurate for an SDDC. This statement was referring to large projects requiring also hardware resources to be bought. Based on this projects entire areas of data center might have been filled with servers, storage and compute.

In an SDDC, projects are still relevant and eventually will even increase popularity since they can be much quicker be realized. This is also referred to as time to market or sometimes, time to value. Since the SDDC is offering infinite resources on demand with a simple mouse click, it is the ideal platform for any project.

In reality, this illusion is only possible if there is a very good capacity planning and monitoring. The monitoring aspects have been discussed so far and are good to keep an overview about the running environment and predict any future potential constraints. The planning is needed to prevent any constraints introduced in a very short amount of time.

The following example might help to better understand what projects are for in vRealize Operations Manager and how they can be used together with vRealize Automation.

A development team decides they need:

- 10 database VMs
- 25 application server VMs
- 100 web server VMs

Those are required in order to test for a specific application scenario. In order to quickly get all this deployed the SDDC is the perfect starting point. So they will go ahead and request 135 VMs to be deployed in a very short amount of time. These VMs will come with different profiles and different requirements.

To make sure the SDDC is not blindly doing anything, which has been requested, approvals have been introduced. In Chapter 5, *VMware vRealize Automation*, these approvals are discussed in greater detail. From a capacity planning perspective, approvals are interesting to prevent sprawl and to make sure that the system can handle the introduced load well enough.

> Besides the cost and regulatory nature of approvals, they are also needed in order to maintain the SDDC resilient and responsive. Imagine what would happen if a user would order as many VMs to bring the SDDCs resources down. All users would be affected. This is another reason why approvals should be taken seriously in order to protect SDDC functionality and guarantee flawless operation.

Additionally, being aware of such massive VM provisioning requests will make it easier to order resources even before the vROps time remaining monitoring feature might trigger a warning.

Projects in vRealize Operations Manager

Lets assume the developers filled in their request to vRealize Automation and this is now send for approval to the SDDC operations team. This team is also responsible for the resource management and availability. As soon as the approval comes in they can use the details of the request to model the data into vROps to see if the capacity will be sufficient for such a project.

For this use case, vROps has its own functionality called *projects*. To model such a project, follow these steps:

1. Open vRealize Operations Manager web UI in your browser by.
2. In the home screen click on **Environment** in the left-hand pane.
3. At the updated view, click on **vSphere Hosts and Clusters**.
4. Expand **vSphere World** | expand the vCenter | expand the data center to finally click on to the desired cluster to view.
5. In the main dashboard click on **Projects**.

At the lower half of this dashboard, there will be a table showing all currently configured projects (if any). If no projects have been configured, this table will be completely empty.

To create a new project, follow these steps:

1. Click on the *plus* sign in the lower half of the dashboard.
2. Provide a valid name, description, and select **Planned – no badges affected**.

> Projects can also be retro-modeled. This is what **Status Committed – badges affected** in the creation wizard stands for.

3. Click on **Scenarios** at the bottom left of the screen to bring up the project modeler.

4. Make sure the correct object is selected, in the example it will be an SDDC cluster. But it can be different virtual objects such as data stores, hosts or even VMs.

5. In the **Add Demand** section drag **add Virtual Machine** in the **Scenarios** area (right next to the left column)

6. Now the project parameters (VM parameters) can be created, fill in all necessary metrics. It is important to try to be as accurate as possible, since the prediction will only be as good as the provided data.

7. In the configuration area (right to the **Scenarios** area) provide all known parameters to model the anticipated VM resource demand. Make sure to fill in consumed versus provisioned correctly. For the databases it is a save assumption that memory consumed equals memory allocated. For the web servers, the memory allocation might be 4 GB but the system might only consume 3 GB. It is recommended to make an educated guess here. But try to stay balanced between to careful and to risky (with **4 GB** RAM allocated, **2.5 GB** is probably consumed).

8. Click **Save** to store the project data.

Once the project is save it will now appear in the **Projects** tab under the project table. As seen in the image, there are some shortcomings with resources for this project. Especially disk space is a problem. The 135 VMs consume way more data store space than currently assigned to this cluster.

Luckily, this might be an easy fix if there is still enough physical storage space available. The solution would be to add data stores to the cluster in order to make room for all this new VMs created.

However, the graph automatically shows the most constraint resource, but it is worthwhile checking also the other resources like memory or CPU to see how they fit into the current environment. CPU or memory issues are much more difficult to solve, since that literally means that hosts either need to be added to a cluster, or their memory or CPUs need to be upgraded (that is very rare, typically organizations add hosts instead of upgrading them).

> In the image CPU demand is not configured. That is because CPU demand (actual Mhz or Ghz the VM needs to run) is quite impossible to predict. If values would be entered here (such as 1.5 Ghz) vROps will calculate that as fixed value the VM always needs. This can lead to a **CPU constraint** info graphic, which would only be true if all the VMs would have exactly as much CPU demand as put into the project. So this setting and model should be taken with a grain of salt.

This is a quick and easy way to identify possible constraints and react in a timely manor to resolve them. In the example the team can add disks to the cluster and give the request from the QA team a go. vRA will automatically provision the VMs on the newly available resources and all the teams are happy.

Ideally this is all completed in a very short amount of time. Given the easy modeling capabilities of vRealize Operations, such calculations can be done literally in no time.

If the project is than realized (the VMs are deployed) it is possible to set a created project from *Planned* to *Committed*. This will than affect the health, risk, and efficiency badges. Also the project can be monitored if the forecast and the actual resource demand possibly match.

Reports in vRealize Operations Manager

Besides the projects to help pro-actively plan for capacity, there is also a reports functionality, which will create custom reports and send them as PDF or CSV attachment via e-mail. There are a couple of preset reports in vROps, but it is also possible to create custom reports to contain exactly the amount of information required to be relevant for the receiver.

Reports customization includes an organizational branding and logos. The most common use case is to send those to the head of operations or even to the CIO level to provide some level of insight into the data center.

They are especially nice if the capacity planning team is not able to access vROps on a regularly base. Reports can be scheduled on a regular basis (daily, weekly, monthly, and so on).

Defining a report is quite simple:

1. Open vRealize Operations Manager web UI in your browser by.
2. In the home screen click on **Content** (icon looks like a little notebook) in the left-hand pane.
3. Click on **Reports**.
4. Click on the *plus* sign under **Report Templates**.
5. Provide a meaningful name to the report.
6. Click on **Views** and **Dashboards** to configure the content of the report.
7. Brows for required Views or add even content from a dashboard into the report.
8. Make sure CSV and PDF is selected under **Formats**.
9. Once the composing is completed, click on **Save**.
10. Now the new report can be run and than inspected in vROps.

Once the custom created report is available, it will show up in the **Report Templates** table.

In order to run the report instantly, click the *Run Template* icon at that top of the reports table (it has a little *green play* icon). Once the report was executed successfully it can be accessed by clicking on **Generated reports (1)**.

At this overview the report will be selectable to download in PDF or CSV format.

Reports can also be scheduled repeated execution. While still in the reports screen (**Content**) do the following:

1. Select the desired report to schedule.
2. Click the little *gear* icon at the top of the reports table and select **Schedule report...** from the drop down menu.
3. In the **Select an Object** screen, select the object the report should run on (for example, a SDDC cluster) and click **Next** to continue.
4. In the **Define Schedule** window, select the preferred weekday, recurrence, time and time zone.
5. At the **Publishing** area, make sure to enter a correct e-mail address to send the report to (or mailing list).

> In order to send an e-mail, vROps has to be configured to use an external web server.

6. Click **Finish** and the report is scheduled for execution.

Views in vRealize Operations Manager

Views are not only available to be put into reports they can also be shown in dashboards. Dashboards are a quick way to display all relevant metrics for a certain topic. Also, they can display a mix of available metrics and data. However, his metrics data to display needs to be available as a View.

Views are the smaller building blocks of vROps information display. As described earlier they can be put into a report like little modules to display desired information. vROps comes with a number of precreated views but there is also the possibility to create custom views on resources, yet not already present.

Designing a custom view is as simple as creating a custom report:

1. In the **Content** screen click **Views**.
2. Click on the *plus* sign in the views table to add a view.
3. Provide a meaningful name to the view.
4. Click on **Presentation** at the bottom of the wizard and select a form of presentation for the view, for example, **Trend**.
5. Click on **Subjects** to continue. Pick an object to get metrics from, for example, **Cluster Compute Resource**.
6. Click on **Data** to select the data to be included. It shows a list of all vROps metrics. For example, **Disk Space Effective Demand %** and **Disk Space Capacity Remaining %**. Make sure that these are not already existent in a preset view.
7. Click on **Visibility** to configure where the view can be used. If desired, it can be added to further analysis to influence the displayed sections.
8. To finish the configuration click on **Save**.

This new View can now be used in dashboards and reports. There is always a possibility to reedit the view if the data is not shown as intended.

Views do add a lot of flexibility to vRealize Operations. Basically they can be seen as Lego bricks adding custom capabilities to fit every organizations needs. Especially when it comes to capacity management, some of this data is not existent in the precreated views. This is a nice way to add this data and even create own reports or capacity dashboards to display these metrics.

Summary

This chapter described capacity management in the SDDC. It was talking about useful techniques to stay on top of the unpredictable nature of the SDDC demand. It also discussed some resource management basics, which are necessary to gain a better understanding of vRealize Operations Manger displayed graphics. Finally it discussed some pro-active tasks like capacity planning. The last section discussed how to use reports and views in order to create custom data providers. Also scheduling aspects of reports where discussed in order to ensure that data can be proactively sent to a capacity management team.

In the next chapter, the focus will be on troubleshooting and monitoring of the SDDC. It will introduce concepts based on best practices and experience to avoid worst-case scenarios. Also it will discuss vRealize Operations from an analytics standpoint to detect anomalies and report those. Furthermore the use of actions attached to alarms is discussed. Finally it will also discuss the importance of a central log management system, in order to be able to quickly identify problems across the boundaries of multiple hardware and software systems. It will show how to configure vRealize Log Insight and provides practical examples on log analysis and dashboards.

11
Troubleshooting and Monitoring

This chapter will discuss troubleshooting and monitoring techniques in an SDDC environment. First, it is important to note that the SDDC itself is a complex environment, which hides this complexity from the user. This is done through a user portal with yet easy-to-request services. Although this is perfect for the end user, it can become quickly very difficult to troubleshoot for operators or administrators. An SDDC is more than just the VMware components such as the portal, the hypervisors, and the virtual networking. It is also using the orchestrator for third-party integration to external tools. A powerful and yet easy-to-consume monitoring needs to be in place for all of these processes and triggers.

If a service deployment is failing, it is important to quickly identify the root cause to fix it. The best case is that it can be found with the error message the deployment generates. The worst case requires a monitoring system that is able to correlate actions to identify a single thread of logs per deployment. That sounds very complex, but this chapter will show how all of this is possible in the SDDC.

Besides monitoring the deployment process of services, it is also important to monitor the health of the deployed systems as well. This creates new challenges for a legacy monitoring system since the use case f the requested service or VM is unknown. This means the monitoring system needs to understand how the deployed server operates in order to detect any failure or problem. A simple threshold-based monitoring system will not be able to deliver this functionality. In fact, the monitoring system itself has to have some intelligence in order to understand the service behavior and when the service is actually failing. This sounds like fiction for server monitoring, but it is the operational truth for the SDDC. The monitoring needs to be as agile and flexible as the platform itself. Yet, the log information management and log handling needs to be lossless. Also, it needs to gather all messages from all used systems in the entire SDDC even if those systems are external to the core SDDC applications. Such systems are **IP Address Management (IPAM)**, **Configuration Management Database (CMDB)**, application installation service, and so on.

Everything that is part of the deployment or life cycle process in an SDDC needs to be monitored. All this information needs to be searchable and process able in a quick and easy way in order to find possible problems before they impact the production environment. All this will be covered in this chapter including the following points:

- Monitoring concepts for the SDDC
- Advanced analytics and monitoring
- Message logging and the recommended log configuration
- Log analysis and why it is important
- Feedback monitoring data to vRealize automation
- Troubleshooting examples in the SDDC
- SDDC self-healing capabilities

Monitoring and analytics in the SDDC

As discussed at the beginning of this chapter, the SDDC introduces some challenges, which cannot be easily overcome with traditional monitoring systems. This becomes clear if one looks at the traditional versus the SDDC way of deploying services and workloads.

In the traditional data center, workloads are often deployed in form of projects. They have a distinct function (web server, application server, database, and so on) as well as foreseeable workload profile. Based on this, the monitoring admin can set a set of thresholds to make sure that the workload is working within its expected range. Normally, these thresholds are CPU usage, memory usage, swapping, disk space, and so on.

A monitoring system is aware of the new server and is associating all these thresholds to the server. If one of these values are violated, it will send a warning or an alarm to the monitoring team or the administrator. This has been used for years in the data center and is a well-known and proven practice.

However, over the past years, the data center complexity has been increased and also the use case of servers is not as clear anymore as before. This trend has been introduced by virtualization. Creating a VM is so easy, it may is not attached to a project anymore. Maybe a developer just realized that one additional VM is needed for testing their code. The creation is quick and easy and all the infrastructure team needs to know is the CPU count, the memory, and the disk size. Given all that flexibility, it is difficult to model each and every VM in a monitoring system, so the systems started to apply default values to the services. Now, the monitoring was not adjusted to the server workload anymore, it was more created with a *one fits all* idea in the background. Examples for these default thresholds are:

- 80% CPU usage = Warning, 90% = Alert
- 80% memory usage = Alert
- 85% disk usage = Warning, 95% = Alert
- 80% net usage = Warning, 95% = Alert

This is an easy profile to apply to all VMs, but it is also one that may create a lot of false positives in an environment.

The risk of false positives

There are two worst-case scenarios when it comes to monitoring a system:

- Not picking up an error leading to an outage
- Reporting a lot of false positives

The first problem can be addressed by having an autodiscovery across all systems in a data center to ensure that all are registered with the monitoring server. Furthermore, it can be handled by applying a default profile (thresholds) to all these systems.

The second problem is somewhat more complex to address and is definitely as dangerous as missing a real outage. False positives are actually monitoring alarms or warnings, which got triggered, but there isn't actually an issue with the VM. An example for this could be, an application server is running at 95% CPU speed, which triggers the CPU alert. But actually, it is required that the application server runs at this speed in order to fulfill its task successfully. A default monitoring profile might report the CPU as critical to an admin. If the profile is not changed this might happen time and time again. These false alarms might lead to an *ignore* behavior of the monitoring admin and a real issue can actually be missed.

Since there might be a couple of hundred (or even thousand) systems in the data center, these false positive alarms can also be a couple of hundreds per day. In all this false alarm noise, an actual alarm might not be seen and therefore may lead to a major outage in the production environment. To fix this noise problem, alarms based on wrong or to low thresholds can be handled by the monitoring admin. If they see that happen frequently, they can adopt the threshold to only report on higher, for example, CPU loads and the problem seems solved.

The silent false positives are far more dangerous and are also quite impossible for the monitoring admin to detect. Imagine that all services are reported as good (green) implying every service seems to be OK. Would anybody say: Hey, that looks odd, let's check the actual condition of all this green services. No, since that is what monitoring stands for. If all is good, all is green. If something is wrong, it turns yellow or red.

This is the other dilemma of false positives, they can also happen silently. Given this, a faulty service might be reported as green. Imagine that the application server suddenly drops to 1% CPU usage. The monitoring system will interpret this as *good* based on the fact that CPU usage is way below 95%. However, the application server might be in deep trouble since it actually stopped working. Maybe the web server is down or not getting any requests, or the software in the application server has crashed. However, all this will be unseen by the monitoring team since the false positive will report it as green.

This is possibly the most dangerous condition since it will automatically lead to the first worst-case scenario: a missed error condition, possibly leading to a production outage.

So in the SDDC, it should be a priority for any monitoring system to prevent false positives. Not only to keep the service quality high, but also to keep and increase the trust users have in the platform. Therefore, a different breed of monitoring system is required, an intelligent one, which is able to learn and understand the default behavior of a workflow. Also, it would be important to find relations between workloads and also different infrastructure types. This ability could help in quickly identifying noisy neighbor issues or other possible side effects.

Management versus payload monitoring

In every automated data center, there are two kinds of monitoring necessary. Management monitoring is ensuring that the cloud suite of systems is running and that no issues are impacting any user. This kind of monitoring may be done by the team running the cloud infrastructure and may be part of their operational procedures.

Payload monitoring is taking place after a service has been deployed and is more around performance and general health topics. Typically, users expect that they can also get an easy report on the health of their deployed services. These services bring different requirements and need to be processed differently. Also, normally the workload is unknown before deployment. This means that it is hard to predict any useful warning or alarm thresholds.

Management monitoring

However, this kind of monitoring needs far more than looking at CPU or memory thresholds. It has to monitor each task or process in the system to ensure that everything works seamlessly together. If there is a hanging task blocking a deployment, it is important to quickly find and resolve the root cause. These are tough requirements to any monitoring systems in the industry. Since there are so many moving pieces in the SDDC, it is the mission of the monitoring tool to keep the overview of all of these elements. In order to do this, actually several systems are required. Not only a dynamic monitoring system but also a very powerful log management and analytics engine is required to handle this task well.

> It is important to highlight that the workloads in the payload cluster will have different monitoring requirements than the SDDC components. In the SDDC, it is key to track all processes and detect any glitches. For the payload, it is important to identify the behavior and report if it changes drastically.

When the SDDC is built and designed, it is necessary to also design the monitoring settings with it. This means that all components in the SDDC should be able to report to a central monitoring system, which can detect and analyze the data efficiently. Furthermore, specific conditions such as workflow monitoring or the third-party integration might be set as well. In this case, the services, servers, and processes are well-known and also their function should be known by the monitoring team in order to supervise them.

So, besides the planning for the services, the creation of the approvals or the implementation of the third-party software, the configuration of the monitoring system is equally important. Therefore, an SDDC design should also always contain a monitoring design.

> It is very important to implement this thoughtfully and in every detail. Detecting errors in an SDDC, tightly integrated in the data center might be a lengthy and cumbersome process. Unfortunately, there is one resource, which is never available during an issue, which is time.

First and foremost all the management systems in an SDDC should be configured to send all their data to the monitoring or log management system. This includes also all the physical devices such as network switches, rack servers/blades, chassis, storage systems, and FC switches, practically, every hardware component the SDDC is using.

Besides the physical resources, also all the virtual resources need to be configured to send their log and monitoring data. This list includes the following:

- All vSphere hosts (ESXi)
- Syslog target
- vCenter /VCSA
- OS logs and tasks
- vRealize Automation
- DEM workers, IaaS server, agents, and so on
- vRealize Orchestrator
- Including workload and system logs, workload debugs, and running states
- NSX
- SysLog forward, messages, and so on
- All included third-party software (IPAM, CMDB, and so on)

It is important to ensure that all parts of the SDDC are consistently and entirely monitored. If one system is not part of this monitoring, it may make a quick error analysis impossible.

Here is an example why it is so important to have all this in place for the management environment:

A user tries to log on to the portal and gets the error message **An error occurred: 12005 – contact your administrator**. Now, the admin team needs to find out what error 12005 might actually be? They put in the error number and the corresponding log on time of the user in the preconfigured log management system to search all logs at this date from all systems in the SDDC.

After the search came back they found that there is a correlating error message in the log indicating that the load balancer for the vRA portal is not coming back correctly. Another colleague logs on the load balancer and affirms that it is not working as it should.

It turns out that they need to reconfigure the load balancer and reboot the two vRA IaaS web servers. After this has been completed, the error disappeared and the user can log in again.

The whole analysis took less than 10 minutes and the fix took another 10 minutes. So from a bad log in to a fully running system in only 20 minutes.

All this would be impossible if the log from the load balancer or the IaaS messages wouldn't be easily searchable. In an SDDC environment, no admin can afford to log on to different systems to look through log files. This method can't scale, and it is also quite impossible to correlate the different log files to an event at a given time. It is possible, but not in a short amount of time.

Payload monitoring

Surveillance of random, dynamic payload services is a different task to accomplish for a classic monitoring system. As described earlier, a classic monitoring system requires quite a good understanding of the application from the monitoring admin. In the SDDC, the owner might not tell the monitoring admin what exactly is installed on a requested VM. It can be a web server, it can be a MySQL DB, or even a container framework. The fact is, the team monitoring the SDDC might not know what the deployed VMs are being used for.

Besides this fact, the payload monitoring is mostly about performance and resiliency. A service requestor will defiantly sleep better if they can look at the status of their server at any given time. Not to check for an outage, but to check the performance of the service and if it is still acceptable. Besides that, the system should be able to foresee unforeseeable issues, such as a VM file system running full. Ideally, everything works without ever touching a single VM. Since the SDDC is all about automation, new services need to be registered automatically with the monitoring system.

> This is clearly proving the challenges of older monitoring systems. A simple threshold setting will lead to false positives or to missed issues and problems. Therefore, it is recommended to use a smart monitoring system, which supports these requirements.

However, payload monitoring can also get complex without the SDDC. There are different techniques to monitor different services. A DB server might require an agent which is able to look into the database and check if all seems valid and working. Same is for a mailserver or other special application servers. It is important to distinguish application monitoring from infrastructure monitoring.

Application monitoring will often require a deep view into the installed service. There are special agents which could monitor how java works on the OS or what processes are running or if a distinct process is still alive. Obviously, these monitoring features will require an OS agent to be installed. This could be done by preparing the blueprint image so that the agent is always deployed. However, it is important that the used monitoring system does support such a pre-installed agent.

> Some monitoring systems require to register the agent with a unique ID. If the agent is pre-installed on the blueprint, this ID might be the same for all deployed services. In such a case it is recommended to install the agent as a post-deployment action, wheter using a software deployment tool or vRA Application Automation.

Also, these things might be tricky to set as thresholds, therefore they require also an intelligent way to recognize errors or at least abnormal behavior of the software.

Payload monitoring becomes quite complex if a service consists out of multiple different applications. The service might be a company's webpage, but the different applications can be web servers, application serversn and DB servers. The whole service might not suffer much if one of the web server or application servers cut out, but if the DB is not reachable, the external website might not work properly anymore. Obviously, this kind of monitoring needs always an understanding for the service and what systems work with each other. It is quite complex to model in a traditional monitoring system, but could still be done if this monitoring system would let an admin set KPIs instead of thresholds.

KPIs versus thresholds

Most applications in a data center are part of a bigger system. This system normally is a service that delivers specific functions to end users. This can be a website, a mail server, an active directory, a content resource management system or any other business relevant service.

Most often monitoring in IT refers to the infrastructure (health, resiliency, performance, and so on). Sometimes, it includes the applications (processes, running services/daemons, responding to queries, and so on). By doing this, typically thresholds are used to qualify the response to then form a simple traffic light indicator (green/yellow/red).

However, this is very hard to be done for an entire service. If multiple servers and applications form a service, when and how is the service affected by a server or application outage? This is a question that can't easily be answered by adding thresholds to all service-relevant instances.

To understand the impact, the issue type as well as the system where the issue occurs might be relevant.

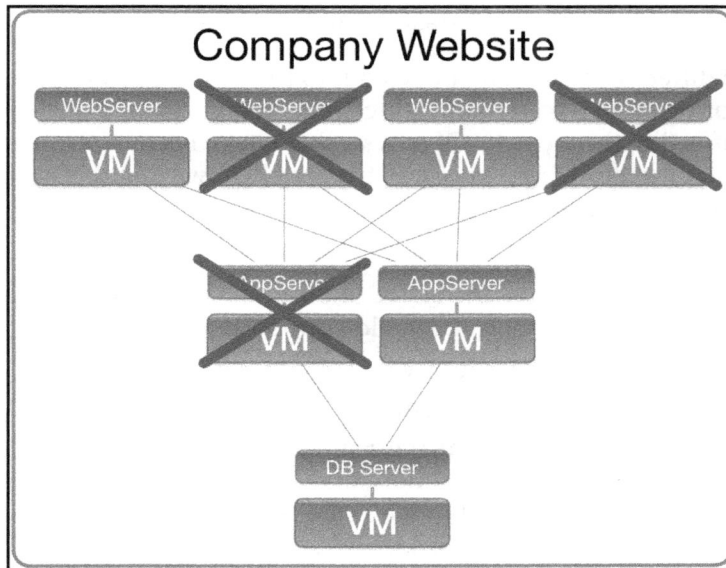

The scenario shown in the preceding image shows a simplified version of a company website service. One of the application servers and two of the web servers are down.

- Should IT be worried if the web service still works?
- Is this already a worst case scenario and the service is not functioning properly anymore?

These simple questions are quite complex to answer. The answer can only be given if the **Key Performance Indicator** (**KPI**) of this service is known. KPIs can be different things and are also often used by the business to describe a performance of a product (sell ability, and so on). However, KPIs become more and more important for monitoring systems as well.

Now, to model the KPI for the web server, it is important to understand what its sole purpose is. In this case, it is quite simple, that is, displaying the company's website. So the KPI for this particular service could be the query response time of the website.

One might think-So how is that different to a threshold? Well, a threshold is a single filter value set on a metric. A KPI is a baseline indicator for a healthy service based on various different factors. In this case, the KPI is not only based on the health of all the infrastructure services, it includes also the network infrastructure as well as other factors.

Given that all this different factors are modeled into the KPI, the IT department (with the help of the monitoring system) can finally judge if an outage like the one described in the picture before is affecting the website. Of course, the outage needs to be fixed, but if ever one has been in a data center when *red alert* is triggered knows that this is one of the worst working conditions. So, the KPI helps to trigger the right alarm and reports the true risk easier to any stakeholder.

Therefore, the monitoring system of the SDDC should also be capable of digesting KPIs or multiple systems monitoring; in short, it should support service monitoring.

> Despite the fact that vROps does support KPIs for services, it is not replacing an ITSM tool, which will perform full **service-level agreement (SLA)** or **service-level management (SLM)** checks. These can be much more complex and include more than "just" the technical aspects. So, ITSM tools will be still relevant in the SDDC when it comes to SLA and SLM checks for the deployed workload.

vRealize Operations Manager

In the VMware suite of products necessary for a Software Defined Data Center, these tools are actually a must. vRealize Operations is covered in `Chapter 10`, *Capacity Management with vRealize Operations* when it came to capacity monitoring. But actually, it can deliver so much more including performance analytic, anomaly detection as well as relational mapping of items. It is also capable of modeling KPIs, and it creates super metrics (metrics consistent out of many others to deliver a single baseline) To complete the set of supporting tools, vRealize Log Insight for log management and analytics makes a perfect add-on to the monitoring toolset. It can handle a very high amount of logs and make them searchable in a quick and easy way. It features the creation of custom log dashboards as well as nice precreated vendor adapters.

Analytics using vRealize Operations Manager

Even though this entire chapter is about monitoring, vRealize Operations Manager is actually a brilliant analytics tool. Besides classical monitoring elements, it makes the analysis of an issue very easy. In fact, it can even understand simple issues and propose a resolution automatically. Before we dive into the world of analytics, metrics, and monitoring AI, it might be good to understand how vRealize Operations Manager is working.

Exploring vRealize Operations Manager anomalies

vROps does report on so-called anomalies. These reflect any behavioral change of a monitored asset. To understand that the new metrics are different than the old measured data, it uses powerful algorithms to build a standard behavior. This standard behavior is displayed as light gray area in metrics graphs.

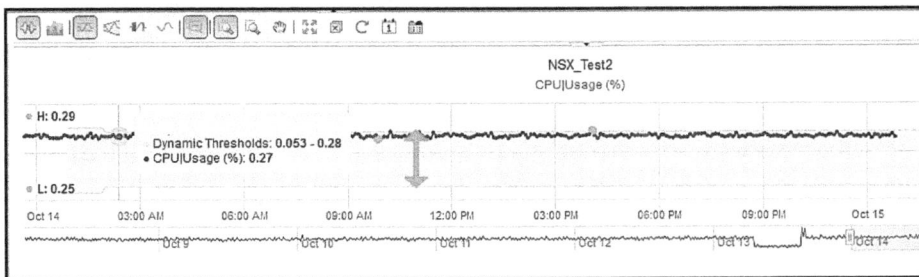

The picture shows a graph where vROps has been able to define a default behavior. In this case, it is the CPU usage in percentage.

The learned behavior is displayed in the graph as light gray area, everything which stays in this area is seen as *normal*. Additionally, there is a box explaining what the learned defaults are. The double-ended arrow has been edited in the picture to mark that area.

Any change of the CPU usage higher or lower than this area is seen as an anomaly. These anomalies can be also seen in the graph in form of little orange dots. Each dot marks a point in time when the learned default behavior was violated by a CPU metrics spike.

An anomaly does not always mean there is an error, but it means that something forced the service to change the learned behavior. Since vROps can't know if this change is good or bad, it is reporting it as an anomaly. However, not every single anomaly gets reported, since that might again lead to monitoring noise and possible ignorance by the admins.

Each day a service runs in a data center might be slightly different. Much like not every day is the same in the office, a data center will have some variance. Maybe there is more traffic on the network, maybe tests are influencing the storage performance. Fact is, a VM cannot behave exactly the same each and every day. vROps does take that into account and is using its own algorithms to measure its own created anomalies count per service. It can be seen by looking at the **Self – Total Anomalies** graph from the monitored object.

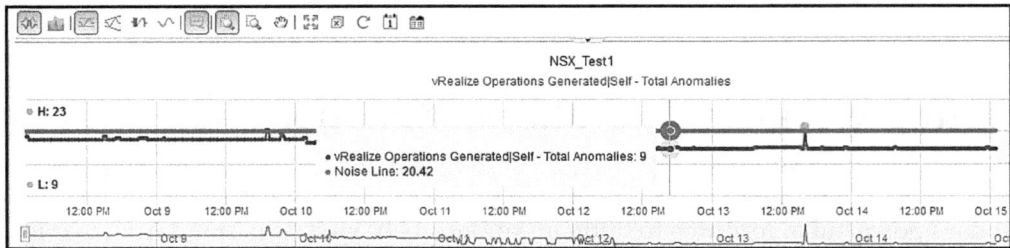

Now this graph has a red top line, which is called noise line. This noise line is calculated by vROps and marks the maximum number of anomalies before they get reported. The noise line is specific to each and every monitored asset. If it is very dynamic, the noise line might be higher. If it is more or less static, it will be lower like in this example.

This is a very smart way of preventing false positives. The noise line can be seen as a barrier to prevent random alerting whenever something is different than the day before. Also, if a systems behavior is changing on purpose and this change is permanent, vROps can learn that as well and takes it automatically into account. It will immediately report the anomaly and the changed state of the service. If the system keeps its new behavior, it eventually will be learned again as the new baseline behavior.

This system could be seen as if vROps sets automatically KPIs for its monitored entities. And in many ways that is true, albeit a manual set KPI should always reflect a business relevance. In the case of the website, this is the responsiveness that is directly affecting how the organization is seen by the audience visiting the website. If one visits a website of a company and the experience is all slow, whacky, and unpleasant, the company might have been perceived by this person in the same way. Therefore, the responsiveness of a company's website might have a direct relation to the overall business.

However, in many ways, anomalies in vROps are treated like KPIs. They share the following same principles:

- Many factors are reduced to one baseline
- Not every metric change affects the overall baseline
- If the overall baseline is affected, there is probably something going wrong

The algorithm to detect the behavior is very powerful and can also handle more complex situations. In fact, vROps uses seven different arithmetic formulas to learn the behavior of a system. The eighth one is used to benchmark the best-calculated behavior from the other seven operations.

An example how all this works might be a paycheck system, which needs 90% of its CPU resources every end of the month, but the other 3 weeks of the month it needs less than 10% of its CPU resources.

Over time, vROps will learn that this behavior is always repeated. Therefore, it becomes the expected behavior of this system. If this pattern somehow changes, vROps will detect an anomaly. Let's assume that it is the fourth week of the month and the CPU is still only 10% used. In this case, vROps will detect an anomaly and will notify the system administrators. In fact, this change might affect the system in many ways so that more and more anomalies get detected, and vROPs then eventually trigger an alert to report the diminished health of the monitored service.

This is one of the many useful functions of vROps, which helps to monitor an unknown environment. If the anomaly count rises higher than the noise line, vROps will display the health of the service as degraded. The logic behind this is that even if it is a very dynamic system, if the anomalies rise to a certain level vROPs assumes that something might has gone wrong and degrades the health score automatically.

Badges and what they describe

The Badges of vROps are briefly described in Chapter 10, *Capacity Management with vRealize Operations* of this book. In this description, their purposes were solely broken down from a capacity perspective. From a monitoring and performance perspective, these badges are important as well; which is why, this chapter features a more detailed description of what they are and how to read them.

As discussed earlier, vROps creates three badges, which are always present at the summary page of any selected object. **Health** is probably the most interesting one from a performance and resiliency perspective, followed from **Risk** and then finally **Efficiency**. Chapter 10, *Capacity Management with vRealize Operations* has covered efficiency to quite an extent already.

The Health badge and how to read it

The intention of this badge is to give a quick and relevant overview of the selected objects' health score. This score is calculated not only from the number of anomalies but also from eventual alerts and warnings occurred so far. It summarizes many metrics to one single badge and will only show a color indicator. The value when the color actually changes is user stable and is stored in the applied vROps policy.

As described earlier, this indicator tries to display in a smart way the health of an object by analyzing more than only thresholds and infrastructure metrics. If the badge is green that means that nothing suspicious is happening based on the learned behavior pattern of the selected object.

If the badge turns yellow, vROps might has detected anomalies crossing the noise line or other events affecting the overall health of the object. These other events can also be indicators known from traditional monitoring like filesystem space. For VMs, vROps can read these values automatically and without the installation of an agent. It will warn the user that the guest file system might run out of space shortly.

If the badge turns red, some serious issues might affect the selected objects. It is clear that the anomalies are way higher than the noise line. Also, maybe other factors may affect the overall behavior of the object in one or the other way. Such conditions can happen if there is a noisy neighbor problem occurring. A noisy neighbor describes a VM that is using its resources so heavy that other siblings (VMs on the same layer / data store, host, and so on) are negatively affected (by its noise).

This often affects storage since some VMs tend to issue thousands of IOs, which leaves others no room for their execution. This can affect the health of all siblings as well as the health of the noisy VM itself. In this case, vROps can not only report the health and the most likely use case of the problem, it will also identify all VMs involved and even correlate the data store. So more than one object's health badge will be affected. It will show all the VMs as affected plus the data store, plus the vSphere host attached to that store. This relational mapping should help the administrator to perform quick corrective actions to resolve this issue.

All this happens without any active threshold configuration. This is what a smart monitoring and analytics tool needs to deliver in an SDDC.

The Risk badge and how to read it

Right next to the health badge, the Risk badge is shown in the summary page. Like the health indicator, its colors / state changes can be set in the vROps policy. This badge tries to look into the future and provide an indication how likely it is that issues might occur. This indication is again based on arithmetic algorithms to foresee the likely future of the object. To accomplish this task, it works with forecasts based on trends and the analyzed behavior. Although this sounds like magic in the first place, it can be explained on a simple example. If we pick up the case of the filling guest file system again, vROps will pick notice that the filesystem is filling up at a steady rate per week. Based on this, it can calculate the date when the filesystem is going to be full. If the trend continues, the risk of a full guest file system is 100% at this date. This, among other metrics, will affect the Risk badge for the VM, and it will also give an explanation how to reduce the Risk.

The Risk is an interesting parameter for capacity management AND monitoring of the system. It is maybe simple on a VM object, but becomes very powerful when used on a cluster object or even an entire data center. But beware, the more objects these badges gather together, the lesser the details will affect the score. Since a filling up VM filesystem might not affect an entire vSphere cluster at any stage.

Whenever a risk is affecting an object, vROps is calculating the score for this badge. The higher the risk, the higher the number, so the risk badge is one badge where a score of 0 is perfect and a score of 100 is worst case. Even though the badges do not show the scores anymore, for this badge the rule is, the lower the better (green).

The Efficiency badge and how to read it

This is possibly the most discussed function of vROps since it has been introduced. This badge is trying to give an overview of used resources. Instead of simply reporting which VM is using how much CPU or memory it will also give hints on improving their configuration. This is called reducing waste. A resource that is configured for a VM and stays unused is seen as *wasted*. The problem is that even though virtualization has some very smart ways of sharing resources, false configured resources will always affect the entire system. There are a lot of books discussing the importance of thoughtfully and correctly configured VMs. The efficiency badge tries to identify bad resource configurations based on the VMs usage of its resources.

An example might be a VM with four vCPUs configured and 16 GB of RAM. Based on its learning of the VM behavior, vROps might notice that three CPUs and 12 GB of RAM are never used (really never, not even all 3 weeks). The system rates the efficiency for this VM down. Of course, this is a simplified example, and there are many other factors than only disk CPU and memory usage.

Although all this sounds very logical, there are unfortunately many factors affecting a VMs configuration. Some maybe performance relevant, but others may be requirements for an installed software. Software vendors started to set requirements for OS configurations since ages; this is true for VMs too. Often these requirements are set to satisfy a wide range of performance cases. The vendors want to prevent that their software might be performing badly in stress situations. Therefore, these settings can sometimes be quite high. Even if the tool is not even touching a tenth of the set resources, they cannot be reduced since those are required to support the software.

Besides that, the behavior of *preallocating* resources have been adopted by users as well. Want to be prepared for any given situation – there might be a moment where all these resources are required and then everyone will be happy that they are available. Although vROps can display that this event might not have occurred in a year's period, there is still the possibility that it might hit the VM in the following year.

Besides these two factors, there is also a third factor that should not be under estimated, cost. If a chargeback / show back model is in place, it might also account a user or business group for used resources. If they choose to burn their money on VMs never using their resources but could just in case – so be it. This is a very common belief in the industry. The user pays for it, so why change it.

Well, the problem with all this is that misconfigured resources are not only a waste of resources and money, but they can also affect the overall system performance. The vSphere hypervisor has to deal with all these configurations in the best possible way. The memory scheduler needs to decide which VM might get access to shared memory from another VM. The CPU scheduler needs to place all vCPUs of a VM perfectly on one NUMA node (if possible). Things like relaxed co-stopping might not save the scheduler always from doing this for all allocated vCPUs for a VM, no matter if only one of them is used.

In the physical world, there is a simple rule of thumb for resources-Add more, get more. Unfortunately, in the virtual world, this could lead to-Add more, get less. Because of all these implications and problems, introduced by the resource waste. This is why vROps tries to limit these configurations to a necessary minimum. It acts to the principle-as less as possible, as much as needed. The Admin team needs to reconfigure the pointed out VMs and decide if these wasted resource can be of a better use for other services in the data center.

This is why, the efficiency badge is always discussed and sometimes ignored. However, try to act as smart as possible with the provided information. In the end, it might lead to a win-win situation.

> Even with the budget example, there might be a win-win. If resources are freed up, more VMs can be deployed, resources are used more efficiently, which leads to a higher VM density that will increase VM payments. For organizations where the cost has only a show back function, this might mean that they can run even more services with the same budget.

The badge itself will reveal its findings by showing a list of resources affected, including some examples how to reconfigure them. It tries to be as intelligent as possible with these recommendations based on the actual resource demand of the monitored service.

Service health information in vRealize Automation

If a user requests a service in the SDDC, it might be beneficial for the user to see if the deployed resource is healthy. Besides the technical benefit, it also has a psychological effect.

The user gets a status right next to the options for that service.

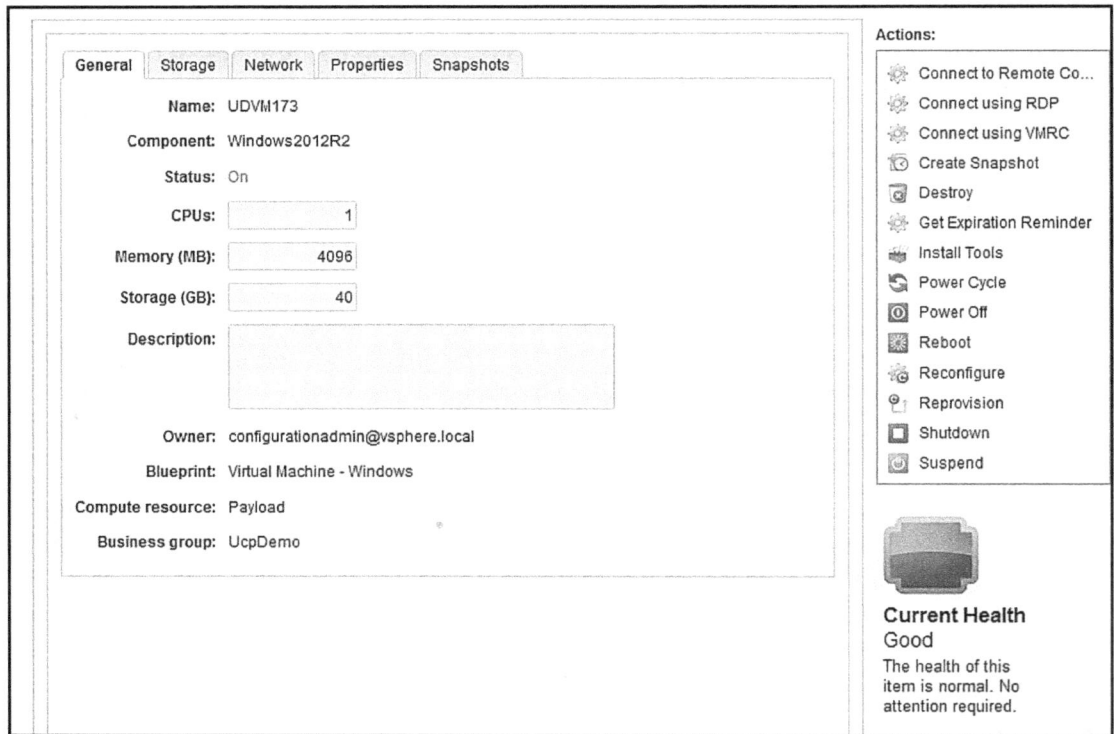

To provide this service, vRA can connect to vROps as a metrics provider. This needs to be configured in vRA using the following steps:

1. Log on to vRealize automation with the system administrator role.
2. Select the **Administration** tab.
3. Select the **Reclamation** menu at the left-hand side.
4. Select the **Metrics Provider** menu at the left-hand side as a metrics provider.
5. Click on **vRealize Operations Manager** endpoint.
6. Provide the credential to vROps. The user does only need to have read-only privileges. It is recommended to create a separate user for this action.
7. Click on **Save** to store this configuration.

From now on, all VMs deployed will display the SDDC health badge in the VMs overview page. The badge will not show any numbers, it will only be green, yellow, or red.

The other use case of this setting is to identify underutilized machines in a tenant and send reclamation requests to the users. This can be done by the vRealize automation tenant admin. The function can be found in the **Reclamation** menu under **Tenant Machines**. In this view, vRA will get a list of machines from vROps where resources can be reclaimed.

Log management in the SDDC

Although vROps is a perfect tool to analyze and monitor any workload, it has its limits. By default, it is not configured as a log receiver or a syslog server of any type. As described earlier, logs are an important part for troubleshooting and root cause analysis. Not only for the core components but also for all the sub asks and workloads required by the SDDC to run smoothly. Many companies do have already syslog servers running since they have been around for years. The typical syslog server is a global target for all other servers to send their logs to. The reason to do this is to speed up the process of analyzing an error since the admin does not have to connect to each affected system to see its logs.

Millions of log entries

Although this sounds great in theory, the reality is somewhat different. Systems can create a huge amount of logs per day. Multiple systems logging to one single server will quickly produce millions or even billions of logged events. For the poor admin, it is literally impossible to look through all these events in order to make sense of the code. Additionally, maybe it is more than one system the admin needs to look through in order to make sense out of the logs. Maybe it is 10 system logs the admin needs to work through and search for events happened at a specific point in time.

All this is quite difficult to be achieved with a standard syslog server, whose sole purpose is often just to store the logs instead of making them easily searchable. Also, log content comes in various different forms and formats for the human being. Mind that it is quite difficult to quickly adjust to different log formats and correlate them to other logs from the same period of time.

This is an example of an error in the SDDC and how it might be tracked using a traditional syslog server:

A VM deployment fails at a specific state, the VM is created in vCenter and also the OS seems to be able to start, but then the deployment stops and the VM gets deleted by vRA.

> Deleting a VM if one or more deployment steps fail is the default behavior of vRA. A function like this makes sure that if something has gone wrong, no leftovers keep space on the system.

All information the SDDC administer has is the time of the deployment and an error message by the system saying: **Could not finish deploying resource, contact your system administrator**.

Now, the SDDC is sending all logs to a central syslog server. The admin tries to read through the logs of this specific point in time. However, albeit all Linux systems send their logs to this server, the windows systems do not. So he has to examine the logs from the windows components of the SDDC (DEM, IaaS server, and so on) separately.

Since their cloud environment is quite large and they are doing around 5-10 deployments per hour there is also a lot of *noise* in the logs from all other deployments.

In order to analyze the error, the admin might have to read through 200 MB of log data. That are more or less 3.2 million characters to read through and look for the error. Not to mention the extra effort to go into the Windows VMs and read through their events as well. If the admin can read superfast (around 250 words per minutes), it might still take more than 34 hours to read through all that logs.

This shows that traditional log viewing and reading in a cloud environment does not scale. The admin needs a system to support him in looking through all that logs and searching for the right entries. Otherwise, a troubleshooting or root cause analysis may take several days if not weeks to complete.

Given that the SDDC is all about performance, agility, and efficiency, such a troubleshooting should not take longer than a couple of hours or a day. But how can that be achieved given all this challenges and the huge amount of logs?

Log management from the big data perspective

Currently, a lot of IT talk blogs and articles are around big data. Typically, the examples for big data are around personalized advertisement. They might pick up the kind of goods a customer buys and based on that an algorithm tries to calculate what this particular customer might be interested in additionally.

Also, everybody who is using Amazon knows the feature where the online store suggests other things one might be interested in. Or, things other buyers of the current article bought as well. All these functions are based on massive amounts of data, simplified and then calculated to provide these suggestions for the end user.

Given the challenges in an SDDC, log collection is also producing massive amounts of data. Although here the data analyst speaks of structured data since log files follow a similar scheme: **Time / Date** | **Machine** | **Severity** | **Message**.

There is always some delimiter between these sections, and there is always a time and a date stamp in each message. The other fields may vary, but the most logs are similar in the way they are displayed.

The following examples show different logs from different systems within an SDDC:

```
Oct 21 00:33:05 vro vco: c1416a88-1b18-4aaa-ae59-3e8ac27ac5f0 prio:INFO
thread:WorkflowExecutorPool-Thread-36 context:
token:4028e58a55a0a3bf0157e424d2be1eed anctoken: wf:Auto_CleanUp_DataStores
wfid:a88ae19f-f92a-4f9d-993b-e8650e8d0831 user: admin@demo.local
cat:WorkflowHandler msg:End of workflow 'LogTest'
(4028e58a55a0a3bf0157e424d2be1eed), state: completed
#####
The computer attempted to validate the credentials for an account.
 Authentication Package:   MICROSOFT_AUTHENTICATION_PACKAGE_V1_0
 Logon Account: VCENTER$
 Source Workstation:  VCENTER
 Error Code:    0x0Enter log examples here
```

Although humans may have difficulties to quickly be able to read different log formats from different systems, a computer mostly does not have these. This is actually the sweet spot of big data: reading through millions of bytes of data. The big data approach is mostly used for unstructured data such as e-mail, social media, all sorts of text events, and papers.

However, the same principles can be used for structured data like logs as well. Since the core use case of big data is to filter reasonable data from the noise and make it accessible to the end user. The same benefit might apply to log management in the SDDC as well: Display a specific point in time and look for a possible error in millions of lines and multiple logs. This is way the SDDC needs a log management tool with these capabilities in order to enable quick trouble shooting and root cause analysis.

vRealize Log Insight

VMware has such a tool, and it is also included in most of the vCloud Suite editions. This tool is often underestimated and can be seen as a very smart member in the VMware product family. It can be deployed in a couple of minutes, and its configuration is very easy and streamlined. In fact, all one has to do is deploy an OVF into the environment, provide a couple of gigabytes for the log storage and the tool starts working immediately.

There are plugins available for different vendors and use cases, but it can also be used without any vendor plugins at all. It is very similar to a syslog server since all systems should send their logs to log insight. But at the same time, it comes with a very powerful log search and index engine to make it possible to search through logs in seconds for specific events or occurrences.

In order to get all logs and events into this capable tool, it comes with ready-to-use Linux and Windows agents. The Linux agent is not a requirement, but comes with nice features such as customizable log locations to forward to vRLI. This is especially helpful if application-specific logs on a Linux host shall be sent to Log Insight as well.

In the Windows world, the agent is necessary to send all the Windows Events to Log Insight in order to process them as well. The agent is quite lightweight and small and can be downloaded from the deployed Log Insight instance directly. The only configuration during the installation of the agent is the hostname of the Log Insight server to send the data to.

SDDC components to add to vRealize Log Insight

Before configuring the log reports or the agents in vRLI, it is important to ensure that the right number of logs is arriving and available to analyze. In the SDDC, it is very important to make sure that all operational important components for are logging into this system. The more data is available, the more complete the troubleshooting results get. Also, do not only think about OS logs, maybe there are other logs and messages relevant as well in order to identify potential issues.

You must have VMware SDDC components forwarding logs to vRLI:

- vRealize Automation appliance syslog forwarding can be configured in the appliance admin menu. There is also a separate setting for vRLI (agent comes preinstalled by VMware).
- IaaS and DEM worker (and agents). The Agent for Windows needs to be installed in order to log in to LogInsight. There is a vRA content back available with preset agent configurations for these components as well.
- vRealize Orchestrator, like in the vRealize Automation appliance, this can be configured in the administrator portal of the orchestrator appliance (external vRO as well as integrated vRO with vRA). There is a Log Insight content pack available for vRO as well.
- NSX Manager and components (DLR, ESG, Controller, and so on) need to forward all their logs to log insight. There is an NSX content pack available as well.
- MS-SQL server holding vRA components DB the agent for Windows has to be installed on the DB host running the MS-SQL DB. There is a content pack available for MS-SQL in order to choose the right DB instance to get logs from.
- vRealize Business Appliance Syslog forwarding can be configured in the appliance admin menu. There is also a separate setting for vRLI (agent comes preinstalled by VMware).
- vRealize Operations Manager appliance Syslog forwarding is configurable in the appliance administration interface.

> Besides these complements, syslog forwarding or the Windows Agent should also be installed on all other Systems the SDDC is integrating to or interacting with. For example, if there is an external IPAM used, it is a must that logs from this systems are available in Log Insight as well. Otherwise, it cannot be detected if there might be an error in these systems since the logs may not exist.

Most of this systems forward their logs in overt to be able to detect an error or issue happening in the OS of the component. However, the vRA DEM and IaaS web server components as well as vRealize Orchestrator have more than just OS logs to offer.

Since a lot of IaaS automation runs through the vRA Windows components, it is important to also get the logs of these automation tasks into vRLI. This is very helpful if a VM deployment might fail at the vRA layer, and it is unclear what is happening. These component logs typically include communication events to vRA as well as communication to the deployed VM.

However, they also include vRA tasks such as resource collection runs and more. To have a complete overview about what is going on insight of vRA it is important to have these events as well available.

vRealize Orchestrator is also a special candidate for log monitoring. Of course, it is important to be aware of the OS of orchestrator and if everything is OK, but the status of the workflows is far more interesting than this. As described in `Chapter 6`, *vRealize Orchestrator*, vRO is a very universal tool when it comes to the integration of the SDDC into the data center environment. It can be used to instruct and automate external systems in order to maintain required processes when a service is deployed. However, this integration is crucial to the functionality of the SDDC. If an external IPAM system is required, but the workflow somehow fails to reserve and acquire an IP address, the VM cannot be deployed. In order to find out what is going wrong, the workflow output as well as the logs from the IPAM system are most helpful.

In version 7.x of vRA, VMware has a very good integration of vRO into Lot Insight. It automatically forwards the ID and output of all running workflows. This feature makes it easy for an administrator to get a holistic view over the entire orchestration system. Given this, Log Insight can be used to filter vRO workflow outputs to find a possible error during any service deployment task.

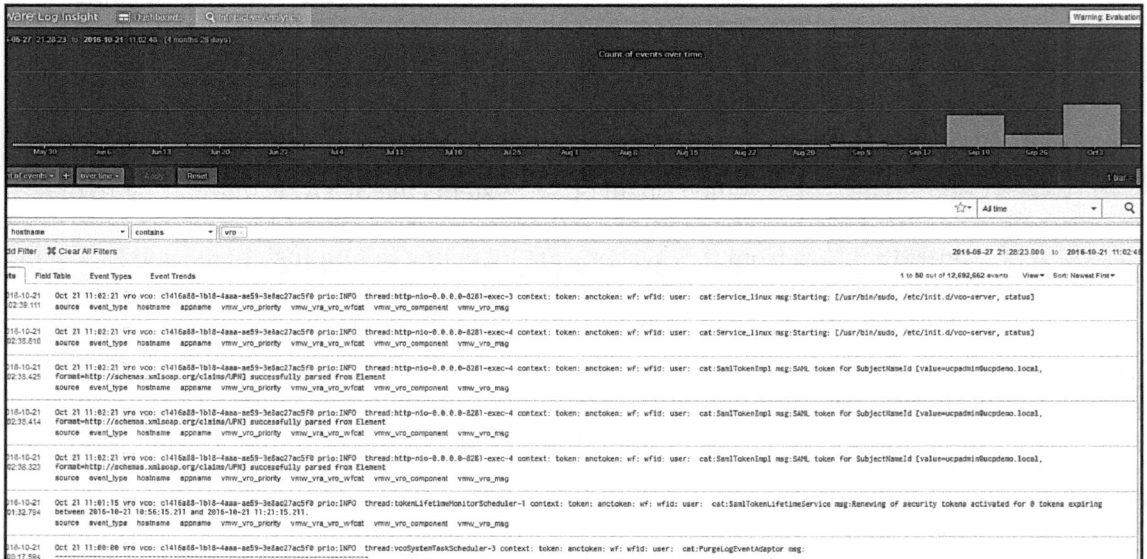

This is not only helpful for troubleshooting any SDDC problems, but it becomes a very nice feature to have if a service designer runs server all workflows to test a new deployment. Instead of checking all of their outputs in vRO, this can now also be done in vRLI. Furthermore, the designer could create a separate view to monitor exactly the workflow runs in real time while the testing is ongoing.

How to analyze logs using vRLI

Once all the log data is flowing in, it is ready to be analyzed. The tool itself can be used for two main functions: Pro-active analytics and reactive troubleshooting.

Most syslog tools are used for Reactive troubleshooting in order to identify error and why they happened. This can be due to an alert from a monitoring system or due to a reported outage. To do an analysis of log data in vRealize Log Insight, it offers the so-called Interactive Analytics View.

Using the Interactive Analytics View

This view shows all incoming logs for the selected period of time. The period can be 5 minutes all the way up to 7 days or even all time. Also, a custom period can be chosen based on a date and time. It also has a bar graphics on top to show the number of events coming in at a given point of time (per minute, 5 minutes, 20 minutes, and so on).

Using this analysis view is very similar to using a web search engine. In a sense, this is exactly what it is, a powerful search engine for your logs.

In the main search window, there are a couple of functions, which are important for quicker search results:

- Under the search bar is a button named **Add Filter**. Use this to further filter the search among specific events, hosts, messages, and so on. Note that more than one filter can be applied to a search query.
- At the right end of the search bar is the time selector. It is important to be aware of the select time frame. Sometimes, it is good to double-check this since it may only show the last 5 minutes.

The area to display the logs also has a lot to offer. It is not only showing the entries, it can be used to build an interactive analysis of logs in order to find things even quicker:

- Select text to look for and choose: Contains or Does not contain this will automatically create a new search with an applied filter on the selected text.
- Select text in a log and choose: **Extract field** This will open a dialog at the left-hand side of the window named **Fields**. Here, a name can be given as well as other parameters like a custom regular expression. Also, if the user has privileges to do so, it can be chosen to whom the field is available: **Me Only** or **All Users**.
- On the left side to each event is a little gear symbol. This allows to look for events like this (or negate it), or it can enable highlighting if the same event occurred in the search. Also, it can be used to set a time range for the shown event. The view event in context mode displays the continuous stream of logs from the source where the event came from.

```
 ➕ Add Filter
                          Show all hidden lines
    2016-10-21 11:44:24.857  [UTC:2016-10-21 09:44:20 Local:2016-10-21 11:44] [Debug]: [sub-thread-Id="14"  context
    2016-10-21 11:44:25.578  Oct 21 09:44:25 nsx 2016-10-21 09:44:25.577 GMT  INFO edgeVseMonitoringThread EdgeVse
    2016-10-21 11:44:27.173  2016-10-21T09:44:23.654Z VRA-DEM vcac: [component="iaas:DynamicOps.DEM.exe" priority="
                             ApplicationID="c4e64999-0fd7-4721-b199-47a3252c3d20" StartTime="Fri, 21 Oct 2016 09:44
    2016-10-21 11:44:27.173  2016-10-21T09:44:26.186Z VRA-DEM vcac: [component="iaas:DynamicOps.DEM.exe" priority="
                             ApplicationID="c4e64999-0fd7-4721-b199-47a3252c3d20" EndTime="Fri, 21 Oct 2016 09:44:2
    2016-10-21 11:44:27.751  [UTC:2016-10-21 09:44:26 Local:2016-10-21 11:44:26] [Trace]: [sub-thread-Id="14" cont
    2016-10-21 11:44:27.751  [UTC:2016-10-21 09:44:26 Local:2016-10-21 11:44:26] [Trace]: [sub-thread-Id="10" cont
    2016-10-21 11:44:27.751  [UTC:2016-10-21 09:44:26 Local:2016-10-21 11:44:26] [VMware.Cafe]: [sub-thread-Id="14"
    2016-10-21 11:44:27.751  [UTC:2016-10-21 09:44:27 Local:2016-10-21 11:44:27] [VMware.Cafe]: [sub-thread-Id="10"
    2016-10-21 11:44:27.751  [UTC:2016-10-21 09:44:27 Local:2016-10-21 11:44:27] [VMware.Cafe]: [sub-thread-Id="9"
                             source   component   context   event_type   filepath   hostname   product   token   vmw_cluster
    2016-10-21 11:44:27.751  [UTC:2016-10-21 09:44:27 Local:2016-10-21 11:44:27] [Trace]: [sub-thread-Id="9"  cont
    2016-10-21 11:44:27.751  [UTC:2016-10-21 09:44:27 Local:2016-10-21 11:44:27] [VMware.Cafe]: [sub-thread-Id="9"
 ⚙▾ 2016-10-21 11:44:27.751  [UTC:2016-10-21 09:44:27 Local:2016-10-21 11:44:27] [Trace]: [sub-thread-Id="9"  cont
    2016-10-21 11:44:28.686  [UTC:2016-10-21 09:44:24 Local:2016-10-21 11:44:24] [Trace]: [sub-thread-Id="6"  cont
    2016-10-21 11:44:28.686  [UTC:2016-10-21 09:44:24 Local:2016-10-21 11:44:24] [Trace]: [sub-thread-Id="6"  cont
    2016-10-21 11:44:32.402  Oct 21 11:44:31 UTILITY dhcpd: DHCPDISCOVER from 0c:c4:7a:74:b6:64 via eth0: network
    2016-10-21 11:44:32.402  Oct 21 11:44:31 UTILITY dhcpd: DHCPDISCOVER from 0c:c4:7a:74:b6:64 via eth0: network
    2016-10-21 11:44:33.407  Oct 21 11:44:32 UTILITY dhcpd: DHCPDISCOVER from 0c:c4:7a:71:5c:a0 via eth0: network
    2016-10-21 11:44:33.407  Oct 21 11:44:32 UTILITY dhcpd: DHCPDISCOVER from 0c:c4:7a:71:5c:a0 via eth0: network
    2016-10-21 11:44:35.492  Oct 21 11:44:34 UTILITY dhcpd: DHCPDISCOVER from 0c:c4:7a:74:b6:64 via eth0: network
    2016-10-21 11:44:35.492  Oct 21 11:44:34 UTILITY dhcpd: DHCPDISCOVER from 0c:c4:7a:74:b6:64 via eth0: network
    2016-10-21 11:44:36.488  Oct 21 11:44:35 UTILITY dhcpd: DHCPDISCOVER from 0c:c4:7a:71:5c:a0 via eth0: network
    2016-10-21 11:44:36.488  Oct 21 11:44:35 UTILITY dhcpd: DHCPDISCOVER from 0c:c4:7a:71:5c:a0 via eth0: network
```

Besides all that Log Insight is also extracting fields from log messages automatically and displaying them as blue links underneath each event. These fields can be extended by the earlier described extract field method. However, an algorithm from log insight is guessing field names based on log content to make the search even easier.

Fields are a very powerful function of log insight since they cannot only be seen and highlighted in the log display view, they can also be used as filters in the search bar. So whenever a new field is identified or created, it will be available as a filter to search through all the logs. This makes creating a complex search quite easy and straightforward.

Creating and using dashboards

Besides the Interactive Analytics View, vRealize Log Insight also offers dashboards. These dashboards can come from plugins, which can be downloaded and installed for various vendors for free, or they can be self-created.

To access the custom dashboards, open Log Insight and click on the **Dashboards** button at the top-left. Then, choose one entry from the **Custom Dashboards** section.

There are two types of custom dashboards: **My Dashborads** (only available for one user) and **Shared Dashboards**, which are available to other users.

Dashboards can be created out of an interactive analytics. They are based on queries of specific events and show their outcome in a graphical manner. An example for this could be looking for specific errors. The dashboard could contain a graphic about all error events.

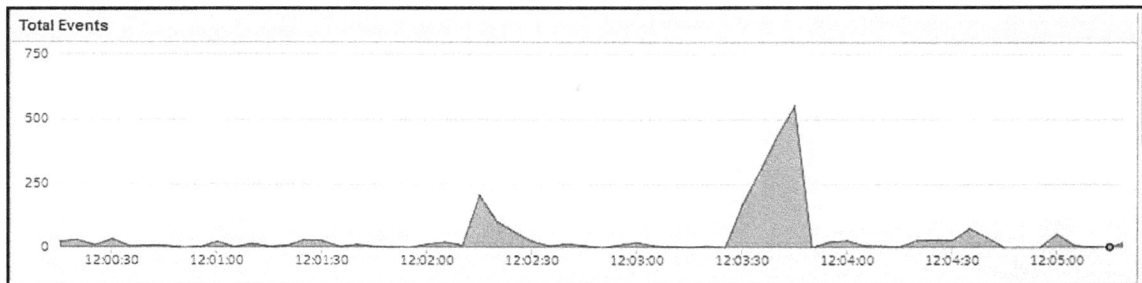

To create a dashboard in vRealize Log Insight, complete the following steps:

1. Log on to vRealize Log Insight.
2. Click on **Interactive Analysis** to get to the log search view.
3. Build the query until the desired result is displayed (add filter, search for specific outcomes, and so on).
4. Next to the search bar, click on the **Add Dashboard** button.
5. Provide a valid name and a dashboard to include the chart in.
6. Click on **Add** to save.

Once the query is available as a chart on the dashboard, it can further be edited. The look and the style of the dashboard can be changed. It can be a bar chart or an area or just a line. Also, the interactive analysis on which the chart is based can be changed any time.

The entire dashboard can be used in presentation mode. In this mode, Log Insight will automatically update the chart contents of all charts based on the selected data time range. Note that this does not work with a custom time range.

This mode can be used to put the update on a monitoring screen in an operations center to see if anything suspicious might be going on in the data center.

The pro-active analytics features

Besides the interactive analytics, Log Insight also has a pro-active component. If some events are way too important to miss them happening, it offers an alert functionality based on a created search.

1. The setup works quite similar like the dashboard creation. All a user needs to do is build the query with all filters applied. Instead of clicking on the **Add Dashboard** button, there is a **Create alert from query** button right next to it.

2. This option enables Log Insight to send out alert notifications to an e-mail account, but also to vRealize Operations Manager in order to log an anomaly. In the case of vROps alerts, the default object (where the alert should occur) can be chosen as well as the criticality.

> In order to let vRealize Log Insight, send alerts to vRealize Operations Manager, those two tools have to be connected together. This can be done in the Administration view of Log Insight under Integration. The hostname and a user for vROps are required to integrate Log Insight. With this, vROps will also be able to direct a user to a log insight query based on vROps objects.

Summary

In this chapter, the monitoring and analytics methods for the SDDC have been discussed. It was not only explained how to use the toolset from VMware, but also that there are new concepts required in order to identify issues before they harm the environment. The mission of all these concepts and tools is to limit the impact on the user. In a perfect world, there will be none, these methods and tools will support the operations teams of an SDDC to achieve this difficult goal.

The next chapter will discuss the need for continuous service improvement. A lot of procedures have been changed in order to make the SDDC run properly, but this is just the beginning. An agile and healthy SDDC is always changing; therefore, it is important to revisit changes from time to time in order to make sure that they are still relevant. This chapter will discuss how to consistently and continuously improve the service quality in order to stay relevant for the SDDC user.

12
Continuous Improvement

This chapter will discuss the continuous improvement process, which is required in order to keep the **software-defined data center** (**SDDC**) working. In Chapter 2, *Identify Automation and Standardization Opportunities* of this book, the principle of automation and standardization was discussed. Also, the business processes in an organization, which need to be adopted in order to support the different requirements of the SDDC. The required changes to make the SDDC run successfully are not static, though. They need to be as flexible and agile as the SDDC itself.

There are rumors that **Information Technology Infrastructure Library** (**ITIL**) is no longer needed in the SDDC since this is now performing all these tasks requiring documentation and control. But actually, the SDDC is an outcome of ITIL. It is the automated way of running a data center, which forces organizations to standardize and to automate as much as possible. The service catalog is what ITIL called the library and offers ready to deploy versions of applications or operating systems. The integration into the CMDB or IPAM is another common fact between ITIL and the SDDC.

Based on this, it is also a good idea to be aware of an important principle in the ITIL framework: Continual Service Improvement.

This will be captured in this chapter, including these points:

- Revisit established services
- Review automation process and service templates
- Recheck business requirements and reapply those to the solution
- Enhance service quality and delivery

Continual Service Improvement

The ITIL describes standard processes occurring in most organizations. Actually, an SDDC is a way of automating ITIL and enforce standardization and repeatable actions across the entire data center. Often ITIL is reduced to a specific toolset or action within the data center, for example, ticketing systems. But that is only a small fraction of what it does. It basically tries to provide a framework to standardize and streamline the delivery of IT services. Furthermore, it also provides options to predefine services so they can be delivered multiple times in a similar format.

Besides that, it also regulates what a change is and what the actions are in order to make changes. Data centers across the globe have made great use of these suggestions in order to streamline their IT tasks and make sure that maintenance can be predicted. Also, this kind of documented changes is necessary in order to prevent any unforeseen consequences when it comes to incorporate patches and updates.

However, before the SDDC all this had to be done with additional tools and often introduced a lot of extra work for the administrator or the operator. Tickets had to be filed and send back and forth before even the first action could be done. Also, some people thought that every suggestion in ITIL is set in stone and needs to be exactly executed as described in the framework within every data center. The idea of ITIL was never to be a bible for IT deployments. The idea was to be a collection of good practices to follow. It was intended to be a framework, not a how-to guide. That means that it holds suggestions on how things might work out, but in the end, everyone has to find out how to adopt these suggestions to their own data center and processes.

Once the SDDC is up and running and all the tools are working in perfect unison they mark the new standard. To get to this state, a lot of processes have either been adopted or complete recreated in order to enable automated service deployment. Processes, which might have been introduced long before the SDDC and have been included because there was no time to change or question them.

Continual Service Improvement is doing exactly this: asking if a certain way of doing things is still the right way to do it. While this is one of the main ITIL principles, it is one of the least used in organizations. However, it becomes very practical in an SDDC.

The graphic explains how the principle works. This model has originally been developed by W. Edwards Deming and is called *The Deming Cycle*:

- **Plan**: This is the design phase of the SDDC. But it can also be seen as the design phase for a new blueprint or service or a project phase for an enhancement.
- **Do**: This typically describes the implementation phase. Basically, this is where the design becomes reality. Either by creating an SDDC environment or by configuring a new blueprint to be deployed automatically.
- **Check**: After the implementation is completed successfully this phase is needed for quality assurance. It will prove if the design and the configuration match as well as if the intended quality target was met. Also, this phase ensures that the design solution is solving the business case as intended.
- **Act**: This is the improvement module. If any deviations are identified in the check phase, those are going to be corrected in the act phase. It is making sure that changes can be implemented into the whole process based on the other three options of this method.

This model has been introduced in order to prevent a cycle rolling back down the hill after implementation. Its acronym is CSI, which stands for a continuous improvement of the offered solution. It requires that a team is working on that schedules, but in the end, it will ensure that the SDDC runs flawlessly.

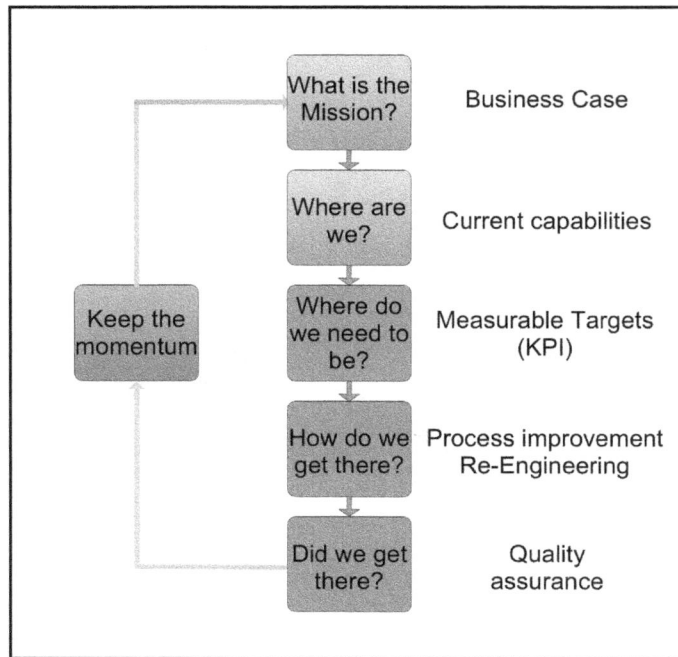

The preceding image shows the constant cycle of improvements in a service. These are the six steps:

1. The business case should always be the driver for the process or project. It is important to understand the requirements and provide the necessary resources or technologies to fulfill them.

2. Before any change is introduced it is impossible to understand all strengths and weaknesses. In order to be able to do effective change, this step should not be underestimated.

3. This phase picks up the requirement from step 2 and agrees with what should be delivered. There might also be newer findings brought into in this step, to further improve the service quality.

4. This is the phase where the processes and tools may need to be changed in order to get to the desired state. It is like a planning phase in a project. This is one of the key phases to understand what changes are required to the processes.

5. By checking the KPIs and performance indicators this step will point out if the goal has been achieved or not. This is an important (**QA**Quality Assurance (QA) step and check, not only single components but the entire implementation.

6. The final step ensures that there is constant change. By getting all results from the former steps it ensures that these steps are completed as often as possible in order to deliver the desired and required outcome.

The reason why it is important to follow this principle can be described with a simple example:

In Steve's organization, it is required to file a ticket before a service can be deployed. The requestor gets a ticket number and this number enables the tracking of the entire process. Now the IT department announced that they will have a self-service portal, which enables Steve to order services on demand using the portal. Steve is quite happy because the another process was clunky and slow.

As he logs on to the portal and requests the first service he is disappointed. The request form in the portal asks him about the ticket ID. He now needs to create a ticket to deploy a service and then go to the portal to put in the ticket ID to request the service which then gets deployed automatically. This is quite an effort for Steve and he is not very happy with the process. While he gets his requested services faster as before, he also has to fill out more forms and bureaucracy has slightly increased to get services delivered.

In this case, the IT organization from Steve has simply adopted the old model to the SDDC. While this is an easy way to include a service without changing it too much, it might not make sense for an automated environment. The solution, in this case, could be that the system is creating the ticket automatically when a user is requesting a service. The auto-generated ticket ID can then be feed into the original system and still be used to track the deployment.

However, this is exactly what is meant by the continuous improvement cycle. Ultimately, it is questionable if the old process is still needed. In the example, all requests are stored in the cloud portal. The portal could be queried for requested information and it also knows the state of the request (successful, failed, in progress, and so on). So the IT department could evolve the process over time to make it easier for the end users as well as for themselves.

By revisiting the purpose and questioning if it is still needed, the IT enters the check phase. The next phase would be to plan the changes and include them into the system. This would be the first of many improvements brought into the system. But therefore the feedback from the users as well as a critical view on present processes is required.

Also, changing processes are normally not doable by one department. Typically multiple departments are influenced when it comes to IT processes. Therefore it is helpful to sync with all parties and decide what the best way forward could look like. In `Chapter 1`, *The Software-Defined Data Center*, of this book, the SDDC **center of excellence (CoE)** was explained. It is a virtual team consistent of multiple data center divisions with different roles in order to run the new automation environment.

The same team needs to work on the continuous improvement and has to work with other teams in the organization in order to ensure that processes around the deployment and integration can be brought up to speed to match the new way of running IT.

Technical assurance

Besides the processes, it is also necessary to question the used technical delivery methods. Are all services delivered using state of the art technologies in order to achieve agility and flexibility?

Sometimes, in order to get the SDDC done quicker, these delivery methods are compromises between the old and the new world. The problem with this assumption is, that if the users accept the SDDC and what it has to offer, they will more and more rely on its deployment quality. If now these deployment modes can't keep pace with the user's demand, they need to change again to fulfill the new requirements.

Good examples for bad compromises are:

- The VM installation method is still used as if it was a physical server (PXE boot).
- The backup/restore is still done as if it was a physical server (OS client, and so on).
- The IP address management is done manually by adding it to a worksheet.
- Each VM gets a static IP based on a specific pattern and use case, no automated IP pools.
- Normally these compromises are done to make the initial deployment of the SDDC faster. But there is a high risk that they are not fast enough changed in order to keep up with the expectations of the SDDC users.

- Once the business is used to the quicker deployments they will start to expand their use of the portal. In many cases, data center automation will increase the number of deployed services. This means, that if there are compromises in place, which will limit this efficiency dramatically, this will be recognized once the SDDC is beginning to grow more and more important for the business.
- In order to prevent a disruption to the service, which might diminish the trust of the users, it is recommended to improve compromised integrations as soon as possible.

Reviewing blueprints

The blueprints are key components in the SDDC. Their feasibility needs to be checked from time to time in order to ensure they are still relevant.

If a deployment from the template is chosen, there are a couple of good practices in order to ensure these templates stay as up to date as possible:

- Update the template OS once per quarter to the most recent patch level. This prevents long waiting times after deployment if the OS needs to download and install a ton of patches.
- Ensure that eventually included software (AV, backup, and so on) is up to date. This can be done while the template is continuously patched.
- If software packages are included, check periodically if the install method is still valid for the most recent version. This is especially important for most Windows installations using PowerShell.
- If XaaS blueprints are used, periodically check if the workflow in vRO is up to date and if the counterpart (the third-party it controls) is still accepting the same commands.
- If a workflow subscription is used, the same principle as for XaaS applies. Also, ensure that if any third-party integrated tool is updated all the workflows relying on that tool are quality checked as quickly as possible.
- Besides the updates and ensuring that the subscribed needed workflows are still working it is also important to review the purpose of the entire blueprint. Maybe it is no longer required in this form. An example could be that the services have changed and instead of installing single VMs now, everyone is deploying entire application environments. Therefore, a single OS template might not be relevant anymore.

- Or the technology has mad a leap and the OS version is no longer needed. Therefore the blueprint needs to point to a newer OS version. All these tasks are part of the continuous improvement of the technical base layers in the SDDC. If there would be no improvement the environment might become outdated quite quickly and would loose its relevance to the business.

Reviewing automation and integration

Automation, standardization, and integration are the base requirements for an SDDC. Chapter 2, *Identify Automation and Standardization Opportunities,* is mostly concentrating on identifying opportunities to automate and standardize in order to make the whole installation and integration of the SDDC possible at all. However, it is also important to revisit these automation tasks from time to time to make sure they still serve their purpose and work reasonably.

A lot of vSphere functions can provide a wide spectrum of automation. A couple of these have been discussed in Chapter 3, *VMware vSphere: The SDDC Foundation*. It is wise to not duplicate an automation principle, which might be already present in vSphere or vCenter. However, vSphere versions will change every year. Even if only the version every second year contains major changes, it is worth checking if any of the custom automation methods can now be done by vSphere.

The side effect of this procedure is that all introduced vSphere features are 100% maintained by VMware. From now on VMware has to take care that the algorithm does not break due to an update or upgrade of the host. This lowers the effort for the operations team and increases the agility and efficiency. Although many people might have been put a lot of work in the automation of certain tasks, it is highly recommended to drop the custom automation in favor of the industrialized one coming with VMware's products.

There are some prominent examples of automation tasks baked into vSphere over time:

- **vSphere Distributed Resource Scheduler** (**DRS**): Moves a VM based on its resource demand to different hosts in order to fulfill those. This happens automatically by a special scheduler, which monitors the demand in the cluster and provides recommendations.
- **Storage DRS**: Automatically migration of workloads between data stores based on criteria like performance or space left (out of space avoidance move).

- **Storage Policy Based Management** (**SPBM**): Instead of matching data stores per name policies can be created to fit the right data store to the requirements of the VM. The technology is based on VMware's VASA adapter, which is constantly improved to deliver even more insights to the underlying storage.
- **vSphere High Availability** (**HA**): It began with a very simple VM restart procedure and has now evolved into a powerful HA toolset. Not only can HA restart VMs from a failed host, it can also monitor the VM heartbeat (based on the VM tools) and restart a VM if it has entered a blue screen or kernel panic. There are even application specific HA adapters in order to restart a process within a VM.
- **Auto deploy**: While it is one of the most complex tools of VMware it provides great efficiency and agility when it comes to the bigger scale installation of ESXi hosts. All it needs is a PXE environment and vSphere Host Profiles to work. Once a new host is started it can be automatically come up with the right vSphere version and can be brought into the right cluster.

While the SDDC might be already built based on this vSphere features and functions, it is recommended to stay up to date with VMware's latest additions and enhancements. Maybe there is a vSphere feature replacing a complex but required automation. In this case, it should be revisited if not the vSphere-integrated automation is a better choice for the previously outlined reasons.

But it is not only the hypervisor, which should be periodically checked. The other tasks where automation was applied on are necessary to revisit as well. An example for this is a changed business case (or an add-on) which may require not the same amount of automation/integration or a completely new approach in order to be successful.

DevOps is one of the candidates clashing with most of the traditional data center integrations. However, since this might be a change the business is asking for the SDDC has to be improved in order to support this use case as well.

But what divides DevOps from standard IT workloads?

The idea of DevOps is to be fast, agile and efficient. There might be 3 to5 different application versions per week. Also, they might use containers or at least a container framework to work properly. As described in `Chapter 9`, *DevOps Considerations*, it is fundamentally different from running traditional IT.

Also, all is about the application. The installation and the OS providing the resources are secondary and definitely, do not concern the developer in any means. In fact, frameworks like **Cloud Foundation** run a proprietary OS as VMs on a hypervisor. On top of that, they use containers to house the application and being able to act as quick and flexible as needed.

IPAM integration is quite useless for a DevOps environment. Also, it does not need a CMDB and would certainly not work well with this principle. These two (automated) integrations are irrelevant to this use case of the SDDC; therefore they should either not be adopted or changed in a way to support DevOps.

While DevOps is a prominent example there might also be enterprise IT changes which might force the team to change or even completely recreate the automation processes. Since the business and the IT are constantly moving, so is the integration effort in an SDDC.

Revisiting the business case

As the implementation of the SDDC might have taken quite some time it is important to revisit the business case and see if it still fits. The business might have changed its demands and therefore the data center automation might also need a change or an update. The initially created service might still be relevant, but there might be new services required to serve other cases. Therefore it is wise to keep the business close to the IT in order to be aware of actual requirements.

In the new SDDC environment, the introduction of new services should be simpler as in the non-automated data center. However, that does not mean that this works without planning and designing. There might be a domino effect if a single blueprint is changed affecting also other systems.

Such a change might be the introduction of a new service, which includes the automated installation of all components. It might be a business system, which can be ordered on demand and is completely deployed by the SDDC. All the requestor has to do is connect to the system and start working after it has been deployed. In order to accomplish this, a number of tasks need to work flawlessly together. The basis will be available in the SDDC. There need to be various other tasks done in order to enable a full-service installation. The software installation might be done using either a pre-existing tool or **vRealize Automation Application Services**. To form this decision all factors should be taken into account. An existing tool might be used because it already has hundreds of applications ready to be installed. vRA might be used because it can also do all the niche installations a traditional tool might cannot. Maybe a mix of both tools is needed to deploy the application as quickest as possible.

The whole idea of a service catalog though is to be flexible and agile. It needs to reflect the actual requirements and desires of the customer using the portal.

Since the business now has a lot of influence on the IT design, it is recommended to have a direct contact with the business to learn about their requirements and plans accordingly. This should not be of technical nature, but to understand what they are planning and what they might need to be successful with their projects.

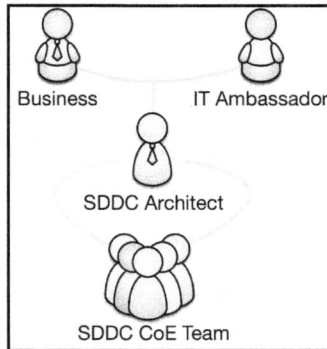

The principle of the **IT Ambassador** (in the preceding image) is maybe close to an internal IT sales person. This might be a good practice to drive the continuous improvement through the new demands and expectations the business has towards the IT. Also, it might strengthen the relationship between those two departments. Since the SDDC capabilities are designed to help the business in succeeding in their daily work the relationship between these parties is very important. A healthy relationship will lead to a good teamwork and make a good SDDC an outstanding SDDC. If the trust can be built that with the help of the IT department there is now challenge the business can't tackle that would be a win-win for the entire organization.

Therefore it might be a good approach to have such a function and to review the business case and the expected functionality at best once a quarter but at least every half year.

ITIL in the SDDC

The creation of an SDDC is far more than only the configuration of a view software tools. It begins with finding the right team for the SDDC operations. This team has to be inter-disciplinary in terms of technology to ensure that all aspects of the SDDC can work flawlessly together. Once such a team is built, it has to identify tasks and processes to either automate or substitute with newer ways of completing IT request. This is not an easy task to complete but necessary since it will ensure that further changes and requirements can be easier fulfilled by the SDDC.

Matching the requirements to the solution

After all of this has been outlined the solution has to be designed in order to fulfill the requirements. This will be the later foundation for the configuration and installation and shall incorporate all features and capabilities the solution needs to offer after it is completed. Compared to other designs, which may only include a single component, this one needs to include all necessary tools and even the integration automation pieces for the entire SDDC.

After the design is set and the decisions have been documented on integration, all the different tools have to be configured in order to form the foundation for the service deployment. Amongst the portal and the orchestration system, there might be network virtualization in the mix. This enhances the speed and flexibility when deploying complex services tapping multiple networks. However, given this capability, it will be possible to automatically deploy entire labs or the most complex services using different networks for application, database or web frontend components.

To be future ready the SDDC should also be ready for DevOps and its changed requirements towards a traditional data center. If the business requires a much quicker application development cycle, there is no chance to achieve this with traditional approaches. However, the agility and automation of the system will also be ready to handle DevOps requirements. This will ultimately help the business to stay relevant and competitive.

Finally, the monitoring and analysis not only for the internal platform components but also the deployed services need to be rethought. Therefore VMware has powerful tools, which can adapt to new situations quickly and learn the behavior of entire applications in order to look for anomalies.

This is a smart way to detect errors, even when there are no thresholds defined. In a changing and quickly adopting SDDC a traditional monitoring cannot keep pace. Therefore, intelligent tools need to be used, which can adopt and learn the data center behaviors to understand what is normal and what is critical. All this defines the SDDC, but it does not mean that this is *set and forget*.

Applying continuous service improvement to the SDDC

To create an SDDC with all its automation and integration processes means that these can't stay static forever. If these principles are incorporated thoughtfully it will lead to a smooth running data center, which delivers exactly the services required to its end users. The built teams running this new data center will be used to this continuous improvement procedure and therefore changes can be introduced much quicker than in the old static data center days.

Since all the automation and integration tasks in the SDDC are created with agility and efficiency in mind, it should also be possible to change those in order to further improve these two major characteristics of the SDDC.

Keep in mind that this is a flexible and agile environment. Therefore it needs to be managed and operated in the same way.

These principles are older than SDDC, but today they are easier to follow than ever. In the time they have been created it was quite complex to automate even the slightest deployment in a data center. Today, with the power of orchestration and network virtualization it is much simpler to automate, therefore these principles should be considered in every data center, but especially in the SDDC.

Summary

This chapter was explaining the need to revisit designs, processes, and services in order to make sure that they are still relevant for the business. Also, it discussed basic principles of ITIL and how it matches to the SDDC architecture and design. It discussed methods and ways to keep the continuous service improvement up and also to create an active and ongoing dialog with the lines of business. Further, it described the need to revisit the created automation tasks as well as the blueprints and services. Since there is constant change in the IT and in the economics these days it highlighted the importance of embracing that change and grow the SDDC with it.

Index

www.ingramcontent.com/pod-product-compliance
Lightning Source LLC
Chambersburg PA
CBHW080907220326
41598CB00034B/5498

* 9 7 8 1 7 8 6 4 6 4 3 7 8 *